GREG CHAPPELL

GREG CHAPPELL

Adrian McGregor

COLLINS

© Greg Chappell and Adrian McGregor, 1985

Greg Chappell is managed by Harry M. Miller
and Company Management

First published by William Collins Pty Ltd,
    Sydney, 1985
Reprinted November, 1985
Typeset by Post Typesetters, Brisbane
Printed and bound by Globe Press, Melbourne

National Library of Australia
Cataloguing-in-Publication data

  McGregor, Adrian
    Greg Chappell

    ISBN 0 00 217485 5

    1. Chappell, Greg, 1948- .   2. Cricket players —
    Australia — Biography.   I. Title.

796.35'8'0924

PREFACE

I arrived in Queensland from Sydney at roughly the same time Greg Chappell arrived from Adelaide. For over a decade, in my capacity as a feature writer, I happened to be present during some memorable moments in his career — débuts as captain of Queensland and Australia, when the World Series Cricket news broke in London, the first WSC match under lights at the Sydney Cricket Ground.

When he retired I wrote to him and he became enthusiastic about a biography provided we essayed a balanced, quality work. To have researched and written that in just six months I must first thank Greg, who endured scores of hours of wearying interrogation with the affability I now know is the man. And Judy, too, who never begrudged a minute of yet one more cricket intrusion.

I am indebted to David Smith, editor of the *Courier-Mail*, for those six months leave, and to Queensland Newspapers Pty Ltd for assistance with photographs. Bob Spence's definitive statistics were of as much value to me in the writing as they will be of interest to readers. Similarly I drew upon Irving Rosenwater's compilation of Greg's career highlights as readers will be drawn to them.

The good offices of Tom Glasgow, of TAA, enabled me to follow Greg's career trail to all points south and Pat Mullins' unique library filled in the rest. Barry Maranta kindly applied his academic eye to the first draft.

Greg's career spanned some of the most controversial years in modern cricket. Often he was at the centre and had an intimate knowledge of events. At other times he was merely an observer. To record every one of those incidents in absolute detail is beyond the scope and intention of this book. Greg's personal impressions are what make this an authorized biography, not a history.

Finally, collaborative works are always at risk for being written under the scrutiny of the subject. We were fortunate that my defence of his underarm pre-dates this book by four years and thus avoids any taint of vested bias. In descriptions of other career incidents Greg, though he did not always agree, not once interfered.

Adrian McGregor 1985

CONTENTS

ORIGINS (1935–1966)

1. Childhood

On 12 October 1952, Greg Chappell, aged four years and two months, a small, slight boy with two prominent front teeth, curly brown hair and large, serious blue eyes, donned cap, pads, gloves and protective box for one of his first cricket Tests. The bowler was his grandfather, Vic Richardson, who at 58 was well beyond his halcyon days as captain of Australia. Vic pegged a few down to his diminutive grandson and when he bowled him, Greg dutifully departed from the crease, carrying his red-handled, Dunlop-Crocket bat, cut-down handle and blade, into the laundry. There he methodically took off his cap, pads, gloves and box, replaced them and came out as a new player. Vic watched, amused by this performance, but by the third fall of wicket he exasperatedly tried to explain to his grandson that the long walk was not necessary. But to Greg the two facets of the game, the reality and the romance, were inseparable, and the Test being played in his head was as important as the balls Pop, his famous grandfather, was dollying up the pitch.

Throughout his childhood and school days Greg retained those Test fantasies, until time turned the dream into a possibility and his skill made it the reality. The other players in this little theatre would make their entrances. Elder brother Ian, then nine, returned from school. Father Martin arrived after visiting his wife Jeanne in hospital where she had just had their third son, Trevor. The Chappells were staying with Vic, Jeanne's father, during the confinement. Martin's arrival would complete the link in the Richardson–Chappell dynasty which for half a century was synonymous with South Australian and Australian cricket.

Vic Richardson's home in Richmond Road, Westbourne Park, an

1

Adelaide suburb of grand old sand-and-bluestone memories, was itself a red brick and sandstone colonial with wide verandahs on every side to ease the heat from the desert north-westerlies which can sear the city, and two fireplaces to combat the south-westerly fronts sweeping up from the Great Southern Ocean. Its expanse of red-painted iron roof, baking in the sun, sat like a sun-hat on its stony substance and graceful stained-glass leadlight windows. Vic bought the house for its large, open backyard, the equivalent of two ordinary house blocks. It included a tennis court where Vic played regularly. That enjoyment was almost cut short when Vic, in his forties, was cutting the vast lawn with an electric mower and ran over the cord. Jeanne, whose bedroom window overlooked the court, saw her father thrown to the ground, his hands locked to the steel handle by the current. Her presence of mind in running to the power switch and not to him saved his life.

Down one side of the yard Vic installed a cricket pitch and played there with his son, Doug, and the neighbourhood boys. Martin Chappell was the son of Harold Chappell, who ran his pharmacy as a shopfront attached to their home on the corner adjacent to the Richardsons. Martin joined in these games but Jeanne first remembered him from a fourteenth birthday party, soon after which Martin left school and went to work. When he turned 16, Martin joined Vic's cricket club, Sturt, as did Vic's son Doug. All three were active cricketers in the same club for several years until Vic, glancing around the Sturt dressing-room one day, discovered that not one of the team was born when he began his first class career. So he retired.

Martin was a regular at Vic's backyard cricket practices and once slogged a ball from Vic through the bathroom window, splintering the glass just as Jeanne's mother, Vida, was entering. There was no long-term impairment of relations, however, because on 26 September 1942, Martin, then 23, married Jeanne Richardson at St Columbus Church of England in the nearby suburb of Hawthorne. The one note of sadness for Jeanne was that her mother, Vida Richardson, had died two years earlier, on 25 September 1940. Martin and Jeanne celebrated their first wedding anniversary, to the day, with the birth of a son, Ian. Not quite five years later, on 7 August 1948, the family doctor walked from his home to the colonial Unley District Hospital near the Richardsons' home to deliver Gregory Stephen Chappell.

Martin and Jeanne had just bought a home in that curious palindrome of a suburb, Glenelg, then a new housing development southwest of the city. The Chappells lived in Leak Avenue, North Glenelg, about three blocks from the beach where the wind blasts in from the Gulf of St Vincent, whipping across the surfless beach, sweeping fine white sand across the concrete esplanade, stunting the shrubs and piling in blows against the trunks of hardy pines. The district later became a holiday spot with amusement parks, fast food and square blocks of flats with names like Gulf View. With its translated architecture it could be Brighton, England.

The Chappells' home, of Mt Gambier sandstone, was three bedrooms and a back verandah on a large block about 23 metres wide. The width is important because it enabled the Chappells to fit a 22 yard cricket pitch across the backyard with space for a three pace bowling run-up. The house itself is dwarfed in significance by the backyard. There, a quarter of a century ago, years before the rest of the world discovered the real benefits of exhaustive, concentrated athletic coaching and training, Martin Chappell dedicated his every spare moment to developing his sons' cricket careers. He rough-sculpted Ian, tempered his technique on Greg, and possibly expected a masterpiece in Trevor.

Martin Chappell was a solid, stocky man, wide shouldered, big chested, bordering on being powerful, an inheritance from his grandfather who was a saddler and leather worker in Moonta, on the Yorke Peninsula in South Australia. He was 175 centimetres, nearer Trevor's size than the height to which Ian, 180 centimetres, and Greg, 188 centimetres, grew. He was an avid cricketer and baseballer, but in 1940, aged 21, he enlisted for the Second World War. By the time he was demobbed Martin Chappell's moment had passed. He represented South Australia in Claxton Shield baseball as a catcher, topped the district cricket averages in 1950–51 and made the State cricket squad that season and the next. But he was never selected to play. Greg vaguely remembers accompanying his mother in the family's Standard Vanguard to his father's cricket matches, but he was too young to recall his style. In later years he heard that his father, an off-spinner, was accused of throwing by his mates. 'There were a hell of a lot of throwers in the fifties,' Greg said. 'It was generally accepted that Dad bent the elbow a bit.' Ian recalled his father as 'a goer, who liked to hook'. When Ian was a teenage baseballer, opponents who had played against Martin would remark to him, 'You're just like your father, hard to get on with and won't give an inch.' Another Ian insight concerned Martin, then about 35, and reaching the end of his cricket career, captaining a Glenelg C grade side of young players at Hindmarsh Oval.

His opponents were West Torrens, captained by a similar team father figure, Gordon Tuck. A young Torrens batsman played the ball down and as it imperilled his stumps, bent down and picked it up. An appeal went up and the lad was given out. Tuck called angrily from the grandstand to Martin fielding at cover, 'Martin, you're not going to let that stand are you?' Martin ignored the call to the dismay of young Ian who was scoring and hoping Tuck did not know he was Martin's son. Driving home that evening Martin told Ian, 'See that kid get out for handling the ball? He won't do that again. It was a good lesson for him.' Silence, change gears. 'And you won't ever do it, will you? It's a good lesson for you.'

Thus Martin's career faded without his ever realizing his great wish, to represent his State at cricket. In that disappointment was nurtured the determination that if his sons had the ability they would never want for assistance or opportunity. To this end as soon as his sons could hold a cut-down bat he began teaching them the fundamentals of cricket. In this respect Greg's story is Ian's is Trevor's and is as inseparable as the brothers were in their backyard cricket play. If it can be called play. Martin began with the basics: forward defence, back defence, an hour of each on the makeshift pitch across the back lawn. Recalled Trevor, 'He taught us that everything we played off the back foot was a development of the back defence, and everything off the front foot, of the front defence.' As a commercial traveller for a pharmaceutical firm Martin often did not get home until dusk, but on weekends and whenever he could after work, he would practise with his sons. Forward defence, back defence, and then mix them up; one short, lifting chest high, the next of fuller length, until it became a sixth sense to the boys to gauge within centimetres where the ball would land. To round off at the end of each session Martin would spend another hour throwing half volleys and long hops to be hit for four. Said Greg, 'He told us it was all very well to stay at the crease but we had to make runs as well, hit the bad balls for four.'

Though he was confident of his own technique Martin followed the dictum that any child trained solely by his parent had a fool for a coach. Thus when each son turned five they began coaching lessons every Sunday morning with a former South Australian country cricketer, Lynn Fuller, who lived five minutes' drive away near the Patawalonga Creek, an inlet, now a boat haven, into Glenelg Beach. Fuller had a turf wicket in his backyard and coached promising boys in the district. To qualify for this coaching was a thrilling coming of age for each

4

Chappell boy. But that week Greg was sitting straddling his backyard fence when he was jostled by another boy and fell on his left arm. He complained of soreness for several days until Jeanne took him to the doctor, who diagnosed it as a greenstick fracture and put it in plaster. Greg desperately demonstrated to Lynn Fuller that with the plaster only from the elbow to the wrist he could still bat, but to his bitter disappointment Fuller refused him permission.

Sunday mornings at Fuller's, while the bells chimed around Adelaide, city of churches, Greg learned his litany. 'Bend the front knee, get the weight forward, get the left elbow up, head over the ball.' It was appropriate that Fuller, in his sixties, taught his pagan religion, complete with wooden sacraments, by rote, rarely explanation. And in the long tradition of the innocents, Greg followed without question, committing his young heart and mind to the idea with which his father had indoctrinated him — that cricket was a worthy object of such love and dedication and that the word, as spoken by Fuller, could be accepted in an act of pure faith. It was not until Greg, together with Barry Richards, began coaching for Coca Cola Bottlers in 1970 that he began to think and explain, 'Get the left elbow up because...' And, as we shall see, only once in the next 30 years did the body of knowledge and faith he possessed in cricket appear to forsake him.

Greg's boyhood was an age of instruction rather than enquiry, so Sundays, 9 a.m. to noon, he followed the kindly, softly spoken Fuller's advice while Martin watched, occasionally dragooned into throwing balls. Fuller's turf wicket was only fully top dressed for half its length and where the wicket ended it fell about 15 centimetres in a smooth, gentle ridge to become plain lawn. After official practice Martin would say to his sons, 'Righto, go down there and defend yourself,' and fire six stitchers off the ridge at their heads and bodies. Neither the Lord's infamous ridge nor the joins in some of the World Series Cricket's two-piece transportable pitches could match the danger of Lynn Fuller's rise. It explains why Ian and Greg were among the last to adopt helmets later in their careers.

Martin was adamant about practising with, and not being afraid of, a hard ball. Ian used to score for Martin's Glenelg C grade side, partially in the hope that one day the team would fall short a man and call upon him. That day arrived against Sturt and the team voted to play 13-year-old Ian. He withstood 45 minutes of a quickish Sturt bowler named Blue Ballantyne and was pleased to score six runs. That night at tea Martin announced to the table, 'You're not playing for the

Cs any more.' 'Why?' asked Ian. 'I batted for 45 minutes.' Said Martin, 'Because you're scared. You backed away from one ball from Blue Ballantyne. If you're scared of a cricket ball you're not playing C grade again until you're not scared.' Ian was devastated because in his mind the most important feature of his innings was that he hadn't backed away from Big Blue.

It was the same with their fielding. Practice with Martin was pelting the hard ball at them from all angles in the yard. Inside the house, unsuspectingly, there would be Martin's shout and a red blur. When Ian took over 100 Test catches and Greg broke the world record with 122 it was not in their blood, it was in their practice. Greg loved it. Martin had no need to coerce him. Only once Greg returned from Fuller's one Sunday lunchtime and headed off. 'Where are you going?' called Martin. 'To play cowboys and indians down the road,' replied Greg. 'No,' said Martin. 'You can go after you've had some practice.' Greg reluctantly agreed and three hours later was still engrossed in practice. No coercion for Greg, but Trevor's memory was of a slightly sterner man. 'He would make you do things properly otherwise you didn't finish,' he said. 'When you had satisfied him, then you could do something else.'

One of Greg's favourite shots was a flick off the hip, played with toes together, both heels off the ground, body slightly forward of upright, whipping the ball off middle and leg over the square leg backyard fence. When Ian attended Fuller's lessons he would obediently block the first two balls and then the third, whack, he would pull it over the on-side fence. 'No, you've got to hit the ball along the ground,' Fuller would remonstrate quietly. And so Ian disciplined the pull from his repertoire not to be re-admitted until a few years later. Then, chasing a tough total for Prince Alfred College, he suddenly pulled a few over the top and wondered to himself, 'Where did that come from? I didn't know I could do it.' When Greg arrived and started whipping them off his hip, Fuller cautioned him, too: 'Hit it along the ground.' But Greg persisted with the shot and after several weeks Lynn gave up, commenting, 'It's silly trying to stop those shots. It's such a natural stroke.' Some 20 years later England captain, Mike Brearley, in his book, *The Return of the Ashes*, devoted nearly half a page to describing just that stroke. He wrote:

> *There's no name for this shot. Very few batsmen can play it ... most people are just nudging it around the corner, but he plays it with*

a free flow of the bat... I think this shot of Chappell's impresses the players more than the public because we know how hard it is to play.

The only batsman Brearley thought could play the stroke as well was the great Sir Garfield Sobers. That shot was absolute proof of sheer, natural talent.

Greg put all that advice and his innate ability to the test in the backyard, first against Ian and then with Trevor. Some of the most bitterly fought Tests between Australia and England occurred between just two players under hot, cloudless skies at Number 4 Leak Avenue cricket ground. Ian, as the eldest, got to be Lindwall, Miller, O'Neill, Harvey and Co., while Greg had to make do with those Poms, Trueman, Statham, Dexter and May. In one day Greg and Ian could complete a full Test series, two innings each and five Tests. No quarter was shown or given and dismissals, especially leg before wicket and caught behind decisions, were constant sources of confrontation. Behind the stumps the side fence was the 'keeper and slips cordon. The fence appealed if the ball was edged between its two cross beams and not wide of one panel of boards. Above that was over the timber catching cordon's heads, below did not carry. The Chappell backyard was dotted with fruit trees, an almond at square leg, another at mid-on, a lemon at deep silly mid-off, a line of peaches along the on-side boundary. Martin tied old wire mesh gates to protect their trunks, which in turn became fieldsmen, and on the full to a fruit tree fielder was out.

Often Greg would find a goodish edge, caught behind. 'Righto, piss off, that bloke's out,' called Ian. Greg was then supposed to walk to the nearby tankstand, write in the last player's score and return as the new batsman. But Greg, being younger, was less inclined to walk. 'No, no, I didn't hit it,' he would say. In the ensuing shouting match Jeanne would know, and Greg knew too, that whatever imperfections of character Ian possessed, he would not lie. It was a signature which caused Ian any amount of aggravation in his later cricket career and it didn't even win for him here because inevitably Jeanne would say, 'Oh, for goodness sake. Greg's the younger, give him a break.' Ian's response to himself was: 'OK, the little bastard won't go out, he can cop this now,' and he'd hurl down his fastest. Greg recalled, 'Once he smacked me three times in a row on the fingers and I was down on the ground wringing my fingers trying not to cry. He came up and I thought, "Finally he's going to show some sympathy", and he said, "Well come on, get up, don't worry about that. The next one will be straight at your head." '

Jeanne's theory that the youngest received the benefit of the doubt foundered against the pads of her middle son. 'I could make Ian give things up to Greg as a littley, but there was no way Greg would give them up to Trev,' said Jeanne. 'Whatever was Greg's was Greg's.' He is a Leo, typically known for their determination bordering on stubbornness, defending their own ground, pride in personal performance and a problem ego. Trevor claimed that Greg would throw the ball instead of bowling and then deny the accusation. Or at the end of Greg's innings Trevor would disappear to pad up and return to find the wicket had been doctored with a watering can. 'How'd those wet patches get there?' he would ask. 'Where?' replied Greg. 'Oh, they're only small patches anyway, they won't affect anything.' Whereupon Greg would make the ball lift off the damp spots and fizz around Trevor's ears. One day Greg made Trevor bowl and bowl and would not go out until Trevor, furious, grabbed a tomahawk from the tankstand and went at Greg. Said Greg, 'I ran around the fruit trees a couple of times and thought, "I can't stay in here, he's going to catch me somewhere".' He took off down the side path, vaulted a 1.5 metre high gate with nary any weight on his hands and ran three blocks before looking back.

The Tests continued under all conditions, mostly with a hard cricket ball, sometimes using a tennis ball with one half shaved bald to give it a wicked swing. When they wore ruts in the crease Greg repaired the damage with a wheelbarrow of black soil from nearby Glenelg Cricket Club's second oval where Lynn Fuller helped out preparing wickets. Greg gradually expanded the black soil area until he had a 3 metre wide, 9 metre long cricket block. Fuller also gave the Chappells an old roller and, according to Trevor, Greg having made the wicket, elected Martin as chief groundsman. Trevor suggested a certain indolence on Greg's part, as evidenced by his aversion to beating the almond trees each year to knock the nuts down. 'Greg would beat for five minutes and then he'd stand back and direct operations. He'd be the foreman,' said Trevor.

Martin also became responsible for the glass-consuming monsters he had set loose in the backyard. First it was the Chappells' back porch glass louvres on the off-side. Then as the boys grew stronger a glassed-in side verandah of neighbour Don Mason became vulnerable to a six over long-off. Mason, who was later elected mayor of Glenelg, was annoyed at first and then grew resigned. 'I've got a good insurance contract,' he would say, and besides, his sons John and Doug, who went to school with Greg, were as often as not involved in the game. Watching those backyard matches, baseball and cricket, Don Mason was not surprised years later when the Chappells were in the thick of World Series Cricket. 'They urged, niggled and barracked each other,' he said. 'They brought the game alive, bit of theatre and showmanship.'

Martin set about caging in the batting crease with chicken wire and proofing his own and neighbours' windows with strategically placed wire mesh gates. A chicken wire Maginot line. 'The way he had the angles organized nothing could get through,' said Greg. 'If you tried you couldn't do it, but the ball would hit the far fence, bounce back against the tankstand, off the brick path and crash, tinkle. Unbelievable.' Once Greg top-edged the ball and it looped over the chicken wire behind the wicket and smashed the window of a block of flats at a closish third man, where a German migrant was having his breakfast. It lobbed in his Weet-Bix and he appeared at the window with cereal and milk and red fluid running down his face. 'I thought, "Oh hell, he's cut his face",' said Greg. In fact the man had also planned bacon and eggs for breakfast and the ball had struck a bottle splattering him with tomato sauce. Greg took off, Ian retrieved the ball, Martin mended the window. Asked once what went into the making of his three champions, the self-taught glazier replied, 'All my spare cash, all my leisure time and about 150 broken windows.'

If Ian and Trevor were not available Greg would play Tests by himself, throwing a golf ball against the laundry wall and playing the rebound, taking the long walk to the laundry, keeping a scorecard, and commentating all the time: 'And Trueman comes in, bowls to Harvey, a magnificent shot, that's four ...' Once during these solo Tests Greg was being Gil Langley, South Australian and Australian wicketkeeper, and he hit the ball over two backyard fences. It was too big for a six, a six was only one fence. After due consultation with his mother Greg awarded Langley a 12.

For fielding practice Greg would throw a golf ball against the brick and concrete tankstand, the edges of which produced awkward and unexpected angles and speed on the rebound. It seems almost trite to remember that Sir Donald Bradman, whose Australian Test run-getting record Greg was destined to surpass, honed his eye as a boy by throwing a golf ball against a similar brick base of a tankstand and hitting the rebound with a cricket stump.

The pounding of Greg's solo matches would drum through the house driving even the long-suffering Jeanne to distraction. Boom, boom, boom, and then relief while Greg stepped inside to listen to a cricket score on the mantle radio before the pounding resumed. Her consolation was, as she remarked, that she knew where her son was. On rainy days he would be underfoot, kicking stuffed socks down the hallway in football matches with Ian, or playing a table top cricket game with cardboard fieldsmen, and a springloaded bowler who delivered a marble at a finger-sized batsman. Ian rigged a hoop on a wall to play indoor basketball and when that palled there was a darts board. Occasionally, sparked by some news event, they would plant jam tins in the back yard and play golf or listen to the Davis Cup and come out with their racquets. The Chappell household rang with sport hour after hour. When Ian left school he bought a half-sized billiard table and they would shift the table tennis table for yet one more outlet for their competitiveness. Their bookshelves held a few Famous Five volumes but the most thumbed were the ABC cricket tour guides, cricket annuals and a particular favourite, *The Fireside Book of Baseball*, which Ian bought. It had a small dice baseball game inside which Greg adapted to cricket and in the summer he would play cricket outside until dusk and then come inside, have tea, and play dice cricket.

This whirl of sporting chaos might have daunted a lesser mother than the daughter of Vic Richardson. Jeanne Chappell could not remember a childhood Christmas Day at home. They were spent watching her father captain South Australia in Sheffield Shield matches at Adelaide Oval. There was no Christmas lunch. 'You could never get a meal at the oval on Christmas Day,' Jeanne lamented. 'It was always fritz [devon sausage] which Dad loved.' Vic was away from home for months on end playing cricket but Jeanne never felt she had a deprived childhood. Rather Vic was an exciting father, not the least because he was a handsome, intelligent and quick-witted man, whose low, cultured voice, with its ringing timbre, made him a famous cricket broadcaster when he retired.

Jeanne played hockey at school and social tennis with other young mothers in the neighbourhood, but she found herself cast, not totally unwillingly, into the role of baggage-girl, washer-woman, car driver and cook for her three sporting sons. She read adventure stories to them at night when they were children but the force of cricket was undeniable. Mornings revolved around the day's cricket prospects and results dominated dinner time conversations. 'It would have been hopeless to push any other interest,' said Jeanne. 'An uphill battle. I'd have been wasting my time.' Martin worked long hours, often not home until 7.30 p.m., and Jeanne insisted on buying a gas fireplace because she tired of fetching the wood herself. They possessed the Australian fear of debt common to the age and bought their first refrigerator when they could pay cash. Holidays seemed rare though Greg enjoyed camping at Victor Harbour, on the picturesque mouth of the Murray River about 80 kilometres south of Adelaide. But Martin did not stint on sporting equipment. The boys had quality bats, bails for their stumps and never wanted for baseball mitts. The Chappells became a two car family — an Austin 7 for Jeanne — in the late 1950s and Jeanne used her new found independence...to watch the boys play cricket more often.

Despite their great sporting bond the boys emerged from the maelstrom of flashing balls with different dispositions and idiosyncrasies. Greg, sharing a room with Trevor, found his younger brother too untidy and asked to partition part of the back verandah with a wardrobe and set up there. When Trevor saw it he wanted in too, so Greg retreated to the original bedroom, alone at last. Greg was organized, Ian was not. Preparing for cricket the next day Greg would pack his bag the night before and leave it at the front door ready to be picked up as he walked out. Ian walked out with a bundle of clothes in his arms, dropping socks as he went and was lucky to have the full set when he arrived. As young boys Ian was almost unfriendly, according to Jeanne. If others wanted to play cricket with him, fine, if not, to hell with them. Whereas Greg always sought company. Jeanne came to know Greg as reliable, rarely rebellious. She could ask Greg to do a chore and it would be done. Ask Ian and he would intend to do it, but if something else took his interest he would wipe the task clean from his mind. Physically Ian and Trevor were strong, whereas Greg could exhaust himself with activity, become pale, bilious and even vomit, and then sleep until lunchtime the next day. Jeanne never had any trouble getting Greg off to bed, but he would rise early in the mornings while Ian and Trevor really wondered why mornings were ever invented.

If Ian wanted to bait his mother he would accuse Jeanne: 'Oh, I know Greg's your favourite.' In later years Rod Marsh took up this humorous catchcry and it never failed to raise Jeanne's ire. 'I really got mad because I don't think I favoured one over any of the others,' she said. 'They all had their share. I think Ian paved the way, and I never did worry too much about Greg. If anything I think it is Trevor who felt the pressure.' One day Ian told his mother: 'You know Greg's not such a good little boy as you think when he's out in the middle.' But Jeanne was always her eldest son's match. 'I know he's not,' she replied, 'and you're not as bad as you think I think you are.'

2. School

The impact of this domestic hothouse of cricket outside the home was, as expected, devastating. Greg was a cricket prodigy. His first school was St Leonard's Primary, a long, narrow, one-storey 1921 building of bright red brick, flying the Australian flag proudly from a short flagpole. It was about 10 minutes' walk from Leak Avenue and if Greg detoured a block he passed a park where, under an old gum tree now preserved in concrete, the colony of South Australia was proclaimed as a province by Captain John Hindmarsh, RN, the Governor, acting on behalf of His Majesty, King William IV, on 28 December 1836. Greg had little interest in such history. His eyes saw only the school's thinly grassed oval, surrounded by fir trees, a timber scoreboard for St Leonard's and Visitors trembling in the breeze, and the concrete wicket with holes sunk for stumps.

At the tender age of eight Greg, still only in grade three, was selected for the school cricket team, a remarkable honour considering his team-mates were in grade seven, aged 11 and 12. It was partly a legacy of Greg arriving just as Ian, who was a brilliant primary school and college cricketer, left. Greg was Ian's brother, therefore was obviously just as good. But Greg's talent outstripped his size. That he was young to be in the team was exacerbated by his being small for his age. He inherited this from Pop Richardson. Vic was coached at Scotch College, Adelaide, by Karl Quist, whose son Adrian became national tennis champion. Vic was one of the smallest boys Karl had ever seen. He described him as, 'knee high to a thimble, but as keen as mustard'. Karl, who played cricket for three States, recalled Vic appearing for school practice one day wearing a tremendous pair of pads. 'He was the funniest sight I ever saw on a cricket field,' said Karl. Vic could only just look over the top of the pads.

'Well laddie, what are you going to do?' asked Karl.

'Keep wickets,' replied the tyro.

'You can't keep wickets.'

'Can't I? You watch me,' said Vic gravely, and as Karl put it, 'The little shaver could.'

Greg's pride at his early selection wilted as the season progressed. Only three times was number eight, Chappell, G., required to bat. He spent the summer fielding and watching his older team-mates. His problems were compounded by the schools using a composition cork ball. The ball bounced so high on the cement wickets that even from a spinner they invariably flew past Greg's eyes. He would occupy the crease for an hour and score maybe 10 to 15 runs while older players, with no technique, would arrive and dash off 20 runs in a couple of overs before getting out. Greg's implacably straight bat meant he was hard to dismiss but he was not strong enough to score. It was difficult to know who was the more frustrated, Greg because he could not score, the bowlers who could not dismiss him, or Greg's team-mates who waited and waited in the wings.

Further inhibitions began to mould his style. He could not possibly get above the ball to drive and his baseball matches were teaching him the instinct that a square cut was a foul. The only way he could score, could produce any power, was by pulling through the on-side. His grip assisted this technical list. Greg held the handle with his top hand well around towards the front so that when he followed through, the natural arc of the bat was over the top of the ball, top spinning it to the on-side. If the habit needed any further reinforcing it need only be remembered that, in the backyard, shots to leg sailed harmlessly into the fruit trees, while to the off-side loomed the glass louvres.

Even then young Greg was serious about his cricket. Once at school a bunch of boys playing red rover kept unintentionally interrupting a match by racing across the wicket Greg and a dozen or so cricketers had set up on the playground grass. Greg warned them, 'We're playing here, you go over there.' Finally Greg ran after a key offender, grabbed him around the neck from behind and pulled him to the ground. 'Listen, don't do that again,' warned Greg. Shades of future streakers and other well-wishing disrupters who earned Greg's wrath on the world's cricket ovals. Next thing Greg was called before the headmaster. The unfortunate boy had dislocated his collarbone in the fall.

Greg always took his bat to school for make-up matches before the bell and at lunchtime. It did not endear him to his teachers, most of whom were women. He began classes hot, sweaty and excited, unsettling the lessons. And well before his classmates caught up with his talent he was allowed Friday afternoons off to play for the school. That meant Friday mornings — woodwork classes — were lost on Greg as he worked on the obsession in his mind instead of the dowel joint at hand. Even if he was too 'ill' to attend school on Friday mornings, he could be relied upon to rise heroically from his sick bed for that afternoon's match. Retribution from Greg's disapproving teachers took strange paths. One madam, in her fifties, insisted he should learn to knit. Greg resisted and her punishment was to make him sit out in front of the class on her lap. She was possessed of, in Greg's pre-teenage eyes, a momentous bosom and he has taken into adulthood terrifying and humiliating memories of being given giant bearhugs which plunged his face into a suffocating cleavage redolent of Johnson's baby powder. The same ample woman, pursuing her knitting campaign, kept Greg in one afternoon, delivering the admonition, 'You stay here and finish that before you go home.' She then proceeded to a staff meeting and forgot all about her captive. Jeanne Chappell arrived at dusk to discover her 8-year-old son sitting in the darkened classroom alone, refusing to touch the knitting material before him. It opens a tiny insight into the oyster of Greg's vision of life. He was defiant, even rebellious, but within the rules.

By the time he was 12, Greg, though still short and slight of frame, had acquired some strength to go with his technique. He captained St Leonard's against arch rivals Glenelg in the final of the local district shield and hit his first century (outside the backyard, that is). The following week he hit another century against Brighton Primary in the semi-final of the greater schools competition and moved into the grand final against Westbourne Park Primary, grandfather Vic's home territory. Centuries were not common among primary school-boys. Indeed the whole team was lucky to make 100. As Jeanne Chappell packed Greg off for the match she reminded him, 'Just because you've hit two centuries in the past two weeks doesn't mean you don't have to concentrate just as hard this week.' Greg won the toss, batted, and instead of building his innings had a rush of blood, went for a big hit over mid-wicket and was caught at mid-on for one run. The real lessons had begun. Greg remembers those matches a quarter of a century after they unfolded as though reading a scorecard in his hand. He has the remarkable facility of reaching back into his memory and reeling off match statistics as though he were Jack Nicklaus annotating the clubs he used in a championship round he had just played.

In those primary school days Greg followed the fortunes of South Australia at Adelaide Oval. He saw Ray Lindwall bowling one morning and was taken with the way Lindwall, whose run-up was so fluid, left a trail of precise footmarks on the dewy green grass. Greg marvelled at such perfection and the next day gathered his puzzled mates for an early morning game on the nearby baseball oval. There Greg was delighted to leave a trail of Lindwall-like footmarks in the grass.

Baseball ran cricket a close second in Greg's heart. Once Greg was refused permission to attend practice for the State schoolboys baseball team in which he was chosen. Enter the enforcer. Unless you have met Jeanne Chappell it is difficult to describe her presence. Someone once said, 'If you've met Ian, then you'll know Jeanne.' She is a handsome, well-spoken, forthright woman who does not flinch from meeting your eye or confronting the truth. Once, while I was driving with her in Adelaide, she inadvertently cut another motorist off. The driver bimped his horn and though Jeanne checked her stroke, what she began to tell that driver would have done Ian himself proud. She descended upon the St Leonard's headmaster. What the hell was going on? She was furious. 'Anyway I won the argument and they let him go to State baseball practice,' she recalled.

Jeanne protested to me that she scarcely knew all the fielding positions in cricket but having watched cricket on television with her I can aver that she sees events on the field faster and with more depth than any commentator I have ever heard. In her Austin 7 she used to drive to Greg's Friday afternoon matches and sit perched in her tiny match-box car, watching and knitting. Greg would see her arrive and ignore her, thinking to himself, 'Hell, I wish I was like all the other kids,' whose parents never turned up. And then after the match, when the rest of the team would slide off for clandestine cigarettes, Greg would trudge over to the Austin to head home. When Martin arrived after work Jeanne would recount to him Greg's performance that afternoon, how he bowled, how out. Then Martin would come and chat about the match to Greg, or he would chat with Greg first and then match that with the facts from Jeanne. 'In later years I was grateful for their interest but at the time I thought it a handicap,' said Greg.

Occasionally in primary and secondary school, Greg would spot a large black Dodge pull up some distance away and he knew that his grandfather, Vic Richardson, would be standing unobtrusively under a tree watching him. Other times, returning home after a school match Jeanne would say to Greg or Ian, 'Did you see Pop at cricket today? He was there until you got your 50 and then he had to go.' Or the phone would ring at home and Jeanne would say, 'Pop on the phone.' Vic would say, 'Well done today,' and then crash, down would go the receiver. Vic declined to get too close to his grandsons' cricket careers. His line was, 'You've got Lynn Fuller, he's a good coach, listen to what he tells you. I'm only going to disrupt things if I start interfering.' But when Ian grew older Vic gave him the odd piece of advice. The first was a trifle loaded: 'If you can't be a good cricketer at least dress like one.' And then when Ian became Australian vice-captain: 'Just do me a favour. If you ever get to captain Australia, never captain it like a Victorian.' He evidently thought them unadventurous. And finally: 'Don't believe that anything is new in cricket. It's all been tried before. Field placings are like fashion. If you hang onto a suit long enough it will come back into favour.'

Considering his undoubted interest it must have been difficult for Vic to remain in the background and yet it was the greatest gift he could have given his grandsons, the freedom to emerge in their own right, unencumbered by comparisons with himself. Only at the very height of their cricketing careers could either Ian or Greg match the fame showered on Victor York Richardson. He was such a superb athlete, not just a cricketer, that in 1925, when he was 30, the Helms Award elected him to the American Hall of Fame as Australian athlete of the year. He was a heptathlete, but only one of his sports, basketball, was Olympic. He captained South Australia in cricket and football (Australian Rules) and represented the State in baseball. He won two State handicap tennis doubles titles, and played golf off a 9 handicap. He once described a week in his life when he was 21: 'I used to do gymnasium on Monday night, strenuous football practice on Tuesday afternoon, then practise basketball that night, play a league basketball match on Wednesday night, Thursday afternoon football practice again, Friday night gymnasium, Saturday morning play baseball, go in with the baseballers, put on my football togs, and come out with the footballers and then go home, have some tea and do gymnasium that night.' In his spare time he played lacrosse. That was the Chappell boys' athletic inheritance.

But cricket was Vic's first love. He captained the first full Australian tour of South Africa in 1935–36. His side was unbeaten although the Springboks had won their preceding series against England. He made a habit of scoring a century for South Australia against touring England teams and held the record for those matches, 231 made in five hours in 1928 including a six hooked off the world's fastest bowler, Harold Larwood, who five years later became the infamous instrument of bodyline. Vic was also a prodigious fielder. In a Test against England in Sydney on 17 December 1928, Vic, fielding at silly point, stole the show even though Walter Hammond struck an imposing 200 that day. Vic intercepted shot after shot so acrobatically that at day's end the players stood back to applaud him as he left the oval. The next morning the *Sydney Morning Herald* asked in a headline: 'Is Richardson Human?' supported by two further cross-heads, 'Richardson the Demi-God' and 'He Could Field Shrapnel'. In the florid journalism of the era, the *Sydney Morning Herald* reported:

If we were Greeks and permitted long Test matches at Olympia, Richardson would be a demi-God this morning with precedence over satyrs and all other earth Gods. We would send maidens of charming proportions to weave flowers in his hair, annoint him with rose water and glycerine and offer him sacrifices of roast pork and devilled peanuts.

When seeking similarities in his grandsons one would have to say Trevor was Martin's son, in build and looks. Ian inherited his father's build, Jeanne's looks and a swashbuckling charisma that was pure Richardson. Vic batted like Ian, full of hooks and aggression, an exciting sight. Vic boasted that he never had any stories published about his evenings socializing after cricket, 'because none of the Press boys stayed up late enough to see what time I went to bed'. In later years Greg was to envy Ian his capacity to drink and fraternize with his team at the bar.

But in other ways Greg was closest to a Richardson throwback. He was taller by nearly 6 centimetres than Vic's 183 centimetres and therefore a seemingly slimmer 76 kilos than his grandfather. Greg has Vic's blue eyes and, like Vic, has a tilt to his smile which shows more teeth on one side, both underplaying and giving an irony to his laughter. Vic's second wife, Peggy Lester, noticed that whereas Ian gave you the truth, like it or not, Vic used guile. 'He knew how to please and so does Greg,' she said. Greg walked to the wicket like Vic, she said, 'Guardsman's straight back, shoulders square, level gaze.' Ray Robinson, in his inestimable work, *On Top Down Under*, wrote that spinners making Vic play forward could curb him. It would have been interesting to see how Vic handled Greg's great left arm spinning adversary, Derek Underwood. Robinson noted that Vic earned a name for producing his best when nothing less would save his side, a burden Greg forever shouldered for Queensland and Australia in his later career. But most interesting of all Robbie's comments was:

Years of leading South Australian teams which were outgunned by NSW and Victoria sharpened his alertness for ruses to steal wins which his side was unlikely to get if matches proceeded in an orthodox manner.

In the light of a later event Greg might not disclaim such a comparison.

When Vic retired he became a radio sports commentator, joining ex-England captain Arthur Gilligan and the man who became the doyen of Australian commentators, Alan McGilvray, in the ABC's coverage of England's first post-war Tests in Australia. Ray Robinson wrote that between them, Richardson and Gilligan introduced biblical and historical allusions into their colourful broadcasting exchanges. Peggy Lester remembers Professor A. G. Mitchell, a leading authority on Australian speech, describing Vic as 'the prince of broadcasters'. Said Peg, 'He had the best of voices, but Jeanne won't agree with me. She thinks Ian has.' Vic and McGilvray were still calling the cricket in Greg's schooldays. If the prosaic schoolboy listening for Test action found McGilvray occasionally loquacious, he also discovered in later years that McGilvray's descriptions of far flung cricket grounds were so colourful and exact that when Greg played Tests upon them he often felt a sense of déjà vu.

By the summer of 1960–61 the Chappells had a television set and Greg watched the riveting tied Test between Richie Benaud's Australians and Frank Worrell's West Indians in Brisbane. When the show came to Adelaide he watched that match until tea on the last day when the family went home on the reasonable assumption that Ken Mackay and Lindsay Kline could not last out the final session and that defeat was imminent. Greg played cricket in the backyard for an hour, turned on the television and was entranced to find the Australian pair still there. 'I can remember Slasher [Mackay] taking it on the body from Wes Hall,' said Greg. 'It was unbelievable.' Gary Sobers and Rohan Kanhai became Greg's idols from that series and when Sobers returned to play Shield cricket for South Australia Greg attended one of his coaching clinics.

That same year, 1960–61, Greg's last at St Leonard's, he was selected in the South Australian State Schools' under 14 team to play in the Australian interstate carnival in Brisbane. Still small, a year or more younger than most of the team, he was absolutely agog at the prospect. The team travelled by train through Melbourne and Sydney, a fantasy for schoolboys on their first eastern States tour. In Brisbane, among the hundred schoolboy aspirants, Bruce Francis was in the NSW team, Bob Paulsen played for Queensland and Rodney Marsh for Western Australia. Greg remembers only Francis, a large lad who looked adult sized to Greg. Although it is Greg's favourite after-dinner speaking subject, his stories about 'a fat kid from Western Australia who was as wide as he was tall' are apocryphal. He does not remember Rod.

That last year in primary school Greg won a half scholarship to Prince Alfred College, a private Methodist secondary school which Ian had just left. But whereas Ian had won a full scholarship Greg's covered half the fees for five years or full fees for three years. Though the Chappells were not pressed financially the additional fees to send Greg to PAC for five years would have stretched them. They opted for Greg to attend the local Plympton High School for two years and take up his fully paid college scholarship after that. Greg was not unhappy. Having been chosen for the under 14 State schoolboys carnival once in Brisbane he was certain to be chosen again the following year in Perth. If he joined Prince Alfred College, a private school, he would not be eligible.

Unfortunately Plympton became the worst two years of his school life. Plympton High was in only its second year. There were no playing fields, few facilities and for all his skill Greg was not chosen in the school first XI. That was the reserve of the Intermediate and Leaving Certificate boys several years older than him. Worse was to come. He was chosen captain of the State under 14 team for Perth and approached the headmaster for the necessary weeks away from school for the trip. 'Yes,' said that worthy soul. 'You can have the time off, but if you go to Perth you repeat first year next year.' Greg's world collapsed. He detested the idea of repeating and so forewent the trip to Perth upon which his whole presence at Plympton had revolved. From then on he longed for the two years at Plympton to pass so that he could take up his Prince Alfred College scholarship.

Ian was making centuries in the district competition, won a cricket bat in a newspaper contest and was starting to attract the sort of publicity that set Martin off compiling scrapbooks. Greg and Ian were so far apart, five years, that they grew up separately, different groups of friends and therefore with little envy or enmity. Greg had room to admire his brother and Ian was sufficiently clear of Greg not to be threatened. The same applied with Greg and Trevor. But in Greg's second year at Plympton, by which time Ian had been selected for Sheffield Shield, Greg's cricket hiatus had become unbearable. He would have wagged school but an infant's school fear that truants were gaoled made it unpalatable to him. Besides, that was never Greg's way. He always observed the rules.

If anything he intensified his backyard practice in those two years. There survives in the Chappell family album a blurred black and white photograph of a young batsman in the backyard taking block amid the wire mesh gates and fruit trees. The batsman's face is indistinguishable, but the stance is unmistakable. Even as a boy Greg settled his body into geometric planes, legs, back and arms forming an isosceles triangle, producing an air of balance and completeness. You could match that photograph against any taken of Greg on his last day at the Sydney Cricket Ground and they would be identical. Much has been read into that stance by those who do not know Greg, to make assumptions and invent expectations about his personality based on that upright, unwavering, inspiring stance. It has its premise in the folklore of a stiff spine signifying a man of character and Greg certainly required that as he endured his years at Plympton. But his love of cricket did not diminish for one moment. If he had need of conviction it was supplied by the headmaster's immortal words when he effectively destroyed Greg's Perth hopes: 'Cricket won't get you anywhere son.'

3. Prince Alfred College

After Greg's last day at Plympton High School he pedalled his bike the 3 kilometres home swept by relief, rode into his backyard, threw his school bag into the air and yelled, 'Prince Alfred College, here I come!' The source of his anticipation was not likely to be the religious teaching of John Wesley but rather his confidence, gathered from brother Ian, that here was a school that gave cricket its proper priority in the scheme of education. He was not to be disappointed.

Prince Alfred College borders Dequetteville Terrace opposite the eastern expanses of the parkland which encircles Adelaide city. A marble foundation stone beside the college's main steps declares itself laid by His Royal Highness, the Duke of Edinburgh K.G. on the 5th day of November 1867. It does not reveal that this act caused a minor brouhaha in its day because a member of Royalty had lent his presence to a nonconformist (Methodist) church school. The main building, a double tower frontage of ochre-hued sand-and-bluestone, with two floors of bay windows, is flanked by two wings with first floor wrought-iron verandahs, which give the whole an embattled appearance. Brass handles open the deep red main doors over which a pane of glass carries the school emblem and its motto: *Fac fortia et patere* — Do Brave Deeds and Endure.

When Greg arrived in 1963 the college could boast 85 years of annual cricket matches against St Peter's, a Church of England college founded 22 years before Prince Alfred. Until 1954 this intercollegiate match, the 'Intercoll', had such prestige it was played on Adelaide Oval. In 1978 the two schools celebrated their centenary of such intercolls and published a booklet of their history. Prince Alfred could point to Joe Darling who, in the 1884 intercoll hit 252 in six hours with blood running down his bat from hands 'torn on the cord handle'. He played for his State aged only 15 and captained Australia in four series against England, winning three. In 1890 a child prodigy appeared, Clement Hill, aged 13, keeping wicket and batting at number 10 for Princes. As a senior student he made 358 retired, and St Peter's annual magazine lamented how 'slack fielding, miserable catching and feeble bowling' assisted Hill's feat. But the St Peter's performance was ameliorated the following week, when Hill, aged 16, playing for South Australia, struck 155 against the touring England side. Hill, a left hander like Darling, went on to captain Australia. Framed photographs of these past heroes lined the corridors and classrooms of Princes in Greg's day. It took the college three-quarters of a century to claim two more players to captain Australia and when it did the college went one better and produced them as brothers.

Greg's scholarship to Princes was at the invitation of the headmaster, Jack Dunning, who was skilled at organizing such funds, especially for potential cricketers. He carried files on such matters in his head, never on paper, and Greg's memory of him was that he could walk into the college grounds and call any Intermediate, Leaving and Honours student by his Christian name.

Dunning was born in North Auckland, studied mathematics at the

University of Otago and won a Rhodes Scholarship to New College, Oxford in 1924. His arrival at Princes in 1949 was a substantial break with tradition. He was a Kiwi not English, a Presbyterian not Methodist, and his field was science, not the humanities. He was not even an Old Boy. But he made a marvellous headmaster. A tallish man, he had a face full of character as though, like the school, he was hewn from bluestone. His 1960s school photographs depict him with his hair parted almost down the centre in the style fashionable in cricket photographs of the 1930s. Indeed, in 1933 he played Tests for New Zealand against Douglas Jardine's touring Englishmen, *Wisden* recording that he toiled hard as a bowler. A 1984 publication, *The History of Prince Alfred College*, contains a photograph of J. A. Dunning, a member of the New Zealand team that toured England in 1937, shaking hands with King George VI at Lord's. If it were not a blasphemy one could say cricket was a religion to Jack Dunning. He hardly missed a ball bowled in inter-school matches and certainly never a match. His office, overlooking the main oval, was framed by two giant Moreton Bay figs, with smaller ashes circling either side. The Head could sit at his desk and watch the first XI practising at the nets by Dequetteville Terrace.

The school coach was Chester Bennett, a thoughtful, patient, bespectacled man with a hairline receding uniformly across the top of his head. He had captained Princes in 1936 and later played State cricket for both South and Western Australia. Bennett encouraged leadership, established a close relationship with team members, taught technique within the capacity of each boy's build but taught all to strive for perfection.

The school chaplain was the Reverend Kyle Waters, a tall, cheerful, articulate churchman with a liberal mind. His wife had attended school with Jeanne Richardson. They knew Victor York who occasionally gave talks to youth groups attached to Westbourne Park Methodist Church where the Waters worshipped. At Princes Reverend Waters held chapel services, taught every student religion a period per week and led prayers and hymns at morning assembly. He knew his boys came from a fairly secular community, that few would adhere to orthodox Christian principles. So with the Christian dogmatics central to his presentation he would, as he put it, 'play the ball where it lay', leading them to a recognition of something beyond themselves and a sense of perspective of their place in the universe. Kyle Waters also loved cricket.

This trinity, headmaster Dunning, coach Bennett and chaplain Waters, created an environment at Princes which adhered to the famous evocation on cricket by Lord Harris, president of the MCC at the turn of the century:

You would do well to love it, for it is more free from anything sordid, anything dishonourable, than any game in the world. To play it keenly, honourably, generously, self-sacrificingly, is a moral lesson in itself, and the classroom is God's air and sunshine ... protect it from anything that would sully it, so that it may grow in favour with all men.

Greg's arrival at Prince Alfred College was a meeting of true spirits. He was still small and outwardly shy. As he put it, 'If I went into a shop and there were five people in front of me and three more came in I'd be the ninth one served.' But Jeanne saw it more as an inner reserve. There was little doubt that cricket was building the youth from the inside out. Said Jeanne, 'He used to walk through the gate onto the oval as a youngster, straight as anything. He looked as though he was confident in himself.' But Princes was also somewhat of a culture shock to Greg. Since it was on the opposite side of Adelaide to North Glenelg, Greg caught a bus into the city and another out to Dequetteville Terrace each day. He was from the wrong side of town in other ways too. Prince Alfred attracted the sons of upper middle class families who could afford the fees, and the old established families for whom Princes was a tradition. There were sufficient boys from Greg's background to make the Plympton High duckling meld in with the swans, but Greg was arriving midway through his secondary schooling, conscious he was a late starter, an intruder. In a way it was like going in to bat, the fielding team turning to face the newcomer, suspicion, perhaps hostility in their body poses, worse still, disinterest, as though he mattered not. That challenge Greg could face. The two weapons in his armoury were that he was the younger brother of Ian, who had captained the first XI, and that Greg knew he was just as good.

The first to befriend Greg was an equally quiet student, Ashley Woodcock, lean, taller than Greg then, and a match for Greg in his talent for, and madness about, cricket. Woodcock was already at Princes, had begun in Ian's last year. On Wednesday mornings at sports practice the first XI players would help Chester Bennett coach the juniors and Ian was their idol. Woodcock knew the Chappell name, and of the family, and was pleased when he heard the younger brother was joining the school. He and Greg struck up a close friendship, based on cricket, which was to last through school, State and national selection and only waned ten years later when Greg left Adelaide for Queensland.

Two other students who knocked around with Greg were Sandy Rhodes, who became a bank officer, and Reverend Kyle's son, John Waters, who became an Adelaide accountant. Rhodes was in Greg's class. 'There was an economics teacher who didn't have much control over the class,' said Sandy. 'Greg used to push his chair around the classroom and sit at various desks. The teacher would look up to ask Chappell a question and do a double take.' Another to suffer was a 70-year-old English mistress who Greg never tired of baiting, stealing her chalk or duster. 'And he'd eat his lunch during the lesson,' said Sandy. 'Not only did he eat it, but we had radiators on the wall and he used to put his sandwiches behind the radiator grill and toast them. After a while there would be this smell of burning toast wafting around the classroom.' But according to Sandy he meant no great harm, was not aggressive in the slightest, and passed English, energized no doubt by his illegal intake of carbohydrates.

Waters witnessed one of Greg's more unusual feats of derring-do. The school library, now the archives room, was lined with a collection of book cases, shelves, rails and ledges which presented a challenge to agile students to circumnavigate without touching the floor. On the wall was a First World War memorial list of names headed by the inscription, 'These Nobly Striving Nobly Fell'. And so did many students, from the thin ledges as they strove for speed. Greg, thin and light and with those long, prehensile fingers which were to take 122 Test catches, clambered like a spider monkey around the walls in record time. It was entered in the back of a special book now lost to posterity but remembered by all who attended Princes in Greg's time.

Greg's academic insouciance was not always unpunished. It didn't wash, for instance, with his maths and form master whose catchcry was that 'manners maketh the man'. He ordered Greg's entire class to stand for a double period once, 80 minutes, because they were misbehaving as he entered. A more cruel habit he had was to arm himself with a piece of wood, usually the crosspiece from the legs of a chair, and call students who didn't know an answer to stand beside him. There, every few minutes, as regular as a metronome, he would ask the question: Got the answer yet? No? Whack! 'Twice he whacked me the whole lesson,' said Greg, rueful at the memory.

John Waters enjoyed Greg's company because 'he knew he was hopeless, or not so much hopeless as he didn't care. He couldn't motivate himself'. Sandy Rhodes agreed. 'Greg wasn't overbright, but nor was he dumb,' he said. 'He just liked playing up, there was a bit of the larrikin in him.' Yet Chester Bennett, who took Greg for history one year, always found him a co-operative, if not particularly academic, scholar. 'I don't think Greg had a sharp word spoken to him throughout his school career,' said Chester. One may suspect Greg's motives in the cricket coach's class yet Kyle Waters also knew Greg as a gentleman in religious classes. 'I never had to discipline him,' he said. Kyle Waters left a large impression on Greg and while it did not send him to church he came to see the good side of Christianity.

For every first XI player who decides that sport will carry him through life there must be a hundred whose dreams fail. It is a tragic selection process wherein only the blessed or lucky succeed. Greg had that certainty. He had no interest in the complexities of algebra. 'Scientific formulas and all the rest of that jargon didn't mean a bloody thing to me,' he said. The same with languages. 'I didn't see that I was ever going to have use for anything but English,' he remarked. Not once did he finish reading any of his required novels or plays. He passed English consistently only because his teachers would accurately predict examination questions and he would concentrate on the areas they pinpointed. Martin and Jeanne rolled with the reports. 'There was no real pressure for us to be dux of the class,' said Greg. 'As long as we weren't the dunce.' Yet Greg, whether because he suddenly found private school standards higher than those of the State school, or because cricket would not let him concentrate, repeated his first year at Princes, his intermediate certificate, replacing science and higher level mathematics with Arts oriented subjects.

On the cricket field prospects were far brighter. Greg played one match in the under 15s and then moved straight into the first XI. The 1963 school cricket photo shows him eye level to the shoulders of the other players in the back row with him. Yet in six out of ten matches Greg was among the two top scorers for Princes. Admittedly Princes were not strong that year, winning only two matches and drawing a third.

In Greg's first year, 1963, Prince Alfred, St Peter's and Adelaide Boys' High School contested a Saturday afternoon B grade Adelaide club competition. It was a tough round comprising many adult players who, but for business or family commitments, would play A grade from which the State team was selected. They took particular pleasure in grinding into the turf toffee-nosed private school cricketers. Three or four players in each school's first XI were up to the standard, but the rest lacked the maturity. Greg came up against many men who had played either cricket or baseball against his father or Ian. 'The old man must have been a fair competitor in his day,' said Greg. 'He'd obviously had a few run-ins with various blokes.' In an early match against West Torrens Greg recognized one player, 'a grown bloody man', who parked himself at bat pad and began sledging Greg from the moment he walked in. 'He abused me, he made comments about Dad, about Ian, just sheer intimidation,' said Greg. 'I can remember thinking: "What have I done to deserve this, I just walked out here." I thought: "You silly old bastard. If you would just shut up, I'm so nervous I'd probably get out." ' The sledging took Greg's mind off his nerves and gave him reason to concentrate. He thought: 'Well, bugger you. The more you talk, the longer I'll just stay here.'

By the annual intercollege match Greg had been promoted to bat first wicket down, a remarkably responsible position for one so young. He hit an unremarkable 19 and 3 in Princes' victory. Chester Bennett's cricket critique in the *Chronicle*, the school magazine, read; 'G. S. Chappell — A young all-rounder of great promise. His batting is correct and resourceful. He is a slow leg spinner of quality and a fieldsman of ability.' But in the same critique he wrote of Ashley Woodcock: 'An opening bat of great promise. His technique is outstanding — if experience gives him a real thirst for runs he could become a great cricketer.'

In Greg's second year, 1964, the three schools left the B grade competition and returned to playing other colleges. Greg was disappointed. 'It was the start of the age when it was not considered good to compete,' said Greg. 'The élite system was thrown out. The idea was to give everyone a bit of fun, even if it meant the best did not improve.' Greg had become the best. By the end of that year he had topped the batting averages with 45, just pipping Woodcock on 42.2. In the annual intercoll he scored 50 and 59. It was the beginning of an era, spanning 20 years of cricket, when Greg averaged 52.20 in all first class games and 53.86 in Tests.

Chester Bennett's subtle presence was beginning to be felt. He had a store of anecdotes from his playing days with South and Western

Australia and the one that had reference to Greg concerned going on with the job. Bennett, like Greg, was given all the technical knowhow as a schoolboy but not the mental attitude to maintain pressure. 'I always felt that 50 or 60 runs was good enough as a player,' Bennett told me. 'I was reasonably mature before it was pressed home to me that was not enough.' And did he impress this upon Greg? 'Oh, very much so.' Greg took him at his word. He scored two successive centuries in eight days and once, with Woodcock, put on 215 for the first wicket. Thus Bennett was able to remark in the 1965 end-of-year *Chronicle*: 'Woodcock and Chappell must rank as one of the finest opening pairs the school has had in recent years. Both are talented batsmen, sound in defence and very correct in stroke play.'

Ashley and Greg knocked around together, staying at each other's homes, practising with Sandy Rhodes who was also in the first XI, and John Waters who was not, but who was their equal in enthusiasm. Greg would catch the bus into town after school with any one of them, scoot down to Adelaide Oval and be admitted free to watch the last hour or so of a Shield or Test match and then catch another bus home. Ashley used to branch out and go to films but Greg was uninterested. Their relationship revolved around sport. Greg supported West Adelaide football club and Ashley Norwood. They made small bets, followed some matches, but preferred playing to watching. Greg enjoyed football, made the school B football squad but was too light to advance on that.

Part of that changed over the summer of 1964–65. Greg spent the holidays feeling lethargic, a puzzle to the family until they realized he had grown 10 centimetres in seven weeks. 'On my first day back at school nobody recognized me,' Greg joked. To his delight he discovered that his years of fending ordinary length balls off his eyebrows were over. By year's end he had grown 17 centimetres and could look over the line of the ball and drive.

But early habits died hard. Greg's batting attracted the attention of Sir Donald Bradman, then president of the South Australian Cricket Association. After watching Greg one day Bradman suggested to Bennett that Greg cease his practice of taking the ball anything up to 15 centimetres outside the off stump and hitting it wide of mid-on. Greg should learn to play it to the off-side. It was eminently sensible advice, designed to eliminate a habit which Greg must eventually correct if he were to reach greater heights. On the other hand Chester could see the same value in that habit as Lynn Fuller had seen in Greg's shot off his hip into the air over mid-wicket. Chester thought: 'If I stop him doing what's natural...' He felt it was better for Greg to hit it for four past mid-on than merely play it to the off-side. But Sir Donald Bradman's advice was not to be lightly ignored. Chester put the problem to his college and cricket superior, Jack Dunning. The headmaster replied: 'You know the boy better than I do. If you think it better he remains as he is, that's what I'd do.' Dunning was intensely interested in his cricketers, would discuss their performances in the staffroom with Chester and occasionally proffer suggestions. If it concerned Greg then Chester would discuss it first with Martin Chappell. 'I knew there had been other people coaching Greg,' he said, displaying admirable politeness as well as wisdom.

Gary Sobers occasionally visited the school that year, as much as anything because Prince Alfred owned one of the best practice wickets in Adelaide. The West Indian awed the boys. Playing for South Australia he made 1000 runs and took 50 wickets in two consecutive seasons, and in 1963–64 had helped South Australia win the Sheffield Shield. Greg pitched his leg spinners up to the great man who was sufficiently impressed to offer encouragement. Yet to Chester Bennett's disappointment Greg did not persevere with his bowling as with his batting. Bennett always wrote of Greg as an all-rounder, but as he commented, Greg's era, the 1970s, the decade of Thomson and Lillee, was not conducive to spinners.

Bennett also wrote at the end of 1965 that Chappell and Woodcock's running between wickets had been a feature of their partnerships. It was true, but there was more to it than met the eye. Ashley and Greg, captain and vice-captain, dominated the school competition in their last year. Their styles complemented each other, Ashley being stronger on the off-side and Greg the on. Opposition bowlers were constantly having to adjust their line to suit whoever was on strike. Greg's and Ashley's priority was to see the team off to a good start and they did this to such good effect that Greg scored four centuries during the year and Ashley two. Greg admired Ashley's sound technique but thought he erred in valuing the perfect forward defensive shot as much as the scoring stroke. Greg's term for it was 'paralysis by analysis'. Woodcock recalled wryly: 'I will say this. As we started to get towards the end of our school career Greg knew how to count to eight balls.' In other words he noticed Greg began pushing the last ball of an over for a single to keep the strike. Woodcock may have been slightly overshadowed by Greg but he was not overawed. He responded in kind. It produced the occasional run-out and some scintillating speed between wickets by the two friends.

As good a player as was Ashley he conceded that Greg dominated the last match of their school careers, the annual intercoll against St Peter's. This match, played on the main oval in front of Saints, was virtually the only entertainment during the last week of school. In those days it was well nigh compulsory for students, staff, the whole school to watch. Parents drove their cars close to the boundaries and pulled picnic hampers and collapsible chairs out of boots. On rugs and under sun hats they watched the match across the green sward, sparkling in the sunshine, while they in turn were watched by Saints' semi-circle of stone and steepled buildings. At afternoon tea the boys donned blazers, manhandled scones and discussed the state of play. Light clapping greeted good strokes or dismissals and each new batsman was given hushed instructions by his coach: 'Call early, back up well, don't rush.'

It ran for four days, as long as modern Sheffield Shield matches, unfolding lazily before its genteel audience, while in the background Princes boys in their creams and red caps or Saints in their blue and white whorled target caps warmed up, the thock of ball on bat beating sleepily around the ground. It was a scene reminiscent of its old world roots, observing traditions a century old even in Australia. The concept was that the match was hard fought, extending the participants, and then after the game that was the end of it. Yet it was such a contradiction. The annual intercoll put enormous pressure on lanky, pale-faced adolescent cricketers. Staff connected with the school in past years placed great store by it. The school *Chronicle* reported it in detail. Old boys turned up, uncles and grandparents. Some boys would have endured eating meals the evening before with fathers who had starred in the intercoll, taking a few wickets, batting better with every passing year. Many in each team would have aspirations to play under-age State cricket. Much rested on this match. Under this pressure boys who had succeeded all season failed in the sunny glare of the intercoll. Parents would introduce themselves to the coaches, umpires in black trousers and white coats would send the adrenalin rushing with a calculated call: 'Six minutes to go'. Students clambered about the scoreboard and positioned the sightscreen while the opening batsmen twiddled and fiddled with every last piece of their apparel and apparatus.

It was in this tense sporting drama, when youths were expected to metamorphose into men before their parents' adoring eyes — and Jeanne was there — that Greg, ice blooded and deadly serious, chose, as he would so often in his career, to produce simply his best. Woodcock was run out for 19 but Greg drove and cut magnificently to build a patient 107 in 220 minutes before being caught just before tea. It was a classic demonstration of what Chester Bennett called 'the Chappell cocoon' — the ability to withdraw from all the shenanigans that go on around batsmen. In Ian's case it was blatant; he would ward off distractions with aggression. With Greg it manifested itself as an aloofness, a withdrawal from the temporal into the cerebral to concentrate on the matter at hand. In later years it would become a deliberate, controlled entry into a state of semi-hypnosis. At Princes it was still an innate condition, less perfect for being so, but still effective. Sir Donald Bradman would have been interested to know that 78 of those 107 runs were scored on the on-side. Of Greg's six fours, five were through the on-side. Three times he hit off-drives and ran three, lacking the power and technique to reach the fence.

When Saints batted they began well but, 'When Chappell was brought into the attack, things began to happen,' the school *Chronicle* reported. Greg's leg-spinners were a mystery to the average schoolboy cricketer. He began with a maiden, and in the next deceived an opening batsman who was stumped. The same fate befell the other opener in Greg's sixth over, stumped. By the end of Saints' innings Greg had 6–61. In Princes' second innings Greg and Ashley looked for quick runs. They put on 97 before Ashley was out for 49 while Greg went out on 76, caught in the outfield dancing down the wicket and lofting. The result was a draw as time ran out for the match and for Greg's school days.

Behind him came Trevor, destined to become a mammoth school-boy scorer, the most prolific run-getter at Princes since Clem Hill. Ahead was Ian, selected that summer for the fourth and fifth Tests against England. The pace was hot for the middle Chappell. Greg was awarded school colours for meritorious performance in cricket in each of his three years at Princes but these honours, and the triumph of the intercoll, were slightly dampened by the Leaving Certificate results which followed. He failed, receiving three passes, in English, Geography and Art. The Public Examination Board minimum stand-ard was four passes. Ashley Woodcock gained Leaving Honours and went on to university to major in history.

Of course, as Jeanne Chappell said, Greg was not interested in further studies. Yet Jeanne devoted her life to supporting Greg's narrow focus to the exclusion of much else. Kyle Waters remembers her fantastic dedication to watching her sons play, 'hour by hundreds of hours'. Once, a few years later, Ian was playing a Test in Melbourne, Greg a State game at the Adelaide Oval and Trevor a match for Princes at the school oval. Jeanne tried to follow the three of them, speeding between the school and Adelaide Oval and listening to Ian on the car radio until she realized she was enjoying none of them and settled down to just watch Trevor. And so, for better or for worse, the greater spiritual realities of life as encapsulated by a love of music, art or literature or any form of human expression other than that with a bat and a ball, escaped Greg's early appreciation, the price paid for the cricketing great Greg was destined to become. But for his end of year address headmaster Jack Dunning, ex-New Zealand Test cricketer, chose as his theme St Matthew's Parable of the Talents. 'Natural and spiritual gifts are bestowed by God,' rang his words. 'You are a failure if you do not use these gifts... You are a tremendous success if you make the fullest use of them.' He did not need to point from the rostrum. It was his imprimatur upon Chester Bennett's prophetic cricket critique, in April 1966, of G. S. Chappell... 'Possibly the finest all-round schoolboy cricketer in my experience... he could go far in the game.'

31

ARCADY (1966–1970)

4. Shield

Greg's transition from college to South Australian batsman was so
swift he scarcely seemed to pause, not to look back in nostalgia nor
to peer cautiously ahead. He accomplished it in just seven district A
grade matches. Within weeks of playing his last intercoll for Princes
he played in Glenelg's semi-final against Port Adelaide. In that match
Port Adelaide's opening attack was Test man Neil Hawke and future
Test player Eric Freeman. Glenelg were 4–71 when Greg arrived, and
not much more when he departed. His contribution was six, sent
packing lbw by Freeman. Ian, at the other end on 30, felt sorry
watching Greg walk off, and remembers harbouring a feeling of
vendetta against the Port attack. He gave vent to this by hitting a
masterly 120.

It was the first time in sport Ian experienced that fraternal bond.
He was captain-coach of the Glenelg A grade baseball team and once
chose Greg, 16, ahead of other aspirants even though he knew what
the criticism would be. Greg collected three hits and one player
confided to Ian later, 'I take my hat off to you. I didn't think Greg was
good enough.' Well, Ian knew that from a thousand backyard matches.
But this vendetta feeling was new. Then it occurred again. In a baseball
match Ian was catcher and Greg on third base when an opponent slid
into third with his feet up high, cutting Greg on the leg. 'I didn't even
think,' said Ian. 'I just whacked my mask down and glove and took off
up to third base.' A team-mate realized Ian's intention, intercepted
him and settled him down. 'That was the first time I remember
thinking, "Well, underneath it all I do realize he's my brother",' said
Ian. But when Greg hit 67 in the second innings of that cricket semi-
final against Port Adelaide, the older brother syndrome was lifted

from Ian's shoulders. 'I thought, "I don't have to worry about this kid. He can play." I almost knew he was going to succeed.'

That Greg did was due in no small part to Ian being chosen in Bob Simpson's Australian team to tour South Africa in the summer of 1966–67. Ian left a vacancy in the South Australian Shield team upon which Greg set his eyes. In October 1966, a month after turning 18, Greg scored 101 not out, 102 not out and 88 in his first three district matches for Glenelg. His 101 was chanceless and he had the good sense to hit it against East Torrens, led by State captain and selector, Les Favell. When Greg teetered on 99 Favell thought to sort out the temperament of the teenager by crowding every available fieldsman within a metre or so of the crease. Greg, unperturbed, played out a maiden over and reached his century in the next. That was enough for Favell.

Greg's next match was for the State against Victoria on Adelaide Oval. On Thursday, 3 November, the eve of the match, he went to bed with a throat infection and awoke the next morning with a stiff neck. He was all things at once, upset, disappointed, nervous, excited and unsure. At 7 a.m. he had Martin bowl to him in the backyard. At 9.30 a.m. he drove distractedly to the oval, narrowly avoiding an accident en route, changed and with a towel wrapped around his throat aproached Favell. The experienced campaigner proffered no sympathy, permitted no histrionics. 'I don't want to hear any more unless you inform me you are not fit to play,' he said and walked away. In retrospect it was just the first of the many lessons of senior cricket Greg was to learn: to take responsibility for himself and his actions.

Greg sat in a corner and weighed his decision. He was desperate to play but feared not doing himself, his team-mates and his family, justice. He went down for another practice in the nets behind the members' stand. His glands were swollen and sore, restricting his head turn to the bowler. He experimented with opening his entire stance and found he could at least face up. A bit of a problem cutting and pulling, but perhaps Victoria would bat first and give him another day to recover before batting.

He came back and took his place in the team, studiously avoiding Favell. South Australia batted first. Favell, with 90, made his characteristic dashing start but the team slumped to 4–178 as future Test opening bowler Alan Connolly ripped through three wickets for 13 runs. Greg came out, scratched around, was dropped at gully by Les Joslin, a future Test batsman, and decided to hit his way out of the cobwebs. Victorian leg-spinner Roger Rayson threw one up outside Greg's off-stump and, as was his fashion in those days, Greg jumped down the pitch and hit it through mid-wicket to the agonized cries of 'Oh Christ!' from Victorian 'keeper Ray Jordan. Anyone unused to Greg's habit — and they all were — presumed they had the makings of a stumping in such a precipitious act. Jordan let Greg know what he thought of the shot for the rest of the over. By the time Greg was out for 53 he had halted the middle order slide.

A similar script developed in the second innings except by then a stiff neck had been replaced by a stiffened heart and Greg, all poise and skill, hit 62 not out including ten fours. He played straight man to a flourishing Favell century and then took over the lead himself directing his number 10 batsman with such good effect they put on 48 together.

That evening at home Martin Chappell could be well pleased. Ian was in South Africa, Greg launched into Shield cricket. Jeanne had rung her father Vic when Greg left Princes and asked him to keep an eye out for a job. An application arrived and Greg became a clerk for Shell Oil. It was that easy in the days of next to nothing unemployment.

Greg was never a problem to Martin, because of his benign personality and because Greg benefited from Ian's rebelliousness. Ian, as the oldest, fought for every freedom and prerogative that Greg and Trevor later enjoyed. Martin hated his sons going out late the day before a match. If they did not get 12 hours sleep they should not play. It all came to a head at 2 a.m. on the porch outside Greg's room one awful night. In nine hours time Ian was due on the field against New South Wales in one of his early Sheffield Shield matches. Martin had warned Ian on Wednesday that week, 'Tomorrow night's an early night. You're playing Friday.' Ian organized two mates to call in on Thursday evening, reasoning, correctly, that Martin would not stop him going out in their presence.

Ian stole onto the front porch about the same moment his father hit it from bed. 'You'll never make runs while you treat your body like that,' shouted Martin. And so it began, for an hour. Said Greg, 'I didn't learn that I shouldn't go out, but I learned that when I came home I agreed with him and got an hour's more sleep.' The corollary to the story is that Ian, only 19, went out that day and scored 149 against Richie Benaud and Alan Davidson, 'just to prove the old man wrong', as Greg put it.

Greg's indiscretions were far milder. He went out one Saturday night, returned late and went to baseball practice the next morning. When he returned at lunchtime Martin was mowing the lawn. He stopped the motor and enquired: 'How was practice?' Good, said Greg. 'How'd you hit 'em?' Good. Why? 'Oh, I just thought you might have struggled to see them, that's all,' and he started the motor and mowed on.

From an early age Greg mixed with adult cricketers and baseballers who smoked and drank and probably did other things too for all Greg knew. And Greg would not have known. Very occasionally he took a girl to a baseball social or cricket dance, but he was more likely to be out with his mates. Martin, who smoked and drank, told him, 'It's up to you what you do, but if you're going to have a drink I'd like to think you could have a drink with me rather than go behind my back.' Greg respected that, but he was not a big drinker. Nor did he smoke. He did not take to cigarettes and counted himself lucky. Some hazy stories emerge from the past, of Greg leaving a party inebriated and driving his car 200 metres along the footpath for a lark. Schoolmate John Waters tells the story because he was in an equal condition, in his own car, on the road, keeping pace with Greg.

Thus when Greg left for his first eastern States Sheffield Shield tour in the summer of 1967 his sole interest was still cricket. This was the adult fulfilment of the dream he had realized when he railed east with the under 14 schoolboys side. But this time he was going to trade blows with some of the idols of his boyhood — Norm O'Neill, Peter Burge and Peter Philpott. South Australian 'keeper, Barry Jarman, warned Greg his 'ticket' on the Melbourne Express was one dozen bottles or beer. Right you are, and Greg deposited his entrance fee in the carriage. But after his first beer he had to admit he did not really enjoy the taste. Said batsman Alan Shiell, later to become one of Australia's leading cricket writers, 'You'll get used to it.' Greg sat back and watched the older blokes polish off his dozen. He was the only fresher to fall for the trick. Another lesson learned.

In Sydney Norm O'Neill, who had been left out of the team to South Africa despite good form, won the match for New South Wales by himself with a magnificent 160 in the first innings. Greg, who scored 68 not out, was the only other batsman who looked capable of playing the unusually slow turning wicket with confidence, mastering New South Wales spinner John Gleeson who took 5–46. One cricketgoer, discriminating for different reasons, was a 14-year-old Sydney schoolgirl, Elizabeth Donaldson, attending her first match with her father. She saw all these young cricketers sliding under the sight screen. Greg was one of them. She took a fancy to him and wrote to him for his autograph. The South Australian Cricket Association forwarded her letter to Greg when he returned from the tour. Greg sent her a modest photograph of himself and thus began a casual, but consistent correspondence.

Greg's Sydney form augured well for Queensland but he trod on a nail while skylarking on the lawn beside the swimming pool at the team's hotel and by the time he reached Brisbane his heel was swollen and blistered. He withdrew from the match against Queensland Country in Toowoomba and by the morning of the Shield match the swelling had subsided. As often happened, adversity caused Greg to concentrate. On 13 January 1967, in near century heat on the Brisbane Cricket Ground, otherwise known as the 'Gabba for its address in the suburb of Woolloongabba, Greg hit his first Sheffield Shield century. His innings stemmed a crisis for the South Australians who had collapsed to 7–77 before the pace of Test speedster Peter Allan. Greg conquered the searing heat and his throbbing foot but, having struck 10 fours and a huge six over the mid-wicket boundary, he was caught trying to repeat the feat. He marched from the field basking in the glow of 104 historic runs and floated into the dressing-room on that high. There, seated, was captain Favell, who, in the best Australian tradition of debunking to disguise delight, muttered, 'Lucky your name's Chappell. If I'd played a shot like that last one the Press would rip me apart.'

Greg's century, dissected, revealed his on-side penchant had changed little from his Princes century just over a year before. Of 104 in Brisbane he scored 72 on the on-side and 32 on the off (Princes 107:78 and 29). Eight of his 10 fours and the six were to the on-side boundary. He received 10 congratulatory telegrams at the ground that day, from friends, Glenelg captain Murray Sargent, and the most expected which read: CONGRATULATIONS ALL VERY PROUD LOVE DAD MUM TREV AND IAN.

But it was not all triumphs. Greg learned more in the four months of that first year in Shield than he had in all his previous cricket. Two lessons came from tough ex-England spinner, Tony Lock, then captain of Western Australia. Greg was facing medium pacer Ian Brayshaw who had been hailed after a very successful previous year. But he had had a lean season up until then. Thus when Greg, on only 4, attempted to leg glance and gave a feather touch to a ball, those behind the wicket went up in unison for caught behind. But the ball also brushed Greg's hip as it passed and Greg had a feeling that umpire Colin Egar could not have heard his lightest of nicks. 'It was just one of those things,' said Greg. 'I knew he wasn't going to give me out. So I just looked up and stood there and he gave me not out.'

The Western Australians were beside themselves and the guilty and embarrassed batsman decided that he would then play a few shots and if he got out to Brayshaw justice would be done. But at the end of the over Tony Lock, fielding at cover, gave Chappell a stage whispered blast about cheating and how the Western Australians didn't play the game like that. He maintained this barrage until Greg's resolve to get out reversed itself into a determination to stay in. 'I thought, "The longer you abuse me, the longer I'm staying out here." ' Greg batted for another 90 minutes and 20 more runs in one of his more forgettable Shield performances. Yet Lock made Greg think through the dilemma of whether to walk and develop a policy. He would leave it to the umpire. He would not walk, New Zealanders take note. Given out, whether he agreed or no, he would go. Given not out, even if he knew better, he would stay and not throw his wicket away in a spirit of magnanimity. He reasoned the decisions, like linesmen's calls in tennis, would equal out in the end. He could thank Lock for that clarification.

The second lesson occurred at Adelaide Oval, again against Lock's Western Australians. This time Lock had the goods on Greg. Always a swift but deceptively casual runner between wickets, Greg was lifting his bat out of the crease and encroaching up the wicket as Lock delivered the ball. Lock stopped in the middle of his action and motioned with the ball towards the stumps with Greg out of his crease. Greg was on 18 and went on to double his score. Sir Donald Bradman was quoted the next day paying tribute to Lock:

> Tony's was a very sporting gesture ... As an old campaigner he could have taken advantage of a young and inexperienced player. He chose to warn Greg whereas he was quite within his rights to run him out.

Sir Donald recalled seeing the Indian bowler Mankad run out Australian batsman Bill Brown in Sydney during the 1947–48 series using this tactic. It became known as Mankadding but has fallen from contemporary use. Tony Lock, on a television show later, was more sanguine. 'If the scores had been closer at the time I'd have done him,' said Lock.

The following season, 1967–68, Greg's Shield honeymoon ended. His first season had allowed him to develop his individuality, to feel uninhibited by constant comparisons. Then Ian, and the rest of the Australian team, returned from South Africa. Ian, a better player than when he left, cast a long shadow. But the rest of the South Australian team too was a formidable list, including evergreen captain Les Favell, Australian vice-captain Barry Jarman, Greg's college captain Ashley Woodcock, Test candidate Ken Cunningham, the Australian Test speed attack Neil Hawke and Eric Freeman, and spinners Ashley Mallet and Terry Jenner, whose names adorned Australian Test teams in the 1970s.

When Les Favell faced Greg in the nets he was intrigued to discover Greg bowling off-breaks instead of his leg-spin. With Ian back another leg-spinner was one too many. Greg was promoted to bat number four behind Ian and thus began the batting order that would eventually serve Australia for nearly a decade. It also consistently threw together, for the first time, the two brothers in partnerships. For all Ian's fraternal feelings and Greg's sibling admiration, they must have suffered from too many backyard Tests. Newspaper reports were dotted with such comments as:

The Chappell partnership was immediately featured by some shocking running between the wickets in which Greg and Ian both had to scramble after mixups.

But Greg produced sufficient innings to continue his climb. Against Victoria he top-scored with 75. A report in the Adelaide *News* said:

No one could have watched Chappell's innings without recognizing the class which stamps his batting ... He has unerring judgement of length, quick reactions and a general air of cool, collected purpose. This enabled him to cope more than adequately with the good ball and wait for the bad ball which he invariably hit on the on-side.

In that 75 he hit 12 fours, only one of which did not come from an arc between wide mid-on and square leg. It prompted Les Favell to comment: 'I just hope he won't lose sight of the fact that there are two sides of the wicket.' Greg's defence was that the Victorians had directed their attack mainly on that side. Their tactic was to hope that Greg would play his favourite off-the-hip shot which sometimes travelled in the air. The Victorians would not be the last team to suffer from trying to exploit it.

Before the State team began their eastern States tour a sterner hand stepped in to resolve Greg's on-side hitting. Sir Donald Bradman, having failed to convince those worthies, Chester Bennett and Jack Dunning, to curb Greg's on-side habit at Prince Alfred College, took matters into his own hands. Sir Donald was chairman of selectors for the team and he and co-selector Phil Ridings used to visit the South Australian dressing-room just before play each day for a cup of tea. Bradman, always private in preference to prolix, commanded such a presence that few of the young players dared approach him. Greg watched him, noticed that he was not tall, wondered how he had dominated the bowlers as he did but sensed, 'He had something ... he was different.'

This day Greg was signing bats on the autograph table by the dressing-room door when Bradman passed. 'Good morning, Sir Donald,' said Greg, holding a bat for something to do with his hands. Bradman stopped and replied, 'I'd change that grip if I were you.' Greg asked what he would suggest. Bradman advised him to hold it as he used to, with the vee between the thumb and the forefinger of both hands pointing straight down the back of the handle towards where the handle spliced into the blade. 'That's the way I used to hold it and I think that's the best way to hold it to be an all around the wicket player,' he said. 'The grip that you've got now is very good for the on-side, but you'll never be a good off-side player with it.' Greg thanked Sir Donald for his interest. Bradman pressed his point. 'It's going to take you some time. Practise. It will feel uncomfortable because you've been doing it the other way but if you persevere you'll become comfortable.' Sir Donald started to walk away and then turned and said, 'I've given this piece of advice to one other player who used to play for South Australia — he didn't take the advice and he's no longer playing for South Australia.'

Greg grabbed two players from the dressing-room. 'Come on, come and bowl to me.' He batted in the nets for half an hour using the new grip, moving the back of his top hand around from the front of the handle. 'Within 20 minutes I started to feel comfortable and I couldn't have gone back to the other way,' said Greg. 'I used it that day.' With such good effect that Les Favell was able to write soon after, 'He is hitting the ball through the covers with a full swing of the bat and still retains his on-side strokes.' The strokeplay had been born which 16 years later would bring him his twenty-fourth and last Test century and would provoke Richie Benaud to eulogize on television:

> Beautiful stroke. What a marvellous way to bring up 100, with a classic cover drive that we've seen so often over the years from this great player.

On the ensuing eastern States tour Greg roomed with Ashley Woodcock who was on his first tour. Greg, now an old stager on his second, initiated Ashley as he had been himself. On their first night Woodcock was so excited he forgot to write out a breakfast order. Greg filled one in for him and Woodcock awoke in the morning to a tray consisting of bran flakes, prunes, smoked cod and anything else unpalatable Greg could muster from the menu.

After that tour, towards the end of the season, Greg hit his second Shield century, 154 against Western Australia, a year since his first against Queensland. One report said Greg had murdered the attack and then had the temerity to suggest, 'Greg Chappell may still go ahead of older brother Ian in the Australian 17 for England in April.' That was never on, but that Western Australian match produced two matters of significance to Greg.

The first was yet another run-in with his old adversary Tony Lock. Greg was facing the last over before tea from Lock and, there being great competitiveness between the pair by now, Greg interpreted Lock's tardiness in finishing the over as designed to annoy him. Which it did. The sixth ball Greg played at his feet and on an impulse, to save time and demonstrate he knew Lock's game, he kicked the ball back to Lock. Lock swung on his heel and appealed to umpire Max O'Connell, officiating in his first Shield game. Greg's stomach hit the pitch. He knew that under one interpretation he could be given out for interfering with the ball. O'Connell ruled not out. 'Why in hell's name not?' asked Lock. O'Connell did not answer. The over was completed and a relieved Chappell walked from the field, wicket intact. O'Connell's ruling was that the ball was still moving when Greg kicked it. Greg was therefore in his rights to prevent the ball from rolling back onto his stumps. Greg survived on a technicality but cricket, as in the High Court, depends as much upon the law chosen to be interpreted as the interpretation itself and umpire O'Connell had proved himself a liberal judge. Ever after Greg kept his feet to himself.

The second matter had a far greater bearing on Greg's career. At the end of a day's play Greg chatted to John Inverarity about his contract to play county cricket with Somerset in England the coming Australian winter. Greg was keen for county experience and had been negotiating with Leicestershire to spend a year in England qualifying residentially to play county cricket. Glenelg captain Murray Sargent, who had played with Leicestershire, suggested Greg live there for 12 months playing second XI cricket for a summer and endure the winter to qualify for the following summer. The idea did not appeal. Greg would have to miss an Australian summer. One summer could swallow him. But in 1968 the county rules were relaxed to permit immediate registration of one overseas player.

John Inverarity had been signed by Somerset but in March 1968 he was chosen in the Australian team to tour England beginning in April. That evening Greg read the Australian team and amidst the pleasure that Ian had been selected he wondered aloud, 'Dad, Invers' selection will leave Somerset in a hole.' Both Martin and Greg knew that it was late in the season for Somerset to find a replacement. Might be worth contacting them, said Greg. Why not send them a telegram? said Martin. Greg did, including sparse career details and concluding that a letter was following. That was Friday. By Sunday Greg still had not written the letter. 'They won't have heard of me, there's no hope,' he told his father. Nevertheless he had said he would send a letter and should, urged Martin. Cogs turned. A former Somerset club executive who lived in Perth knew John Inverarity and had heard about Greg's 154 against Western Australia. His opinion prompted a phone call to Greg from the Somerset club a week after he posted his letter. The terms were six months' cricket, April to September, air fares paid both ways, accommodation provided and £1000 salary. Was he interested? Was he! It was more than his annual wage as a clerk. 'I was so excited, they could have offered me anything,' said Greg. 'I would have paid to play.' A contract followed, was signed and on 11 April 1968, a week before Easter, Greg flew out of Australia and into a new dimension of his cricket career.

5. Somerset

The feelings of a Glenelg 19-year-old, 188 centimetres tall but nowhere near a man, innocent to the wiles of the world and yet no naif, boarding an Air India flight to become a semi-professional cricketer nearly 20,000 kilometres from home, may be easily conjured. He was an explorer into his own future, an adventurer into his boyhood fantasies. He was too excited to feel brave or sad. To be paid to play cricket was not work, it was bliss. Events had transpired so swiftly that it was all he could do to grasp each passing moment. No time for anxiety. At Adelaide airport Martin was bursting, while Jeanne was betwixt and between. She had been through it all six years earlier when Ian had sailed off for a year in Lancashire League. She remembered that well enough. Ian had caught the train to Perth to embark. 'He just walked onto the train, didn't even turn around and wave goodbye,' she said. And that was it. So she could not be as concerned over Greg. Anyway it would have been wasted on Greg. He could not wait to get there.

The realities of international flights in 1968 soon descended on him. The aircraft was crowded; his long frame grew cramped in the narrow seats; they were delayed in Bombay in frightful heat and humidity; he did not want to risk eating or drinking; there was no room to lie down; he could not sleep sitting up; he wore a jacket and tie because no one told him better. He had the sense not to drink alcohol but after nearly 36 hours he finally fell asleep exhausted over Amsterdam. That gave him an hour's sleep before landing at Heathrow in London. Somerset secretary Richard Robinson, captain Roy Kerslake and players' representative Fred Rumsey, who played an occasional Test for England, welcomed him at the airport and they set out for Somerset.

The trip passed in a dream. There was lunch at a hotel in the regatta town of Henley-on-Thames and Greg's first English half pint, then across the windy plains of Wiltshire and Stonehenge of antiquity to Jane Austen's Bath on the Avon, where they met the Somerset club president, Bunny Longrigg. None of this tourism registered on Greg, by now in a torpor of jet lag. They drove through Somerset, flanked by the Bristol and English Channels down the long chin of England's west country to Torquay, about 300 kilometres from London, where Greg had been invited to stay over Easter with Roy Kerslake's parents. Greg had supper and then excused himself. He had landed at Heathrow at 8 a.m., it was now 9 p.m. He had slept one hour in the past 48. 'I'm sorry, I've got to go to bed,' he said. Coming from an Adelaide summer Torquay felt freezing. He welcomed his winter pyjamas and an electric blanket, the first he had ever seen. It had one heat, hot. He switched on, turned off the light and crashed. At midnight he awoke, soaked to the skin with perspiration from the blanket going full bore. He turned it off, climbed back into bed still clammy and slept for 24 hours. He slept all Good Friday and awoke for dinner that evening. The next day, Saturday, he stood in freezing weather watching the local Torquay soccer team and by that evening the combination of exhaustion, overheating and supercooling had produced the expected result. He was ill for a week with a sore throat and then finally made it to Taunton, headquarters of Somerset cricket club.

Taunton, with a population of 35,000, about the size of a major Australian country town, was the market town for Somerset. On Wednesdays local farmers brought their sheep, cattle, poultry and produce to sell in open stalls in the centre of the town. The markets were right opposite the Crown and Sceptre Hotel, a middling old English pub which became Greg's home for the next six months. It had half a dozen rooms upstairs, a couple of cosy bars downstairs, and a dining room. Though quite old it had ceilings which accommodated Greg's height. On later visits to England Greg struck, literally, 500-year-old hotels which induced in him a wary stoop to avoid their massive, low ceiling-beams.

The hotel was run by a middle-aged couple whose family had grown up and left and they welcomed Greg as an Antipodean son. Breakfast was part of the accommodation and lunch was provided at the Somerset County Cricket Ground 200 metres down the road. Dinner he ate out, often at an Indian restaurant opposite the hotel. It was the perfect arrangement for a young man unwilling to cook, iron and mend for himself. In return for their kindness Greg taught the couple's pet mynah bird a few Aussieisms such as 'G'day', and 'How'rya goin'?' Later the bird learned Greg's jocular morning greeting, 'G'day, why don't you get rooted?' The latter bemused his hosts until Greg explained the dialect, after which it was greeted with much hilarity when it croaked the welcome to others not in the know.

On his first few days Greg walked the quaint town. At a sports store built on a bridge over the River Tone, which runs through the town, he bought his first track suit for pre-season training. At home he had trained in his cricket gear but here in April, early summer averaged only 10°C. The team often played soccer or ran, and, as Greg was to discover, they played so much cricket no one wanted to get their creams dirty unnecessarily. But before he played Greg began to undergo a mild education of manners in the old country. The secretary Richard Robinson and captain Roy Kerslake had met Greg at the airport and shown him every consideration. He referred to them as Dickie and Roy. Then one day in Robinson's office the good secretary remarked to Greg, 'I don't mind you calling me Dickie when we're in private, but when it is in front of the other players or the members, it is Mr Robinson or Mr Secretary. The same goes for the captain. It's captain or Mr Kerslake. Not Roy. Some of the club members have mentioned that they have heard you calling him by his Christian name.' Greg was astounded. What had he struck here? He was only 19, but Kerslake looked only in his late twenties and Robinson in his thirties. Les Favell had been old enough to be Greg's father but he had been Les to Greg.

What Greg had struck was the remnants of the English sporting class system based on gentlemen and players. It is exactly the sort of irrational snobbery which makes Australians gag. It is just one of the hundred reasons that Australian–England Tests for so long carried such intense feeling. The struggle, from Australia's view, was for equality. An international, inherited, sporting class struggle. Greg went to Kerslake and asked for confirmation. He did not want to upset anyone, least of all his captain. 'Don't worry about that,' said Kerslake. 'Roy is my name and that's what you should call me.' That was fine with Greg. He relaxed. He called Kerslake Roy from then on and Robinson he did not call Dickie. He did not call him anything. He was pleasant, waved to him, acknowledged him and greeted him, but he never ever called him by name or title again.

Apart from that hiccup Greg was delighted with the club so that he was easily able to handle another custom he discovered. The English did not invite acquaintances home for a meal. That was reserved for friends. For anyone less it was, 'Let's have a meal in the pub.' Greg only made it to two or three Somerset players' homes. He did not mind. They were not being rude. Instead there were three pubs close to the county ground of which the Crown and Sceptre was one. He preferred it because the hotel had cold lager on tap, an unusual innovation in those pre-Fosters and Fourex invasion days. Not that Greg drank a lot, but the downstairs bar solved any thoughts of social loneliness.

He practised at indoor nets all April with an occasional foray, sun permitting, outdoors, where he found the ball disconcertingly able to beat his bat. His leg-spinners were hardly put to the test, which was just as well because he had trouble gripping the ball in the cold. The first few weeks of the county season were miserable, cold and bleak with an incessant drizzle which he never actually felt but which saturated clothing unnoticed. In these conditions he played his first county match, against one of the giants, Yorkshire, at Taunton.

Still playing then, not as fast as of yore, but still immensely strong and experienced, was Freddie Trueman. Greg had read, heard and knew all about Trueman. Hadn't he had to make do with the man in his team when Ian always took the Australians in the backyard? Trueman walked into the Somerset dressing-room before the match, greeted the players he knew, espied all the new faces including Greg's, and began counting and pointing, 'Mmm, that's 2, 4, 6, 8, 10 — that's 10 scalps for F.S. [Fred Sewards Trueman].' A brazen piece of cricket conmanship, predicting he would scuttle the new bunnies in each innings.

Yorkshire and later England captain, Brian Close, took two successive wickets. Thus Greg, coming in at number five, made his English county début on a hat-trick. It all happened so quickly he was still putting his first pad on when he heard the call. It was mid-afternoon but by Australian standards of light it seemed evening. He avoided the hat-trick and then prepared to face up to the legendary Trueman. Gerald Pawle reported in the *Daily Telegraph*:

> *Somerset were struggling but Chappell stood firm. It took him 20 minutes to get off the mark, but in the fading light he proceeded to play with the most attractive assurance, driving Trueman to the on for four and hooking him to the square leg boundary, and making one superbly timed shot past extra cover off the militant Close.*

Those words disguise the following. The pitch was moist, tailor-made for seam bowling of which Trueman was the master. Trueman's first ball was well up, pitched on leg stump and Greg, scarcely believing his luck, fairly leapt at it to play his favourite on-drive. The ball became the near perfect outswinger, its only flaw being that it swung sufficiently to miss Greg's outside edge and the off stump as well. Greg retrieved his feet, adjusted his dignity, and drew a large breath, promising himself not to make that mistake again. He looked up to see Fred flick his long black hair out of his eyes and pose, legs astride, hands on hips and growl, 'Bludy hellfire!' in his broad Yorkshire accent. To the last two balls of that over Greg made the same error and was relieved to hear the call of 'over'. Reflecting, Greg concluded that if he had been playing well enough he would probably have laid a bat on those outswingers, or more exactly an edge, and have been caught behind. It was not encouraging.

Trueman's next over Greg fended at and missed a few more deliveries before he got a thick edge down to third man for his first county run. As Greg ran past Trueman the veteran addressed him, 'You've more bludy edges than a broken piss-pot, lud!' As nervous as Greg was he could appreciate Fred's wit. It was all that he had expected from the legendary sledger. Another over and Greg did something different. This time he managed an inside edge down to fine leg and Fred reached into his full repertoire, 'I'll bet I know where thee learnt cricket, lud, bludy Edgbaston!' Greg then took an unprecedented step. Peering into the Stygian gloom he appealed against the light. One of the umpires looked incredulous. 'You must be bloody joking, son. It's not Australia, you know. If we don't play in this bloody light here we don't play at all.'

The members' bar at the ground was right behind Trueman's arm and it was so dark the bar lights stood out like a beacon across the ground. 'Right,' said Greg. 'If we're going to play in the dark I want it all dark. So can you get the lights turned off in the members' bar? I can't see the ball.' Not for a moment did Greg believe they would grant his request, but he was sure it would rain harder any minute, so bugger it, he would waste a bit of time. The umpires were taken aback at the 19-year-old Australian's audacity. They conferred, cantered off and had the lights turned off. The members, possibly even those who objected to Greg's impertinence in calling club officials by their Christian names, then drank in the dark.

The match continued and Greg had reached 14 not out when the rain became heavier and they all went off. But not before Trueman had galloped in and bowled a bouncer by which time the pitch was so soggy and slow the ball just sat up and looked at Greg who accordingly dispatched it for four. Trueman glared and uttered the immortal metaphor, 'Like bowlin' fookin' doughnuts on a fookin' shit-heap.' And then, as a Parthian shot, 'Wait till I get you at Scarborough, lud, I'll knock your fookin' head off.' Scarborough was one of Yorkshire's home grounds so Greg walked from the wicket wondering to himself: 'This will be good fun, playing six months of this!' In fact Fred's time was almost past but John Snow was to keep Fred's bargain.

Greg's initiation was not finished yet. After a swift declaration by Yorkshire Greg came in late the next day and hit 30 runs before rain set in properly. Since it was nearly stumps anyway Greg retreated hastily to the Somerset dressing-room, a dingy old pavilion since replaced. It consisted of a one-man bath, for the captain, and a huge communal bath. If you did not make the communal bath first you were in with everybody or worse, in after everybody when the team's grime had settled nicely on the lukewarm surface. In his brief time there Greg had learned the tricks. He dropped his gear and jumped into the bath first. Just as he relaxed the Yorkshire captain, Brian Close, stuck his head around the corner and called, 'Right, lads, going,' and was gone before Greg could speak. Hell! He leapt from the bath and started drying himself swiftly. A second later Somerset opener Roy Virgin appeared urging Greg to hurry. The Yorkies were out in the middle. Greg threw his clothes on still wet, tripping on his jock-strap, pulled boots on without socks and with half-buckled pads made it to the dressing-room doorway which led down a tunnel past the visitors' dressing-room onto the ground. Standing in the doorway were Close, John Hampshire and as many other players as could fit given they were in a state of hilarious collapse from Greg's desperate, dishevelled state. The umpires had already called the match off.

Two matches later Greg began to put together the calibre of innings which would make the English press notice that another Chappell had arrived apart from Ian, who had just landed with Bill Lawry's 1968 Australians. Somerset drove to Gravesend to play Kent led by Colin Cowdrey, yet another name from Greg's backyard scrapbook of memories. On a turning wicket left-arm medium paced Kent spinner, Derek Underwood, took 7–46 to decimate the Somerset innings for 134 runs. Some English writers would later boast Underwood could bowl kryptonite to Greg's Superman. Greg was one of his victims there, stumped Alan Knott, but only after Greg had hit 61, nearly half his team's score. Greg's confrontation with Underwood was characteristic of their battles to come in situations when Greg was running out of partners. He hit nine fours and one six, punching Underwood off his back foot and driving with a free swinging bat. Having witnessed this piece of defiance *The Times* cricket writer, John Woodcock, was moved to write:

He alone took advantage of what few half volleys there were. So far the snares and problems of English cricket had not had time to undermine his play and it is to be hoped that they never do so. Correct in defence and positive in attack...he should serve Somerset well.

Greg was about to serve Somerset even better but first came a match against the touring Australians. Greg had only been in Somerset six weeks and here was brother Ian with his friendly smile. They had both come halfway round the world to play their first match against each other, discounting the odd thousand or so in the backyard that is. But all was not comradely in the match where Ian and Bob Cowper scored a century each, putting on 233 for the second wicket on a complacent Taunton pitch. It was reported that Somerset 'bowled with philan-thropic inaccuracy and fielded with pedestrian fallibility' which begged the question of why acting captain Brian Langford delayed bringing on Chappell to Chappell until the latter was 127. Perhaps they feared a brotherly conspiracy and so it seemed when Greg's second leg-spinner became a full toss. Ian pulled it into deep mid-wicket where Roy Virgin, running in too far, misjudged and dropped it. Greg groaned, Ian grinned and hit a later ball for six in exactly the same direction. In return Greg hit 44, including a six and six fours. At lunch Ian introduced Greg to Jack Fingleton, former Test batsman of the bodyline era and a respected cricket writer. Fingleton, who died in December 1981, became a staunch admirer of Greg.

That night Greg accompanied the Australians to the Rose and Crown Hotel in nearby East Lyng where they played skittles, an old English game from which ten-pin bowling must derive. It was a relaxed evening. Greg stayed in the background, still a novice in that company. But he did not stare at them and imagine himself in their shoes. Somehow Greg had his head down so hard in those creative years that he never quite consciously married the two ideas, the dreams of his boyhood and the actuality of his fast realizing them. There would come such a moment, but not then.

Greg's usefulness to Somerset had doubled when he won the club's single wicket competition the previous week. From the time he had grown 18 centimetres between the ages of 16 and 17, Greg had trouble landing his leg-spinners consistently. In this single wicket champion-ship he did not risk them and resorted to seam bowling to contain his opponents. Somerset coach Bill Andrews and team-mate Ken Palmer encouraged him. The height that had deprived him of leg-spin was made for seam bowling. He practised the art but bowled leg breaks to the Aussies that week. Three days later injuries in the team to play Gloucestershire forced Greg to the mark. He responded with 4-37, including the prized wicket of South African Mike Procter. It was such a tidy display that the local correspondent felt obliged to check with Greg. Had he never bowled seamers before? 'Never,' grinned Greg.

His bowling was never to approach the standards of his batting, or catching, but it made Greg the complete player. Bill Andrews remarked afterwards, 'One day you'll open the bowling for Australia.' Greg laughed it off but eight years later, on 27 December 1976, in the first Test against Pakistan in Adelaide, Greg opened the Australian bowling with Dennis Lillee in Pakistan's second innings. The cause was Jeff Thomson's disastrous shoulder injury while fielding. It happened again, in March 1982, third Test against New Zealand, second innings, in Christchurch. This time it was Lillee who broke down. Chester Bennett would have been proud. He had always wanted Greg to be an all-rounder.

Greg's seam bowling was just another instance of his fortune in selecting Somerset. In one of the major counties he would have been overawed and overlooked. Somerset could use whatever talents he possessed. Small headlines began appearing: 'Chappell Gave Notts Fright With Seamers,' and 'Chappell Finds Success With His Seamers'.

In the ensuing matches Greg travelled through, yet hardly had time to notice, nearly every county in England. They played 16 other counties and played six days a week. Because Somerset is so far west most trips involved heading east towards London to join the major motorways for all points north and south. On one trip they played Yorkshire in Scarborough on the north-eastern coast in a match beginning on Wednesday. Somerset being the lesser side usually spent a lot of time fielding and Yorkshire wrapped the match up late on Friday afternoon. The team then drove to London, through the Friday evening peak hour traffic and reached Hove at midnight. The next morning, Saturday, they played Sussex, lost the toss and fielded. Greg's memory is of hedgerows and motorways and a travelling companion called Bill Alley who talked and talked.

Alley was an expatriate Australian who had lived in England so long he had qualified to play county cricket even when a seven-year residency was required. He had played Sydney club cricket in the 1930s which put his age some 30 years above Greg's. But for all his years away he was still aggressively, insistently Australian. The Somerset team was delighted to shunt Greg between themselves and Alley whose favourite and oft-used epithet offended their senses. There was no team bus. Senior players were given a car allowance and Greg drove with Bill in his Hillman station wagon. Alley would talk non-stop and Greg was happy to listen.

'He never taught me a thing,' said Greg, 'but I learned a hell of a lot from him.' Alley was an excellent seam bowler but Somerset wicketkeeper, Dickie Brooks, fancied himself at taking Alley's medium pacers and used to stand up at the stumps. Bill took this as an insult but would say nothing and proceed to bowl his seamers with computer accuracy. Alley loved bowling maidens. If five balls yielded no score, the sixth was always wide down the leg-side where the batsman could not score. Maiden over. But with Brooks up at the stumps Alley would bowl the sixth ball two yards faster and it would hum past out of Brooks' reach, four byes. 'Now piss off back where you belong, son,' the irascible Alley would call.

'He wasn't the sort of bloke everyone loved but he was a character and I liked him despite the rough edges,' said Greg. 'I could probably relate to him better than the Englishmen could.' Greg also roomed with Alley on trips and although he never made bed before midnight himself, he always beat Alley there. 'He used to drink gin and tonics and he'd be up until two or three in the morning, standing and talking,' said Greg. 'Only twice he beat me. Once I came back very late from London and I'd lost my wallet and had to wake him to borrow the taxi fare. And another time I came in and he used to sleep on his back with the sheet pulled up to his face with his big hooked nose hanging over the edge of it. He just opened one eye and said, "Where've you been son?"' Alley's rough Australian accent had not conceded one tone to the decades of dialects it had been exposed to in England.

At first Alley was protective of Greg and invited him home several times. Alley regretted having never played for Australia when it was quite obvious he was worthy. That season he was one of only four Somerset batsmen to score over 1,000 runs — 1,219 to Greg's 1,163 — and was fifth highest wicket taker — 36 to Greg's 26, although in each case Greg's average was better. To Somerset, Alley was their long-serving, expatriate, problem prodigal. As Greg improved with every game Alley inevitably began to recognize Greg as a contestant for the title of resident Australian but he remained friendly. As it happened that was his last year in county cricket. The next season he became a county umpire.

As the season progressed Greg's social life stagnated. Playing Saturday, Monday and Tuesday one match and then Wednesday, Thursday, Friday somewhere else was death to female friendships. In June in Leicester he braved a local disco, fronted a likely lass and, though no dancer himself, took to the dance floor with her. Just Greg's luck, the next song was 'Yummy, Yummy, Yummy, I've Got Love In My Tummy' by the 1910 Fruit Gum Company. Worse, his partner crystallized into a disco queen possessed of all the suggestive actions appropriate to the title of that song. It was all too much for a clean living Aussie lad. Apart from such encounters he maintained his occasional correspondence with Elizabeth Donaldson in Sydney who was cleverly avoiding any admission which might reveal her schoolgirl age. Not that Greg was much of a writer. He preferred to ring home every fortnight than write a letter. He occasionally dashed off a postcard, 20 words, love Greg. He was accused at school of reducing essays to a précis so in a few minutes on the phone he would check in, still alive, how's everybody?

The big difference between Australian and English cricket he noticed was the lack of fraternization between teams off the field. Greg had found in Sheffield Shield cricket that the custom was for the batting side to visit the fielding side's dressing-room where the day's competitiveness could be talked about and forgotten. Not everyone pursued it, but enough did. In county cricket on the last day the travelling team had to hit the motorways for the next match. But even during the match it did not occur. Greg did not know his opponents any better at the end of three days' play than at the start. Until Warwickshire. The match was sponsored by Harvey's Bristol Creme Sherry and at the end of the first day both teams were invited to a cocktail party in the players' lunch room. After speeches most headed off for home or the usual pub meal. Greg, unattached, was one of five players who remained, along with John Jameson, Rohan Kanhai and Dennis Amiss from Warwickshire.

Two cases of creme sherry later the five players had broken the ice sufficiently to encourage them to adjourn to a nearby hotel. Greg drank four glasses of alcoholic apple cider on top of the sherry and sitting on a stool in the warm bar talking to his, by now, great friends Rohan and Dennis, he was as good as gold. But the toilet was a 50 metre walk across the carpark and in that distance the comparatively freezing cold precipitated the alcohol in Greg's blood. His head spun, he was ill. He wisely decided he had talked enough cricket and headed for home, the Crown and Sceptre. He bounced along the street walls until a car beeped beside him — Mike Barnwell, a Somerset team-mate. If Greg was heading home he was going in the wrong direction. Did he want a lift? At the hotel the front door was shut and double locked. Greg had never been this late before, never unlocked that double lock and never in this condition. A police car cruised up and shone a light on him. 'I live here,' explained Greg and then, 'Thank you very much constable,' when the bobby unlocked the door for him. Once inside he could not double lock it again, latched it and staggered upstairs to his room, threw his clothes off and carked it. What the tea lady discovered when she arrived at 7 o'clock the next morning, with silver teapot and pottery milk jug, remains in the annals of her eternal gossip but Greg was not fond of apple cider for months afterwards.

Greg's county career continued apace, but he was not heeding Chester Bennett's Prince Alfred advice that anything less than a century was not enough. Against Nottinghamshire he faced his boyhood hero, Gary Sobers, when Somerset were once more facing a two-day defeat. The occasion loudly demanded a long, dedicated innings, but Greg chose to prove his fighting spirit by the bold, brief disastrous route. He scored a rousing 51 in 90 minutes before being caught trying to hit the great West Indian out of sight over mid-on. Next day he made amends, taking 4–20 with his seamers.

Each match brought new famous names for Greg to engage, none more so than against Middlesex, including future England captain, Mike Brearley, and Test players Fred Titmus and Peter Parfitt. Titmus was rated one of the best off-spinners in the world then and he caught Somerset on a slow turning wicket at Weston-super-Mare, 30 kilometres from Bristol. Somerset lost both their openers for just two runs. Greg announced his intentions with three tremendous sixes which promptly retired the seam attack in favour of Parfitt and Titmus. Greg had not played much first class off-spin. Australian wickets rarely favoured the genre. Eric Hill reported in the Bristol newspaper, the *Western Daily Press*,

> *Titmus and Parfitt at times looked quite amused as the young Australian smoothed, steered, hammered, drove, cut and hooked them out of sight with a tremendous selection of strokes. It was a fantastic effort and when at last he mis-hooked Parfitt straight up*

in the air all but the 11 Middlesex men must have prayed that Murray would drop it. He did not.

Only two other batsmen reached double figures for Somerset but Greg hit 148 in 180 minutes, his first county century. Minutes after walking from the field, captain Kerslake awarded him a county cap for meritorious achievement, an honour many county players achieve only after years of playing. Greg was just nine days from his twentieth birthday.

His growing reputation preceded him to one of the last matches of the season, against Sussex at Hove, featuring such luminaries as Ted Dexter, Tony Greig and John Snow, the England fast bowler who would wreck Bill Lawry's Australians in Australia in 1970–71. Ted Dexter wrote in his book, *Bradman to Boycott*:

> *Now it was just this kind of budding young cricketer [Greg] whom the stormy John Snow would usually make it his business to teach a short, sharp salutary lesson.*

If Snow needed any incentive it came before the match when several of the Somerset players innocently described Greg's Middlesex century to Snow and said, 'You want to watch this bloke, he can hook.'

Dexter could have pre-empted events. Snow was by far the fastest English bowler Greg had faced all season. In one over he top-edged a Snow delivery behind square leg and Dexter, at mid-wicket, made ground but dropped the catch. 'I should have been out then,' said Greg. Instead the next over Snow bowled a quick, straight, angled bouncer and on a damp pitch Greg hooked through the ball early, timing his face perfectly. The ball cannoned into his right eye, splitting his face above and below the socket. He staggered away from the wicket clutching his bleeding eye and tottered into the arms of Tony Greig, at gully, who lowered him to the ground. They unbuckled his pads and his batting partner, Roy Virgin, pushed his chubby face close to Greg's. 'You all right?' he asked. 'Yeah,' Greg groaned. 'The next bloke that says I can hook can get rooted!' Carried off, first aid room, ee-aww in the ambulance and stitches in hospital, eight above and seven under the eye. Greg stood up to leave, his legs buckled and he was kept overnight for observation. That evening his Somerset team-mates visited and left and then John Snow appeared bedside. 'Sorry about that,' he said with a small smile, but Greg absolved him. 'It wasn't your fault. That's the chance you take.' They chatted for 10 minutes and Greg found him quietly spoken, intelligent, a nice bloke. But obviously the clergyman's son and poet was a different man on the field.

That injury sidelined Greg for two matches and instead of following the Somerset camp back to Taunton Greg arranged to meet them for the last match at Essex. He booked into a private hotel in London. It was only his second free visit to that great city. He knew about, but avoided, Kangaroo Valley, haunt for working-holidaying Australians in Earls Court. He was not interested in Buckingham Palace, or West End theatres. He was there to see the Australians play their final Test at The Oval. He saw Bill Lawry walk out with Australia in trouble and sensed immediately that he would hit a century. And so Bill did but Derek Underwood cleaned up the Australians on a wet pitch and won England the series.

Greg saw Ian again, at the Waldorf in the Strand where the Australians traditionally stay and relaxed with John Inverarity and Ashley Mallett before heading off to Chelmsford to play Essex. In his final innings, his first since his eye injury, he came out to bat once more in descending gloom. West Indian fast bowler Keith Boyce tore in and second ball let go an enormous beamer which Greg picked up only at the very last instant, throwing his bat in front of his face to ward it off. If the umpires could have peered closely enough they would have seen Greg turn ashen but instead they called stumps. And so Greg concluded an extraordinary season of experience as he began, walking off in the gloom, but undoubtedly aware that in only a short space he had begun to fulfil a great promise.

Before heading home Greg, Ashley Mallett and John Inverarity accepted an invitation from Frank Russell, of the London Cricketers' Club, to play against the British Army team in Germany. After two days' cricket Greg and Inverarity embarked on a lightning eight-day tour of Europe in a luxurious Mercedes they hired. They slept in the car, were caught in a storm, stripped off and dried their clothes from the Mercedes windows while careering down the Rhine Valley motorways stark naked.

Greg had good reason to be carefree. From the British Army headquarters in Mönchengladback, 24 kilometres from Dusseldorf, he had rung home. That month, September 1968, the Australian Government held a ballot for national service call-up. Greg had registered before he left Australia and, like thousands of other young Australians, had counted down the days anxiously. Greg knew little about the army and less about the Vietnam war in which Australia had become hopelessly enmeshed. He hated the idea of his destiny being decided by so random a method as a lottery. If his marble dropped he would stay in Somerset; they could stick the army. He rang his father. 'You missed out,' said Martin. At last Greg came home.

6. Judy

In the Australian summer after Somerset Greg displayed his first curiosity in anything not surrounded by nets and requiring a protective box. His pen friend Elizabeth Donaldson in Sydney had let slip that her older sister, Judith, was Miss Roselands, 1968. Greg, having divined Elizabeth's relatively tender years, was intrigued by Miss Roselands. Next time he wrote he offered Elizabeth and her family tickets to the Sydney Cricket Ground when South Australia played New South Wales. Elizabeth's father collected the tickets from Greg at the Travelodge in Bondi. That evening the Donaldsons drove Greg and Ashley Woodcock to the Bulli Pass to see the fairyland of lights of the south coast stretching beneath them. In the car was Judy Donaldson, 19, green eyes, long blonde hair, *retroussé* nose and a pleasant contralto voice which immediately put that rather introverted pair, Chappell and Woodcock, at ease. Judy found Greg shy, somewhat handsome. To Greg, Judy was personable and obviously beautiful. But the pair kept their glances to themselves, each respecting that Greg and Elizabeth, who was with them, had been writing.

Greg marked that New South Wales match with a century and though it would be nice to say it was for Judy, in fact it was for the Australian selectors about to choose 15 players to tour India and South Africa later that year. Greg lost his synchronization at first on the altered bounce and pace of Australian wickets after Somerset. Added to that he felt constantly listless, the legacy of glandular fever he had contracted towards the end of his Somerset season. Late one evening, after a welcoming home party at Leak Avenue, Jeanne Chappell had discovered Greg sitting with an icy bottle of beer clamped between his knees. 'My feet are hot,' explained Greg. That night he rose to put his head under a tap. A local doctor diagnosed a mild fever from a stomach upset, possibly contracted on his way home. But that week Greg had a medical checkup for a new job with AMP Insurance and the medico found an enlarged spleen. A blood test revealed the disease. Somerset had been his first occasion away from home. No Martin watching his hours, Jeanne his meals and health. Fascinating cricket conversations wheeled into the small hours of the morning in cosy English bars. And then there was cricket, driving and more cricket.

The cost of this mild hedonism should have been Greg's standing down for a month or so at home. He did not and the disease's insidious weariness sapped him for weeks. But home living slowly repaired him and he had gradually compiled an undeniable *curriculum vitae* for the Australian selectors, chaired by Sir Donald Bradman. Greg was initially overshadowed by brother Ian who put up sensational scores in the first four Tests against the West Indies, averaging 89.5 and eventually being named Australian cricketer of the year. But by season's end Greg had accrued 707 runs at an average of 50.5 to finish seventh in the Australian batting averages.

His name was being mooted for possible blooding against the West Indies in the fourth and fifth Tests and, failing this, he needed only to score well in the final Shield match against New South Wales to join Ian for India and South Africa. He produced 102 and 51 not out to help secure the Shield for South Australia and was rewarded with the headline: 'G. Chappell Grip on Tour Place'. It seemed a foregone conclusion. The tourists would be the 12 who played the West Indies, plus Greg and two others. But as the South Australian team waited at Sydney airport to fly home they heard news which took the cheer from their Shield celebrations. Greg missed out. Stunned players gathered in groups. New South Wales spinner, John Gleeson, who was chosen, looked surprised as he waited for his flight to his home in Tamworth, northern New South Wales. Greg had been as severe on him as on any other bowler during his two winning innings in the match just completed.

The next day, 4 March 1969, the South Australian newspapers all but ran the news in black borders. 'Greg Chappell Shocker' said the *News* street poster. Keith Butler wrote in the Adelaide *Advertiser*:

A Victorian birth certificate is obviously a gilt-edged invitation card to Australian cricket selection. Victoria has six players in the team... South Australia, the champions, have three.

Butler, excusing himself if he sounded parochial, then ran brief comments from three other major Australian dailies. The *Sydney Morning Herald*: 'Irvine fortunate... Chappell dreadfully unlucky';

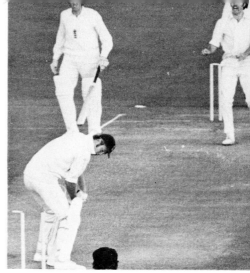

Left: Greg Chappell and the former Judy Donaldson sign the registry after their wedding at Bexley Methodist Church, 10 November 1971
Above: Greg clean bowls Tony Greig, second innings, first Test at Manchester, 1972.
Below: Greg catches Basil d'Oliveira at The Oval, 1972. Bowler is Ashley Mallett, wicketkeeper Rodney Marsh. Australia's win there tied the series

Top left: Greg employs his backhand
sweep to hit a four through slips
during his 181 against Essex on the
1972 UK tour. West Indian crowds
loved this unorthodox shot, but so
did bowlers because it occasionally
got him out

Top right and centre: A famous first
Test as captain. Greg hooks Michael
Holding for four during his first
innings century against the West
Indies at the Gabba, 1975–76.
Lance Gibbs congratulates Greg on
his second innings century in the
same match. In his first Test as
captain Greg made a century in each
innings, a unique feat in cricket

Right: With ABC general manager,
Talbot Duckmanton, after Greg was
chosen Sportsman of the Year, 1976

Left & below: The Battle against Underwood. The Jubilee Test at Lord's, UK tour, 1977. Greg square cuts Derek Underwood and Tony Greig does a jig watched by Mike Brearley and 'keeper Alan Knott. Underwood finally bowls Greg for 112 in the second Test at Manchester on the same tour. On the right surface Underwood was one of the few bowlers who could contain Greg

Top left: Mike Brearley applauds Greg's century at the MCG, second Test, 1979–80. Greg respected Brearley as a captain more than as a batsman

Top right: Greg and Judy after he was awarded an MBE in 1979 for his 'outstanding cricket ability and gentlemanly approach to the sport'

TWO CRISIS YEARS

Above: 'How are you at bowling your underarms?' Greg's memorable question to brother Trevor at the MCG, 1 February 1981

Centre right; The underarm. Brian McKechnie blocked it and threw his bat in the air, thinking, 'Oh God, this is not cricket, you know'

Right: Greg, grim-faced, leaves for the SCG on 3 February, for his first public appearance since the underarm. He is carrying the first of what became a flood of telegrams supporting him

the *Age*: 'Selectors rocked cricket...'; the *Australian*: 'Chappell...a shock omission'. Robert Gray, Sydney cricket writer, said:

> *I don't know what Greg Chappell has to do. He is an infinitely better player than Jock Irvine... His omission is one of the biggest bombshells our cricket selectors have dropped in a decade.*

Jock Irvine was the quite promising Western Australian batsman whose only mistake was to be chosen ahead of Greg. He had averaged 52 runs against Greg's 50.5 but his experience was on the fast, true WACA ground in Perth whereas the Australians would face spin in India and seam in South Africa. Greg had a second string in his bowling and he was recognized already as one of Australia's finest fieldsmen. It is no disrespect to Irvine to say that Australians perceived in Greg a potential champion which they did not see in Jock.

Greg was bitterly disappointed but managed the right words. 'There's plenty of time for me...better players have missed out over the years.' It was not as innocent a remark as it sounded. Martin Chappell confirmed the allusion. 'We didn't bank on Greg's inclusion because it had happened before with Ian.' Ian was overlooked for the Australian team to tour the West Indies in 1965, coincidentally after he too had scored a century against New South Wales.

Soon afterwards Sir Donald Bradman, while making bonus presentations to South Australia's Shield cricketers, gave some inkling of the rationale behind Greg's omission. He told Martin, accepting an award on Greg's behalf.

> *The Australian selectors have come in for a deal of criticism on Greg's omission from the team to tour overseas later this year. As a selector I can't comment. But maybe next summer when this lad is making centuries here in Australia, some kind writer might write and say how much better it is than carrying out drinks amid riots in Bombay.*

Subsequently Greg was grateful he did not go to India but at the time he was intensely disappointed and it was not helped by a faint but lingering doubt that other factors may have contributed to his omission. That doubt came from his grandfather Vic Richardson. Although the doubts were caused by tensions which occurred half a century ago, it is necessary to air the past in order to understand the present.

In February 1934, Donald Bradman moved to South Australia to take up a position with a stockbroking firm. He went to England as vice-captain of the 1934 Australian team, captained by Bill Woodfull, who was making his final tour before retiring. It was clear that Bradman was captain elect. It was likely also, but not certain, that he would have been groomed for this position by being awarded the South Australian captaincy for the 1934–35 Australian summer. However, Bradman fell ill in London in September 1934, at the end of the Australian tour, and stayed in London until April 1935, missing the whole of the Australian summer.

Vic Richardson did not make that 1934 England tour. He had been captain of South Australia since 1921, a record period, and remained captain during the summer of 1934–35 while Bradman was convalescing in London. The Australian team to tour South Africa was selected in the winter of 1935 and the team left the following October. Richardson was chosen as captain and he led the Australians to a much acclaimed series victory over the Springboks.

During that summer, while Richardson was away, Bradman captained South Australia to win the Sheffield Shield, and at the start of the following season, 1935–36, he was retained as captain. He missed the first State match through a family bereavement and then assumed the reins. Richardson played only a few matches under Bradman before retiring from State cricket. Richardson was extremely hurt by his removal from the South Australian captaincy. He felt it had been accomplished behind his back while he was on national duty, that he had given a lot to South Australian cricket and deserved better. He was not without support among senior players. 'As a matter of fact some of them thought it stank,' recalled Peg Lester, Vic's second wife. Richardson did not blame Bradman. His sights were set on various forceful figures behind the South Australian Cricket Association. But it was inevitable that Bradman became associated with the episode in his mind and he confided his grievance to Peg Lester some time after they were married. That feeling, if not the chapter and verse of the episode, filtered through the Richardson–Chappell family and emerged refined as an unspecific uneasiness about Bradman.

Bradman's version of these events, the skeleton of which he once told Ian Chappell, is that before the South African tour, Bradman, advised by his doctors not to undertake a strenuous tour, consulted a member of the Australian selection committee. This selector confided to Bradman that, if available, he would be chosen and made captain.

The selector also made it clear that Richardson's batting would not earn him a berth. Further probing revealed that if Bradman was unavailable Richardson would be selected as captain because he was by far the most suitable alternative leader. Timing thus was of the essence. If Bradman did not withdraw, he and a vice-captain would be named. If Bradman subsequently withdrew, it would then be very difficult for the selectors to call Richardson in as captain when he was not even in the original selection. Bradman withdrew and Richardson's captaincy became history.

These events are reproduced to clarify whether Bradman himself seemed of a mind to play any Machiavellian role in Vic's overthrow from the South Australian captaincy. It would appear that the State selectors gave scant respect to Vic's length of service for the State. He was a phenomenal sportsman even at 42 when he was replaced by Bradman. With hindsight one wonders why they did not give Vic the option of stepping down with dignity, rather than cause his ignominious fall from successful Australian captain one moment to mere State player the next. But cricket officialdom has never been known for its sensitiveness or even awareness, and they would pay for it dearly when a commercial revolution overthrew their monopoly half a century later.

There is one more element. In private life, and socially, Vic and Bradman never enjoyed any great affinity. They toured England together in 1930 but Bradman, as a teetotaller, was not one of Richardson's friends at the bar. There was no apparent animosity between them. When Vic published his life story in 1964 he autographed a copy and gave it to Bradman who accepted it with grace. Sir Donald, as president of the South Australian Cricket Association, issued the invitations to the opening of the Victor Richardson Gates at Adelaide Oval in 1967. In public each was unstinting in their praise for the other. Two years before he died Vic told a television interviewer, 'Bradman's record speaks for itself, the greatest run-getter and the greatest exponent of batting that you could possible think of. I don't think we'll see the like of him again.' But privately he would say, 'He had the best figures but I'd rather watch McCabe any day.' In that same programme Bradman named Vic as one of the four greatest fieldsmen he had ever seen, and probably the best of all at silly point. What he did not say, but has noted privately, is that on Vic's triumphant South African tour he averaged only 16.8 runs per Test innings and finished tenth on the Australian Test averages.

Too much could be made of what may simply have been disparate personalities but for the friction having been discovered by Vic's grandsons. One day Ian attended a reception for the touring New Zealand team at his old Prince Alfred headmaster Jack Dunning's home in Adelaide. Ian saw Dunning walking out to say goodnight with Vic, Alan McGilvray and Bradman. Ian hastened behind to say goodnight to Vic before he left but heard Vic turn the conversation to offer a gratuitous slight to Bradman. Ian stopped in his tracks and decided against saying goodnight.

Thus Ian became alerted to the friction. Greg, as he became older and interested, occasionally drew Vic out to talk about Bradman. One of Vic's favourite sayings was, 'If you can't say something nice about someone you shouldn't say anything at all.' Vic would invariably praise Bradman as a player to Greg but proved elusive when pressed for more. Thus Greg too, by that default and from other comments he occasionally heard in the family, became alerted. I have no doubt that Bradman could comment at length on these events but with Richardson deceased it is not presented to promote debate. It is to show that Vic's slight antipathy to Bradman caused his grandsons to watch Bradman and his influence carefully. Subsequently Greg was glad not to have gone to India, but that did not mean he should not have gone.

In April 1969, Greg flew off for his second season with Somerset. Whether because of his tour selection setback or because he had now played cricket non-stop for 12 months, cricket yielded very slightly in his interest. He actually took a holiday. He flew to South Africa to board the P & O liner *Oronsay* from Capetown to Southampton. Boarding the liner he ran into Graeme McKenzie on the gangplank. McKenzie was returning to England to play for Leicestershire before the India–South Africa tour. He invited Greg to join him for the day visiting the vineyards at Stellenbosch, near Capetown, where Springbok Test player, Eddie Barlow, worked. McKenzie had been on board the ship since Perth, knew all the young passengers and within half an hour Greg knew them too. For two weeks he relaxed, visited the casbah in Casablanca, a bullfight in Lisbon, played deck quoits, deck tennis, but never deck cricket.

The second Somerset season Greg was older, sought more privacy and was not quite as hellbent on social debilitation as in 1968. Somerset wicketkeeper, Charles Carter, knew a family in a small village, Bishop's Lydeard, eight kilometres out of Taunton. On their farm the family rented three cottages named after flowers, Honeysuckle, Rose and Lavender. Greg and Carter shared Honeysuckle, two storeys, two bedrooms and bathroom upstairs, and kitchen, dining and lounge down. The cottages backed onto the farm and one morning as Greg was washing up he gazed as cows grazed the new meadow right up to his kitchen window. Somerset county is thought to have taken its name from 'the summerliness of the air' and just then on the radio came the pop song 'There's Something in the Air' by Thunderclap Newman. If Greg hears it now it transports him to that somnolent moment. Cottage companion Carter had a London girlfriend who occasionally visited weekends and Greg invited one or two Taunton girls he knew for a dinner party. Other times Carter went to London and Greg, assured that the cottage was too far from Taunton for passersby to drop in, rested. He read, watched television or went for leisurely drives in his car through the back lanes of Somerset's rural verdure, kilometre upon kilometre of rich meadow land.

Under this less taxing regime Greg's cricket prospered. He scored the season's first century in the John Player one-day league, racing to 100 in 88 minutes to defeat Surrey almost singlehanded. Of that one-day century it was reported:

> This tall lean Australian was soon driving the ball with a wristy flourish and quite destructive power to most points of an arc between cover and mid-on.

The next day, a county match against Surrey, he was applauded all the way to the wicket for his previous day's performance. Surrey's Test medium pacer, Geoff Arnold, bowled him for a duck four balls later. Greg had developed his off-side play, assisted by every Shield and county bowler who plugged away outside his off stump to restrict his scoring.

Another score of 76 for Somerset against the touring West Indians had Gerald Pawle of the *Daily Telegraph* making the comparison:

> Anything short was punished with a merciless severity which reminded one of Bradman in his heyday.

Another writer concluded:

> He is tall, elegant and classical... You might imagine Chappell to have been a member of Maclaren's Harrow side until you hear him call for a run.

However Greg saved his best for his twenty-first birthday. Somerset organized a cocktail party for him at Weston-super-Mare, scene of his first county century the previous season. The day before, 6 August, Greg took Worcestershire apart. In three and a half hours of precise hitting he reached 144 including 21 boundaries. Alan Shiell in the *News* office in Adelaide read it on the cable service and rang Martin Chappell at home. He and Jeanne had already sent a present, now they would add a cable. 'We'll be holding a party for him when he arrives home next month,' he said.

One sees Greg at this stage, frame hardening into adulthood, slim and sideburned, dark eyebrows prominent on a narrow face, pictured with the mayor of Weston-super-Mare and the Somerset club president, an Australian hardwood standing loftily between two soft English ashes. With Bill Alley retired to umpire, Greg's medium pace seamers were in more demand than they had been the previous season. He took 45 wickets, twice the next best season figures of his career either in England or Australia. Included in those was a best ever performance of 7–40 against Yorkshire at Leeds, two weeks after his twenty-first birthday. 'I enjoyed that,' he said, against the team which had given him such a hot welcome to county cricket the previous season.

Despite those particular triumphs 18 months of continuous play had sated Greg's appetite for cricket. In his first year he had felt a vague unease about his obsession. He had rung Martin and asked him to look out for any job with more future than a clerk. His father had come up with selling insurance for AMP and they signed Greg on, enlarged spleen, glandular fever and all. Now, back in Somerset, he found his county incentive waning. Six and seven day a week cricket was teaching him bad habits. He began thinking 'Oh well, if I don't get runs today, I'll get another hit tomorrow, or the next day.' It was eroding the foundations of a substantial reason for his success, his mental discipline.

But it was more than that. One day, gazing around the dank dressing-room as yet another day was rained out, it struck him. 'I saw these blokes, late thirties or 40 and they had little else in life other than cricket,' he said. 'I thought, "I don't want to be sitting here in 20 years' time, wondering what the hell I'm going to do." ' The thought almost threatened him. They were all nice blokes, good company, good friends, but cricket had become a soporific surrogate for employment that might stretch their intellects. Greg counted their talents. Some went on the dole in winter, another carried parcels for British Rail, yet another worked part-time in a skin and leather factory. There were exceptions. Captain Roy Kerslake was a solicitor, opener Roy Virgin worked for the county council and was learning local administration. They had education, qualifications and careers which enabled them to indulge their sport. What did Greg have? An excellent on-side and improving off-side technique, a safe pair of hands and a tidy bowling arm. 'I thought, "Jeez, when you boil it all down, cricket's good fun but it's not the way you want to live your life." ' And thus cricket, the holy grail, tumbled harmlessly and irrevocably from its pedestal and fell at Greg's feet.

He considered a correspondence course in business studies. He had the hours, sitting in dressing-rooms, playing cards or reading while the rain tumbled down on the cricketing workshop floor. But the hours were broken and sporadic, not conducive to study and he had never been a star scholar anyway. He could end up messing up both, study and cricket. Then for the very first time he fine-tuned the two cricketing images he had long held in his mind, his boyhood dreams and his rapidly improving cricketing self. 'What I'd really like to do is to represent Australia,' he thought. 'If I do that I'm going to get enough cricket over the next 10 years to satisfy all my cricket needs.' Instead of cricket being an end it became a means of creating, along with work and a family, an enjoyable life. Those other aspects were beginning to gel too.

During the season he had continued writing to Elizabeth Donaldson in Sydney but it was the memory of sister Judith that stirred him. He considered writing to Mrs Donaldson to explain his plight. He did not have the heart to write to Elizabeth and say, 'Sorry, I'd rather write to your sister.' Meanwhile, like a rather corny, but very romantic soap opera, Elizabeth had found a boyfriend — whom she subsequently married — and she, in turn, was wrestling with how to mercifully end her longstanding correspondence. As Greg pondered, a letter arrived from Judith: 'Elizabeth has a boyfriend, she has asked me to keep up the correspondence.' Did the cool, collected batsman's heart leap with joy unfettered? Greg replied to Judy with a line which, in the light of later events, we may interpret as ringing with poetry: 'You are not the least person I had expected to hear from, but you were the last.'

Greg concluded 1969 in Somerset with 167 more runs than his first season, at a princely 0.4 of a run better average per innings. That ended the apprenticeship, thank you. He flew to New York, was ripped off by the cabbie driving him into the city and spent a careful three days avoiding subways and suspicious alleyways. He rode a lift to the top of the Empire State Building where he had seen old King Kong climb with Fay Wray and caught a baseball match, the New York Mets versus the Atlanta Braves, at the Mets stadium. From that voluminous childhood tome, *The Fireside Book of Baseball*, Greg knew the teams intimately and enjoyed it. But, on his own, he cut short the visit and moved on to Los Angeles which he left even sooner, and spent a week in Hawaii, catching wavelets at Waikiki on a hired board. Then on to Sydney where he stayed a few days with the Donaldsons.

This time there was no subterfuge. Judy had only assumed Elizabeth's pen-pal role a month before Greg arrived. In the ensuing few days her past unfolded. She was born on 26 November 1949, 15 months after Greg. She had attended St George Girls High, and her family's interest in tennis left her with memories of smelly sandshoes, ant-bed courts and afternoon teas. Her religious upbringing was Methodist, and through that she acquired a love of music. She sang in the church choir and began her Bachelor of Music degree at Sydney University until sister Elizabeth, who has much to answer for in Judy's life, entered her in the 1968 Miss Roseland's beauty contest. Judy won, beating, among others, Penny Plummer, who went on to become Miss World. Judy declined the Miss World opportunity, accepting instead a two months modelling safari around Australia and to Manila and Hong Kong. The glamour spoilt her for the austerity of classical music study and she had graduated as a teacher when Greg met her.

Greg's reaction to her was singular. He never doubted that he would marry her. 'I just knew she was something special,' he said. 'I knew I could look from then until I was 65 and I was never going to find anyone that I liked more.' It was a remarkable fixation given Greg's background. He was from an all boys family, had been educated at an all boys school, and had graduated in the school of an all male Sheffield Shield and English county cricket. He was shy anyway and before Judy had not known any girlfriends for any length of time, of any great note. Yet he asked Judy to fly to Adelaide for his delayed twenty-first.

He offered to pay her fare but being a well brought up young lady and wishing to avoid any presumption of obligation she charmingly declined and paid herself. Back home Jeanne Chappell was amazed. She knew nothing of the friendship. 'Of course you know what mothers are like,' she said. 'You think people have got two heads, don't you? I mean in those days we thought, "Fancy bringing somebody from Sydney, that dreadful place. Weren't they all women of ill repute?".' But Jeanne had more pressing problems. She was catering for a hall full of 250 people. Judy flew in the night before. Greg introduced her to Ian and Kay Chappell on the way from the airport and they finally arrived quite late at Leak Avenue, North Glenelg. Judy opened her suitcase and Jeanne, peering in, wondered, 'Why on earth has she brought all this?' There were tea towels, table cloths, sheets and pillow slips. Judy looked stunned. 'It's not my suitcase,' she said. Judy had collected a hostess' glory box, packed in an identical suitcase. It was midnight, too late to track it down. Jeanne held up one of her own nighties. Judy was tall, but too thin. Then Jeanne had the answer. A pair of Greg's pale blue shorty pyjamas. Said Judy, posing, 'Mum always wanted a boy.'

The next night Judy felt the full force of the cricketing world which dominated the Chappells' life — Test, State and club cricketers, school friends, baseballers, Martin's cricketing era, Vic Richardson and his ilk, the whole Chappell–Richardson clan, all steeped in that sacred game. Vic made a speech, told a few risqué jokes at Judy's expense but, even more embarrassing, predicted she would soon become part of the family. Said Jeanne, 'He carried on a treat, I've never known him like that.' Judy liked him despite, or perhaps because of, his predictions. 'I don't know whether he had these strange powers or not, but he knew,' she said. She was not to meet him again. The party was early in October and Vic died on the thirtieth. The family telephoned the news to Ian in Bombay where he had begun the tour that Greg had missed. Greg was saddened. Just as he was reaching an age to enter an adult relationship with his grandfather, Vic was gone. But a new season had begun, the cricket cycle continued, and as Vic's complete career closed, Greg's was about to bloom.

It began with his selection in the Australian Second XI that toured New Zealand early in 1970. Queensland captain Sam Trimble led the side which contained, in Greg and a young tearaway bowler from Perth called Dennis Lillee, two of the three names that became the heart, lungs and brain of Australian cricket. The three unofficial Tests were rained out but Greg's determination going out to bat impressed Trimble. 'Something about him set him apart from the others,' he said. Wicketkeeper John Maclean, also from Brisbane, had struck up a friendship with Greg. Maclean had no doubts: 'He was a class above the other young fellows even though it was quite a good side,' he said. Sam Trimble topped the tour averages with 84, but Greg, who passed

25 in nine out of his 11 innings, was second with 60. Greg enjoyed the tour. The cricket was above Shield standard and therefore conformed with his new-found career goals of attaining Test level. He was especially conscious, after Somerset, of being an Australian among Australians, most of them young and ambitious like himself.

For two weeks on that tour, Greg and his team-mates led a gullible Dennis Lillee on a merry round of deceit, fakes and lies which would fill this book in the recounting. Dennis, watching Greg sniff a wine's bouquet at lunch one day, leant across and whispered, 'You'd be a bit of a toff wouldn't you.' Greg looked offended and replied he worked for McWilliam's Wines, at which Dennis withdrew and apologized. Dennis checked, found Greg worked for Coca Cola and challenged him with it. Yes, Greg used to work for McWilliams, now he worked as a Coke taster and he explained how he never swallowed a mouthful, always spat it out. What did Dennis do, asked Greg. Dennis was a bank teller. 'So was I,' said Greg, 'until I got caught with my hand in the till.' Lillee's eyes widened in wonder.

Next day Greg recounted this to Graeme Watson and Dave Renneberg. 'It's true,' said Greg. 'We've got a bloke here we can tell anything, we may as well do a job of it.' The end of a two week shaggy dog comedy came when Dennis finally caught on and yelled, 'You bastards, you've done me.' Greg laughed, 'Dennis was one of the most naive blokes ever to come into cricket but we never ever put another thing over him. From that day onwards he became the most cynical. He wouldn't believe anything you told him unless it was in black and white.'

If all was light within the camp, it was not without. When they arrived in New Zealand the Australians found cricket the poor cousin of Rugby football. The New Zealand cricketers were equable and friendly, the conditions less so. 'The fact we were an Australian Second XI meant nothing to anybody,' said Greg. 'If we'd been a third grade Rugby side from the back of the bush we'd have been received better.' A rough Rugby mentality intruded. In hotels drinkers would notice the Australian accents and wander over for an argument, never a conversation. 'They didn't want to talk about cricket, they wanted to talk Rugby because they knew New Zealand could beat Australia at Rugby,' said Greg. 'They'd rather have a fight than a feed,' he added, varying the usual alliteration. They found some hotels risky to enter late in the evening. These hotels had linoleum or tiled floors and plastic bar or table tops, all designed to hose and sweep the broken glass, beer slops and blood away because the Australians saw a fight a night in such places. They normally stayed in or found hotels of a higher class than those described and were well looked after.

Australia was partly responsible for the reception. The New Zealanders felt aggrieved they were considered worthy of only a Second XI visit. This in turn rebounded on the New Zealand cricketers who were treated as nobodies. A decade later when Richard Hadlee had become as well known at home, through televised one-day matches, as Dennis Lillee in Australia, cricket began to approach the popularity of Rugby. 'One of the tragedies was that we had a country so close to us with conditions very similar to English conditions and we didn't use them,' said Greg. 'It was stupid. Both countries could have got a lot out of it.' Greg vowed after that first trip he would never return. Yet he did, half a dozen times, and his cricket life was to become inextricably entangled with New Zealand.

While Greg prospered in New Zealand, Australia foundered against South Africa. Australia defeated India 3-1 but it was too much to then ask them to take on South Africa. Graeme McKenzie, carrying a debilitating virus managed 1-333, Ian Chappell, whom Gary Sobers had described the previous summer as 'one of the great players of today,' averaged 11 runs a Test dig. South Africa won 4-0. Sam Trimble noted sagely, 'That other tour wouldn't have broken Greg, but it wouldn't have given him the confidence he got from New Zealand.' Greg had completed one of the most thorough cricket groundings possible. If Australia needed him, he was ready.

CONFIRMATION
(1970-1973)

7. First Test

The inter-city express from Melbourne to Adelaide rocked through
the dawn carrying the South Australian cricket team returning from
a Shield match against Victoria. At Murray Bridge, nearing Adelaide,
the porters picked up a bundle of Adelaide *Advertiser* newspapers and
folded them under the doors of the sleepers. It was 17 November 1970.
Eric Freeman was the first to rise, around 6 a.m., and read the
Australian team to play England in the first Test in Brisbane in 10
days' time. Among the 12 named was G. Chappell.

Freeman spread the news. The corridors rang with calls of the good
word. Not just Greg, Terry Jenner too, and of course, brother Ian. For
Greg it was a moment to savour as the express thundered into the
early morning. He was 22. He had enacted this idea so often as a boy,
but even when he made his State's team, four years earlier, he did not
really think he was as good as the likes of Doug Walters, Paul Sheahan
or Ian. But since that moment in Somerset 18 months ago when he
had taken stock of his assets his fortunes had risen with his confidence.
Three unofficial Tests against New Zealand and now the ancient foe,
England. At home telegrams flowed in, from Somerset vice-president
Alf Coulson, from Murray Sargent as always, and from that irrepressible step-grandmum Peg Lester, to Martin and Jeanne: CONGRAT-
ULATIONS TO YOU AND BOYS 2 UP AND 1 TO GO.

But Brisbane withheld her favours from Greg for a later phase in
his life. He was in the Test 12 but it was a toss-up whether the
selectors went for an extra bowler, Terry Jenner, or an extra batsman,
Greg. Deciding twelfth man is a painful experience. The selectors do
not name him normally until just before the start of play. A week of
anticipation can be dampened at the twelfth hour. At a team lunch at

the Brisbane Cricketers' Club looking out over the 'Gabba's oval of grass, Greg sat next to Jenner, both only a few seats away from the captain, Bill Lawry. A basket of bread rolls was knocked to the floor, Greg bent to pick one up and Jenner simultaneously skewered the identical roll with his knife. 'Take it easy,' said Greg, 'I've got to play cricket tomorrow.' Bill Lawry quipped quickly, 'Oh, it wouldn't make any difference.' It was either an unlikely joke about a knife wound not affecting Greg's batting or he was already slotted for twelfth man.

Greg carried the drinks and watched Rod Marsh make his Test début to the parochial discontent of a Brisbane crowd who thought that their John Maclean should have been chosen. With Brian Taber and Gordon Becker in South Africa, Maclean had been chosen as number three wicketkeeper to go to New Zealand with the Second XI. Taber became the scapegoat for their Springbok trouncing and Marsh jumped from fourth ranked 'keeper to the top job. 'I guess the raw talent he had must have showed out,' said Maclean, generously philosophical. Greg felt sorry for the reception meted out to Marsh. 'I think he got as big a surprise as anyone else that he got picked,' said Greg. 'He might have hoped he would get a game, but I think deep down he thought it was a surprise choice and perhaps he wasn't sure in his own mind he was ready for it.' Marsh missed a couple of catches that later in his career would have been a breeze. Doug Walters and Ian Chappell kept telling Marsh, 'You're due to catch one soon,' which Marsh took darkly until they explained it was the team joke for dropped catches.

The second Test starting on 11 December, Armistice Day, was the first time Perth had been allocated a Test. Nearly 85,000 spectators approved the choice over five days but Greg made the match equally memorable for himself. On Perth's fast track Jenner made way for Greg batting at number seven. Early on the third day, 13 December, Australia, chasing England's first innings of 397, was 3 for 105 when Doug Walters was caught behind off Peter Lever, 4–105.

Greg strapped on his pads as Paul Sheahan went in. Now the nerves set in. Greg always slept well, but this morning he had awakened early and not gone back to sleep. Today he was to bat. No one spoke to him as he carefully attended to the silver buckles on each pad. It only takes a minute, but the waiting can become an eternity. The Australian attitude to baptisms is Spartan, isolation leading to survival. No time for the metaphysical, just dry mouths, knotted stomachs, iron sphincters. There is no help in life at the crease therefore none tendered before. The team was tense and withdrawn. John Snow was beginning the careful dismantling of Australian batting confidence as surely as Mike Procter and Peter Pollock had in South Africa — except Snow was probably even better. He had Keith Stackpole and Lawry in just 18 balls. Ian Chappell and Ian Redpath recovered and then again a collapse. Greg scarcely had time to grow nervous. He had just sat down after putting his pads on when Sheahan was run out for two. Australia 5–107.

Greg was sorry for Sheahan, and the team, but glad that his own trial by waiting was so blessedly brief. As he walked out he felt dazed, by excitement, by nervousness, by the occasion, by the crisis. Sheahan had crossed in his run out so Greg assumed his place at the bowler's end to experience Test cricket. What he saw was like the taste of brass in his mouth. Conditions were good for pace bowling. Ian Redpath was defying the attack. England was concentrating on him because he was the senior player. They were working him over feeling that once he was gone they could isolate Greg and they were through.

The longer Greg watched Redpath the more he learned about Test cricket batting, how Snow bowling for his country was not Snow bowling for his county, how Test tension raised everything into the realm where each action contained the intention of perfection. Snow was nearing that. Very fast, sometimes three balls out of eight short and driving up into Redpath's armpits or past his face. Said Greg, 'Redders just ducked and weaved and occasionally got hit and every time he stood upright he swayed back, the old Adam's apple poking out, and he mouthed down the wicket to Snow, "Get —." He didn't say it loud but Snow saw it and smiled to himself and went back and bowled. They didn't exchange a word but Redpath must have got 100 bouncers that day.'

Greg watched this tremendous battle from close quarters, felt the guts emanating from 22 yards away and was drawn into a contest which had become a metaphor for a young man experiencing trench warfare watching his senior officer lead him into fire. Redpath, in an act of sheer will, would not be intimidated and that became Greg's inspiration to hang in with him. If it meant that much to Redpath, it would not mean less to Greg. 'All I could hope to do was stick around,' said Greg. 'Not much was expected of me, I probably didn't expect much of myself. Just hope we could get close to 200.' What Greg did not fully realize was that he had chosen to follow over the top one of Australia's most fanatical cricket patriots.

Greg knew all about the English attack of Ken Shuttleworth and Peter Lever. He had played and made runs against them on their own county cricket dunghills. They were neither awesome in anticipation nor actuality. Shuttleworth and Lever were sharp, but not express. Snow was. Snow was the first bowler that Greg, or any of the team, had faced who bowled continually short. 'He was into the armpit all the time,' said Greg. 'But he never bowled it short enough or wide enough to give you room to hook or cut. It was always just short and into your body with a couple of blokes in close, one in front, one behind. And he kept you under pressure. He'd get you back and back and back and then pitch one up wide outside off stump and you felt so relieved you got overexcited and tried to drive and risked being caught behind.'

Greg took no such risks. The bowling was so good he set his mind to simply getting behind the ball and keeping it out. He was not concerned about getting off the mark. A duck was no worse than 1 and that was his score after 40 minutes. After 67 minutes he reached double figures. It felt like hours. Greg's height allowed him to stand up and drop Snow's short risers at his feet. He attempted no aggression against him, just waited to tire him, to see him off. By tea Greg had felt his way to 48 as he and Redpath, like sand through an hourglass, imperceptibly piled runs together. After three hours Greg reached 50, acknowledged a good round of applause and sensed the balance of power changing. The moisure in the wicket had dried out, the bowlers, having almost broken through except for this last redoubt, were tiring. The England captain Ray Illingworth began to show his frustration, driving his bowlers for the vital wicket which in turn caused them to flag and stray down Greg's leg side.

Brer Greg was born and bred under that on-side blackberry bush and as they bowled to his strength he gained confidence, picking up short pitched balls and hitting them over mid-wicket. It was the shot that Lynn Fuller had decided not to curb years before. 'Settle down,' cried Lawry to himself and anyone else within earshot. 'Take it easy. You've got a chance to get 100. Don't muck it up.' Ian, sitting with Lawry, reassured him, 'Don't worry. That's just a natural shot for him. He's got here playing like that.' Ted Dexter watched Greg and later wrote in his book, *From Bradman to Boycott*:

It was quite uncanny that he could time the ball so well in that area, on the half volley, off a length and short of a length, off his legs

*and off his hip . . . no single stroke since the famous Compton sweep
so flummoxed the bowlers and exercised the minds of tacticians in
the England side.*

Greg swept from 48 to 92 in less than an hour after tea. The new ball
meant only that it sped more quickly from his bat. He made no
conscious decision to switch into top gear. 'We'd broken the back of
their bowling,' said Greg. 'I felt the opportunity was there to push the
scoring along. Any chances that came along I was going to take.' And
then he himself almost gave a chance. Once more Snow bounced Greg
who had hardly hooked all day. But with the scoring racing along a
hook was Greg's reflex action. He hit it high on the blade and the ball
careened straight towards fine leg. As soon as he mishit it Greg fell
into a sweat of chagrin. 'Oh no, to go this far and mess it up now!'
But he had hit it so high on the splice that it did not carry, falling 9
metres short of the fine leg fieldsman. Greg reproached himself, 'I've
had that little bit of luck, I'm going to make sure of it now.' He hadn't
given a chance up to then, and now though nearing the end of his
tether, did not give another.

On 99 the clock struck five in Perth, 7 p.m. on the east coast of
Australia, and the ABC, which had been televising this historic
innings, interrupted the cricket to read their evening news bulletin.
In thousands of armchairs from Brisbane to Melbourne, viewers
reached for their telephones. They included three people who would
play important and varying roles in Greg's future, Judy Donaldson in
Sydney, Barry Maranta in Brisbane, and David Richards in Melbourne.
When the telecast was resumed Greg was 104. 'Unbelievable,' said
David Richards, who eventually achieved a position in Australian
cricket where he could say, 'That's all changed a bit.'

In that time Perth's inaugural Test crowd had swamped the pitch,
congratulated Greg with the beat of a hundred backslaps and trod all
over the pitch, that delicate skin, until Greg moved like Pied Piper off
the wicket square to prevent damage. He was exhausted, mentally
more than physically. He had batted four hours and with Redpath
pulled Australia out of the woods. When he was caught for 108 a few
minutes later, it was clear a batsman of quite stellar qualities had
appeared in the Australian firmament. Greg's own reaction was relief.
As dressing-room congratulations washed over him he contemplated
that if he had not gone to Somerset, had not known these England
bowlers, he would never have made his century. But even more he

knew that if Redpath had got out, he would not have lasted himself. He had only to glance wicketwards to see Redpath still there battling it out. Ever after Greg said that he had known several players who would die for the baggy green Australian cap, but only two who would kill for it. One was Ian Redpath. Statistics did not move Greg. That he had joined an élite list of 10 Australians to have scored 100 in their first Test — the last being Doug Walters five years earlier — mattered less than that he had come in at 5–107 and left at 6–326.

At the end of the day Richie Benaud led Greg across the ground for a television interview and the departing crowd turned and applauded Greg all over again. After the interview Benaud said, 'Look, if I can offer any advice at all, no matter what happens in the rest of your career, whether you're having a good run or a bad run, don't ever stop playing your shots.' Benaud was much respected as a players' man. When Walters had performed the same feat Benaud was on hand to advise, 'Congratulations, don't sign a thing until you see me.' Walters recalled in his book, *The Doug Walters Story*, it was the best advice he ever got. Greg thanked Richie and, as we shall see, took Benaud at his word.

An analysis of that 108 revealed that only 21 runs had come from off-side shots. The rest, 87, including all his 10 fours, were on-side shots. If anything his list to the left had become more pronounced since his younger days, but in truth the England bowlers had bowled there and that is where he hit them. What matter anyway when the Adelaide *Advertiser's* next morning street poster, in black and scarlet, read: 'S.A.'S GREG "A GREAT"'. John Woodcock wrote in *The Times* that Greg's last 60 runs, scored in 70 minutes, 'must rank among the most irrepressible ever made by a young batsman in his first Test match'.

Greg uttered the throwaway line that perhaps now he would be known as Greg Chappell and not Ian Chappell's brother or Vic Richardson's grandson. But he was never ever annoyed about that. He was as proud of them both as Vic would have been of him and as Ian was. In fact with that century Greg instigated a new approach from Ian to his own batting. 'I started to play my best when Greg came into Test cricket,' said Ian. 'I had this little bloke I used to beat up in the backyard and suddenly he's playing better than I can and I better get off my backside.' Up until then Ian had been playing well enough to stay in the Australian team, but now it seemed new standards of excellence were being set. 'He gave me the needle,' said Ian. 'I think my record as a batsman before then averaged about 40 and afterwards as Australian captain, about 50. It became a hell of a lot better.'

Two days after Australia drew that Perth Test, Greg faced England again, batting for South Australia. South African Barry Richards, who was working with Greg for Coca Cola, and Ashley Woodcock, put on an opening stand of 247 in the first innings. As admirable as were their centuries, they did not match Greg's in the second innings. He scored 102 in 118 minutes in a glorious display of free wheeling, free hitting, as though he had taken up where he left off in the second phase of his Test century. His last 50 came in just 35 minutes and his last 10 scoring shots to his 100 were 4, 4, 6, 6, 1, 6, 2, 4, 1 and 3. Those three sixes were off Derek Underwood, two of them off successive balls, the first over wide mid-on and the second among the members at square leg. The third he pulled to reach 95. It is as well to remember such rampages before naming Underwood as Greg's nemesis. It was easily the fastest century of the first class season.

That innings compounded a misinterpretation Greg had made of Richie Benaud's advice after Perth. In the next three Tests Greg's scores were 15, 2, 3, 20 n.o., and a duck. Greg got himself out trying to play his shots too early. 'I misconstrued Richie's advice a bit,' said Greg. 'He meant basically I was a stroke maker, always play your shot. Left unsaid was that I still had to remember to build an innings. That part I forgot until the last Test in Sydney.' Greg could not expect to walk in first up as though he had just scored 100. Of course if we beam back 10 years that was the warning he received from that wise coach, Jeanne Chappell, after he had scored his two successive primary school centuries. But some lessons must be re-experienced to be remembered.

John Snow dominated the rest of the series. He noticed that Greg, with his on-side propensities, was moving right across the stumps and exposing his leg stump, which is where Snow clean-bowled Greg once. Greg countered by changing his guard from middle stump to leg stump, but that was after the event. Snow was simply too quick for the Australians. Graeme McKenzie was not as fast and did not bowl as many short-pitched balls. Doug Walters in his book reckoned Snow was three yards faster than Australia's Alan (Froggy) Thomson. Greg, in later years, rated Snow's accuracy for his pace as second only to Dennis Lillee's and the equal of West Indian Andy Roberts'.

At season's end Greg and Ian took a bucket of baseballs down to Greg's old Plympton High School cement wicket nets and practised playing short-pitched balls. They used baseballs because when thrown they skidded a little before lifting, whereas cricket balls tended to jump unrealistically. They learned the footwork, the balls to stand up and play, to hook and to let go. But like Greg's changed guard, it was all after the horse had bolted.

Greg also learned on that tour the England players had their own problems. At first they could not pick John Gleeson's spin. Every third or fourth over of Gleeson's was a maiden. England had team talks about how to play him. 'They played him as though he was bowling hand grenades,' said Greg. Basil d'Oliveira told Greg that during one Test he walked down the pitch to his partner and said, 'I've just cracked his wrong 'un.' His partner replied, 'Yes, I knew when we started. But don't tell those bastards in there,' nodding towards the England dressing-room. Such was the atmosphere among some of the England team. Others, John Edrich, John Hampshire, Peter Lever and John Snow, were regular visitors to the Australian room for friendly drinks.

From their occasional remarks Greg pieced together the factions in the England camp. Ray Illingworth was captain but there was a feeling that Colin Cowdrey should have been. Illingworth commanded the support of the north England players except for those who felt Geoff Boycott should be captain. 'There seemed to be two or three blokes who thought they would be a better captain than the bloke doing it,' said Greg. 'Which is something we have never had in Australia- ... well, that's not entirely true.' Despite any disharmony off the field the English players' county professionalism brought them together in Tests under Illingworth's shrewd guidance. He read the game well, attacked when necessary, bided his time if need be. 'There were probably better cricketers than Illy,' said Greg, 'but none of them more competitive or determined to win.'

Bill Lawry's captaincy reached its nadir, in some critics' eyes, in the fifth Test. He declared late on the second day with Rod Marsh on 92 and within a few blows of becoming the first Australian wicketkeeper to score a Test century. 'I felt for Bill,' said Greg. 'He was agitated — you could see him pacing up and down the dressing-room. He wanted to declare and he wanted Rod to get his hundred, but he didn't want him to take all day over it.' Illingworth marshalled his bowlers, several overs passed with few runs scored. Ten to 15 minutes stretched taut Lawry's anxiety. In the end he called, 'Righto, that's it. Come in.' Said Greg, 'With hindsight I think Rod would feel Bill's decision was made in the best interests of the team.'

The sixth Test in Adelaide saw Bill Lawry start to acquire the firepower to match Snow. Dennis Lillee played his first Test and took five wickets in the first innings. But by the seventh Test in Sydney, England led 1–0 and Illingworth was poised to become the first England captain since Len Hutton after the war to win a series in Australia. Lillee had arrived too late for Lawry. Greg thought Lawry bowled Froggy Thomson into the ground. 'Froggy was built like me, didn't have a lot of strength or stamina,' said Greg. 'Bill used him as a stock instead of a shock bowler.' Nor had Lawry much faith in Ashley Mallett who became a trump card for Ian Chappell in the 1970s. But the intangible seemed that Lawry had spread a stony touch over the team. The cricketing electorate, remembering the success of Benaud and the front running of Bob Simpson, wanted winners.

In replacing Lawry with Ian Chappell the Australian selectors treated Lawry like the losing captain of a volatile Third World soccer team. They did not stone him, but they obliterated him from the Test scene. 'I can understand the selectors wanting a new broom, to make it easier for Ian to take over the reins,' said Greg. 'But I'm sure Bill would have respected Ian's position and vice versa. I know Ian would have been delighted to have had him in the team for his batting.' The man who replaced Lawry, Ken Eastwood, aged 35, from Victoria, scored 5 and a duck in the last Test. 'I think if Bill had played we could have won in Sydney,' said Greg. 'He was still one of the better batsmen around.'

Greg's form recovered in that Test with 65 and 30, but the Test became memorable to Greg for other reasons. John Snow, for all his bowling venom, was a quiet man on field, but an antagonism had developed between himself and umpire Lou Rowan. It came to a head in Sydney because Snow felt Rowan was no-balling him unfairly. Greg was at the crease when the action occurred. 'Snowy never said much to other players, but he was having a go at Rowan which was most out of character for him,' said Greg. Illingworth bought into the argument from his close in bat-pad position and Rowan, in Greg's opinion, became emotionally involved. Rowan told Illingworth, 'You get on with your captaining and I'll do the umpiring.' It was stock aggro dialogue.

In the closing stages Terry Jenner was hit in the head by a Snow delivery. Greg at the other end saw it all clearly. 'Terry was working on the numbers' theory,' said Greg. 'As soon as it left Snow's hand Terry convinced himself it was short, but it only came up waist high and Terry ducked straight into it. Terry was just as much at fault.' The crowd was incensed. Illingworth took heed and told Derek Underwood to field at fine leg. 'You better go down to third man,' he told Snow. No, Snow wanted to return to fine leg, right in front of the noisy Paddington Hill crowd at the SCG. Illingworth insisted, Snow resisted, came to grips with a spectator, and cans rained onto the ground.

Illingworth led his team from the ground leaving Greg and Dennis Lillee, who came in after Jenner's dismissal, at the crease. Dennis walked up to Greg and asked: 'What do we do?' Said Greg, 'I've got no idea. I know those last in possession have got a better chance of winning than anyone else, so we better stay here.' They watched the umpires disappear into the pavilion where they gave an ultimatum to Illingworth that unless England returned the match would be awarded, as Greg's instinct told him, to Australia. England returned and won the match and the Ashes. It was a dispiriting experience for Greg, in his first Test series, begun with such promise.

England left Australia to their Shield devices where for South Australia Greg had moved up to his favourite batting spot at number 4, behind the openers and Ian. Strangely the brothers, for two of the best batsmen in Australia, had not yet put together a large partnership. 'One of us would get out straight away,' recalled Ian. 'I think our highest was 32 for a long time.' They did not exceed that in the last Shield match of that season, against New South Wales at Adelaide Oval on 26 February 1971. Ashley Woodcock opened with Barry Richards, who made 55 and then Ian and Ashley took the score to 239 before Ashley was run out. 'It was my fault,' said Woodcock. 'I was 95 and on the last ball of the over I hit the ball to mid-on for a single trying to keep the strike. That would have taken me to 96 to start the new over.' Woodcock trudged to the dressing-room, passing Greg who was next man in. Woodcock showered and changed then heard a roar from the crowd unlike any he could distinguish. He rushed upstairs just as Ian Chappell was walking off. Everyone told him, 'Don't go back down to the rooms.' Ian and Greg had both finished ingloriously at the same end. It would not be safe for man or beast in that dressing-room until Ian settled down. Ian's version: 'We both ran one,' he said. 'Then I ran back down to him and he still wouldn't run. So I had to turn back and got out by a foot at the other end. He ran one and I nearly ran three, that's how much time we had.'

Two years later in a Test against the West Indies at Barbados Greg turned a ball down to fine leg and delayed running until it had cleared a fieldsman backward of square leg. Ian had called 'Yes' and ran like there were two in it all the way. He was well into his second when Greg, slower to start, was just turning. Greg, running to the 'keeper's end saw the fieldsman had the ball in hand — few West Indians have poor arms — and called 'No!' Said Greg, 'Ian was at full pelt and he had to put the brakes on and he had no hope.' Ian was run out for 72. Greg went on to score 106, perhaps to atone for the run out. 'He wasn't too happy,' said Greg. 'But he was even less happy in Adelaide three years later.' Fifth Test, January 1976, against the West Indians again with their superb arms. Ian: 'He hit a bloody full toss straight to Viv Richards at mid-on and ran. I got out by a long way, which I mentioned to him.' Greg's explanation: 'The last ball of the day, I meant to hit the ball wide of mid-on and called on where I meant to hit it. Instead it ran straight to Richards who fired it back to Deryck Murray over the stumps.' Murray actually dropped the ball, but took the bails off anyway and Ian was given out. 'It was a bad decision, but it was a worse call,' admitted Greg. 'Did he give me stick! He just stormed straight off and reached the dressing-room before I did. I heard the bat go down, locker doors slamming.

"Nice bloody call!"

"Sorry . . ."

"Sorry!"

"Sorry I spoke."

"Get —." '

It was not that Greg was a bad runner. He was good, and quite quick. Playing winter touch football in Brisbane in later years it was said he ran like a whippet. Said Ian, 'Call him selfish or call him smart. I was a dunce because if someone called "Yes" I used to run, whereas if I called "Yes" and he didn't feel like running, he didn't run. Those couple of occasions were diabolical.' Greg found it inexplicable. 'I was involved in half a dozen or so run outs in 151 Test innings for Australia and of those I had to run Ian out twice.' Mind you Greg was even handed. That half dozen includes three occasions when he himself was run out.

Ashley Woodcock had an experience too. Way back in their last intercollege together, he and Greg put on 58 before Ashley pulled the Saints' offspinner through mid-wicket to the man on the fence and called for the run. 'I got halfway down and Greg said "No". It was my call. I went back and was run out.' Greg went on to make 107.

Was is coincidental that Greg twice scored centuries after such misfortunes? There was a feeling among cricketers that Greg became a ruthless individualist at the crease, battening down to become invulnerable. The run out in cricket is the only form of common dismissal where the batsman is at the mercy of his partner. Both Ian and Greg were held in some awe by their colleagues in this regard. They valued their wicket so much, defended their territory so fiercely that no one wanted to be responsible for a disaster. 'If there was a line ball situation you knew who wasn't going to be run out,' said Ashley Woodcock. 'Chappell I. or Chappell G.' Mind, that comes from Greg's friend who has already confessed he had been run out trying to keep the strike. Nevertheless it was with the mischievous hilarity born of great relief — that they were blameless — that the South Australian team watched Greg run Ian out in March 1971. Having been part of the Australian team that lost the Ashes only two weeks earlier, it became a humourless season's finale for Greg.

8. Married

In the winter of 1971 Greg set off from Adelaide in his Holden Kingswood for a two-week holiday in Sydney with Judy Donaldson. He drove non-stop, arriving so exhausted and disoriented he could not find her home in Bexley and finally had to telephone for directions. 'I can remember that evening talking and watching television with Judy,' said Greg. 'I couldn't focus. I couldn't have been talking too well either. I was a zombie for two days.' Judy's holidays did not coincide with Greg's. It had been the same when Judy visited Greg in Adelaide, rushed visits, followed by long letters and costly phone calls. The previous summer Judy drove to Brisbane with her parents to watch Greg against Queensland. Trevor drove up with Martin and Jeanne and Greg rewarded them all with a century in each innings. It was Judy's first taste of Brisbane at its tropical worst. They walked from their Kangaroo Point hotel to the 'Gabba each day in steaming, thunderous heat. 'We soon learned if you had a shower it didn't matter whether you were wet or dry after it,' said Judy. That was the sort of distance the young lovers had to traverse to meet. It was too frustrating. The 1972–73 tours of England and the West Indies were in sight. 'It would be 18 months before we could spend any decent time together,' said Judy. So in August, two years after Judy had first written to Greg in Somerset, they were engaged and the day set for 10 November 1971.

It was a midweek wedding because Greg finished a Shield match the weekend before and had a club match the weekend after. From the absolute outset there was never any question what would have priority in their lives. The wedding was in the Bexley Methodist Church where Judy had sung in the choir. Ian was best man, and the cause of it all, erstwhile pen pal Elizabeth, bridesmaid. Quite a few cricketers attended, Brian Taber, Kerry O'Keeffe, Geoff Davies, and Richie Benaud and his wife Daphne who had been sponsoring Judy in the Miss Australia Quest only to see their charge whisked from the field by Greg. At the reception Greg bore with the speeches manfully, his toes curled painfully tight in his shoes. In his brother-in-law's shoes actually. Greg had packed his dinner suit in Adelaide and forgotten his black dress shoes. It was either brown casuals or fit his size 10s into size 8½s. The newly-weds spent that night, Wednesday, at the Top of the Cross at the Travelodge, flew the next day to Adelaide and moved into a house about a kilometre from Leak Avenue.

Two weeks and two days after their wedding Greg was in Brisbane, twelfth man for Australia in the first unofficial Test against the Rest of the World XI which replaced the cancelled South African tour of Australia that summer. Greg was 23, Judy 22. Marriage was a cultural reverse for Judy. On Sunday mornings she had sought perfection of the spirit in the house of the Lord, not a perfect on-drive behind the house on a lawn. She was uplifted by classical music where there appeared none in the Chappell house. Whatever Greg's artistry with the bat his interests did not embrace the arts of piano and chorale. From the moment Judy arrived in Adelaide music slipped from her life. She moved from sharing with a sister to an extended, male oriented family, from being waited upon at home to waiting upon Greg. Judy adapted, assisted by Jeanne and Kay Chappell, Ian's wife. Judy Donaldson disappeared to emerge as Mrs Greg Chappell. It was that complete because nothing in Judy's life could compete with Greg's involvement with cricket. They did not discuss the expected duration of his cricket career. 'She knew I was pretty committed, that it was a big part of my life,' said Greg. 'I didn't know how long I would play. The way things were looking early that season it wasn't going to go much further.'

Greg's scores had been unimpressive but he felt he was striking the ball well and was genuinely surprised when he was made only twelfth man. The Perth match belonged to Dennis Lillee who took 8–29 in dismissing the Rest of the World for only 59 runs on one of the fastest wickets Lillee ever had the fortune to tread.

Greg carried drinks and listened to the consternation in the World dressing-room. Gary Sobers was captain but it was Rohan Kanhai, one of Greg's sherry drinking partners in Taunton, who responded to Lillee's challenge. Kanhai, a champion batsman in his own right, privately disapproved of the monopoly of media attention heaped on his countryman Sobers. He was a proud, sometimes fiery, small man and considered the World XI's first innings lacked courage. 'He really got up their skirts,' said Greg, who heard it all from his non-player's chair. 'In the second innings Rohan stalked onto the ground with steam coming from his ears,' said Greg. 'Dennis hit him in the throat with one that took off and I thought, "That's the end of him". But he made 118 out of 279, as good an innings as you're ever likely to see.'

Christmas Eve, 1971, Greg spent in the Wrest Point Hotel, Hobart. He and Ian were there to shore up a Combined XI, mainly Tasmanians, against the Rest of the World. There was no pressure about the match and the night before Greg joined World players Intikhab Alam, Asif Masood and Zahir Abbas of Pakistan, Englishman Richard Hutton, son of Sir Leonard, and South African Hylton Ackerman in a singalong, 100 verses of Robin Hood with Intikhab cleverly keeping the beat with two coins on a window.

Greg carried that bonhomie onto the field, scoring 19 and 23. Greg confessed, 'I got myself out going for shots, that was how I justified it to myself and anyone else who wanted to listen.' Despite these scores Greg was selected to play in the next international in Melbourne starting 31 December. While in Hobart he received a letter from his father enclosing a clipping of a 29 November newspaper article by respected Adelaide *Advertiser* writer, Keith Butler. Martin wrote, 'Butler makes quite a lot of critical comment about your cricket. I don't believe all of it but perhaps there is enough in it to at least have a look at what you are doing.' Butler wrote:

> *Greg Chappell is no longer the certainty to tour England that he was a year ago. This has been due, in part, to his Australian selection — a selection which restricted him to a non-combatant role in the first two Tests.*

He wrote that Greg had not grabbed his limited opportunities and listed his season's scores: 4, 11, 26, 8, 14, 19 and 23.

Chappell should make every effort to bury opposing bowlers each time he walks out to bat and not be carried away by trying to entertain.

While Chappell was scoring a light-hearted 19 and 23 in Hobart at the weekend two of his big tour rivals, Ian Redpath (118) and Paul Sheahan (61) had their heads down grinding out runs against NSW at the MCG.

The time is overdue when Chappell must appreciate that selectors are impressed by runs.

Butler then listed Greg's 1970–71 scores after his 108 Test début and concluded:

Add this season's scores and Chappell emerges with the statistics of having played 14 innings for only 240 runs. And Greg for a player of your quality, it's not good enough!

Greg's first reaction was anger, but his father's words gave him pause. He had a meal, returned to his hotel room, locked the door, turned out the light and sat in a chair and thought. In the stillness a stream of consciousness began running into words and flowing into ideas ... nine out of 10 times the bowler did not bowl magnificently, he got himself out ... how to prevent the inevitable happening as long as possible? ... what was he thinking on his bad batting days? ... he was impulsive, doing something he hadn't even thought about ... on his good days there was a pattern ... on his bad there was none ... he didn't get out the same way all the time ... the only similarity was that he brought it about himself.

That was a start. At least Greg had admitted he had a problem, was no longer pretending that all was well with a batting average of 17 runs over the 14 innings Keith Butler had annotated. To stop those impulsive bad habits he had to replace them with a good habit. He had to programme himself with the right thought processes. That was where he arrived after an hour in the dark. He took it further.

How did he play best? ... playing straight, he did not cut or hook a lot, he was a driver ... full face of the bat he was taught ... to develop that habit he needed a positive thought to occupy his mind as he occupied the crease ... play straight, watch the ball, play straight. Play straight.

And so Greg composed his mantra. If he was bowled a half-volley on the leg stump he would drive it no squarer than mid-on. A half-volley on the off-side, no squarer than mid-off. He would not think about the gap just in front of square leg or another behind point where he could get runs because that conditioned his mind to wait to play a shot there. That was a bad habit because if the ball did not land where he could hit to those gaps he would not score. Worse, he would eventually try to hit the wrong ball there because that was where his mental processes were guiding his feet and eyes.

Next day Greg began practising his theory, basically driving the ball in a vee sector through the end of the nets. He tried running a blank tape through his mind to eliminate all extraneous thoughts, but that was impossible. So it was back to play straight, watch the ball. 'That didn't mean I played only those shots,' said Greg. 'I'd been training for 20 years and could play all the rest by instinct. It wasn't difficult. But by uncluttering my thoughts I allowed my mind to play every ball on its merits and signal my hands and feet correctly.'

It worked instantly. In Melbourne he scored 115 not out, proof that he had practised it first ball to last. From that Greg learned a little more, to vary his levels of concentration while batting. 'As a kid I used to get sore hands from gripping the bat so hard all the time,' said Greg. 'But there was no point in concentrating while the bowler walked back to his mark.' Bobby Simpson had told Ian the same about slips fielding. If he concentrated flat out for an hour he would be exhausted. Better to relax between each ball, then bear down again at the bowler's delivery stride.

From Melbourne to Sydney for the fourth international starting on 7 January. Here Greg made 197, again not out. A report of the innings said, 'Greg's century was almost faultless. He drove formidably ...' The two consecutive centuries cemented his place in the approaching tour of England, but just as important were further developments in his philosophy.

After each innings, when batsmen are always left alone to make peace with their dismissal, Greg lay on the massage table and reviewed the good moments of a good innings, what mistakes he committed in a bad and how to eliminate them in future. If he had no time in the dressing-room, then before he slept that night. 'I'd trained so much for the the physical side I knew if I could get the mental side right I'd be OK,' said Greg. He extended it to other areas which would increase the odds in his favour. What did John Snow do that was predictable, or later, Andy Roberts or whoever? He began practising against them in his mind, searching for early warning signs, imagining their styles, their deceits, and how to counteract them.

'That practice was better than any net practice,' said Greg. 'A lot of nets is unrealistic, blokes bowling who never do in a game and true bowlers never going flat out. A lot of it is almost irrelevant.' Sometimes he could not stop other thoughts intruding. But 99 per cent of the time it worked. Said Greg, 'Physically there were a lot of players who had as much or more ability than me — Paul Sheahan, Doug Walters and later Martin Kent, all beautiful strikers of the ball.' But Greg sorted out a better mental approach to accompany the physical and that separated him from the rest.

About 10 years later in Brisbane a friend invited Greg to a seminar on the power of the mind. Greg paid $200 for four days to discover that psychology, through a system called alphadynamics, had come up with an approach to life that Greg had employed in his cricket for a decade. Empty your mind then fill it with the task. It was gratifying to Greg to have his self-taught psychology confirmed, but by then he had scored another 50 first-class centuries as proof for himself.

Acquiring that mental discipline completed the full cloth of Greg's batting education. What had begun with Martin, through Princes, Shield, county and Test, was now rounded by his own unique intellectual capacity. It was the beginning of Greg Chappell the master magus who could, whenever the mood took him, erect a force field of mind and technique against which bowlers battered themselves hopelessly. Said Ashley Woodcock, 'You'd hear players in the district scene say when Greg came out, "Oh jeez, here's another 100 coming up." He was the type of guy with such pride in his performance that even if it wasn't a Test he would produce the goods. Sometimes, you know, he was near perfection.'

Yet perfection is an illusion. As part of his conversion to the power of positive thinking Greg decided to censor the newspaper input into his mental computer. If he had a bad day he did not need to have it confirmed, emphasized and aggravated by reading it the next day. 'All it was doing was getting me upset and angry,' he said. 'So I decided if I had a good day, fine, read the papers, all positive stuff. But to have that negative input beating an already battered ego, you didn't need it.'

And this Greg adhered to from then on. He respected some writers — the venerable Ray Robinson and later on, ex-Australian captains Richie Benaud and brother Ian, until the pair took a tumble in his estimation. And there lay the flaw in the facets of his shiny new diamantine philosophy. It was Keith Butler who alerted him to the peril of his scoring sportiveness at Christmas 1971. Perhaps Greg may have awoken to it himself anyway. But by declining to receive all shades of feedback he became somewhat like the general who would hear only good news and thus never learned of his own imminent defeat. Cricket is not war and the only damage Greg's self censorship inflicted was that he never desensitized himself to criticism. If he were to lead an unimpeachable cricket playing and an impeccable cricket political career, then there was no harm in pursuing such a closed door policy. But in years to come Greg would stand at the epicentre of some of the biggest storms to rock contemporary cricket. And he suffered badly for not having inured himself with a thicker hide.

The Rest of the World tour was memorable to Greg for one other reason — Gary Sobers' 254 in the Melbourne international, possibly the best Greg ever witnessed. In the first innings Sobers came in late in the day and made it obvious he thought the light too poor. Greg, fielding at mid-on, agreed. 'The umpires should have come off,' he said. Instead Lillee let Sobers have a short, quick ball and he was caught behind for a duck. He was furious, with the umpires, with Lillee, with the Australian team. He slammed his bat on his pads as he stalked off, the only time Greg ever saw him angry ... until he strode back on again in the second innings with such a dour mien that Greg, an arch reader of physiognomies, knew they were in for something. Greg was in his first season with Somerset when, in August 1968, he heard how Sobers, captaining Nottinghamshire against Glamorgan, became the first man to score 36 runs from a six-ball over. Six sixes. If Sobers was inclined. 'In Melbourne, his first two scoring shots were fours in front of point,' said Greg. 'They went past gully at 100 mph. He gave Dennis a real pizzling.' Over 150 of his runs came in fours and sixes.

Another feat, rendered almost unnoticed by Sobers, was Graeme Pollock's century. Greg, fielding at covers, was fascinated by the way Pollock leaned effortlessly into his drive. Greg would move forward to cut the ball off only to have it seemingly accelerate past for four. That evening he sought out Pollock and picked up his bat. How heavy was it? About 3 pounds, said Pollock. Greg had been using a conventional 2.4 pound Gray-Nicolls bat since he signed with that manufacturer in 1969 while at Somerset. 'Graeme played basically in front of the wicket with a full face, perpendicular, not too much cross-bat,' said Greg. 'That was the way I played, so I thought it might be worth giving

85

it a try.' Greg ordered a heavier bat, 2.8 pounds, then 2.12 pounds before finally settling on 2.10 pounds which he used ever more.

The Rest of the World beat Australia thus paving the way for more lopping of dead limbs from the Australian team to tour England. Lawry was gone, Redpath would miss as would McKenzie. But Greg, with his two undefeated centuries, topped the Australian batting averages with 106.25. He was a certainty.

9. UK

A tall, lean figure, clad in a green tracksuit with gold trimmings, emerged from the centrally heated warmth of the Waldorf Hotel into the 5 a.m. snapping chill of a London morning. He turned right out of Aldwych up Bow Street to Covent Garden and ran back through time amid the noise and dialects of the market tradesmen. This was years before the jogging craze swept the western world, but the English always were tolerant of eccentrics. They ignored the runner as he veered right towards the Kingsway. This was Greg, on his first day in England with Ian Chappell's 1972 Australians. Either excitement or circadian dysrhythmia had woken him early and sent him on this run.

There was certainly sufficient to speed the pulse. From the moment the team had gathered in Sydney for blazers, sweaters and caps, and to be allocated tour roommates, a current of anticipation accompanied their every gesture and glance. They were a young team, the worst ever to leave Australian shores according to the English press. No Lawry, McKenzie or Redpath. John Snow, poet-turned-comedian, thought it a good side, 'provided you were playing for England'. Ladbrokes, Britain's big bookmakers, were quoting England 6/4 and Australia 3/1. The spirit of the underdog was already uniting them. Some had been before — Ian, Doug Walters, Keith Stackpole and Paul Sheahan — and others, Bruce Francis, Ashley Mallett, Jeff Hammond, Dennis Lillee and Greg, had English experience. But for them all this was something different. Greg was 18 when he first played with Somerset. Now he was nearly 24. Then he was an apprentice, now he was a journeyman, a member of the cricket crusade Australia launched against England every four years. Instead of a visitor to the 1968 Australians at the Waldorf Greg was a 1972 colour bearer.

As he jogged down Kingsway towards that hotel it was still early. He headed off down The Strand, cut left beside the Savoy down to the

Thames and ran along Victoria Embankment as far as Westminster Bridge before halting, breath condensing into evanescent clouds, and retracing his path back to the Waldorf.

Practice at Lord's was not until 10 a.m. What would he do for the next few hours? He was not alone in this thought. Downstairs most of the team were eating breakfast, wide-eyed victims too of the time change. Greg joined them, rough, sun-scarred antipodean faces, their stares, used to the limitless distances of home, seemed to ricochet off the solid confinement of the old world dining room. They were young crusaders carrying with them the eternal hopes of cultures and continents of aeons past, that the blood of the new world would prove superior to that of the parent. Crusaders and yet pilgrims, for England was where cricket had begun, where the sport at which they had chosen to excel had a pedigree as sound as any of the other institutions with which Britain abounds and is bound.

The Reverend Canon Lawrence Jackson, archdeacon of Coventry, rounded to this tradition in his speech welcoming the Australians at a lunch given by the charitable Lords Taverners at the Cafe Royale on 25 April, Anzac Day. A superb raconteur, he had the Australians in stitches before concluding seriously:

> I happen to feel that there is nothing which belongs so much to England and the English way of life, than cricket. And in a world which is so full of violence and topsy turvey values, I look upon cricket as a great sort of 'ein fester Berg', as Martin Luther would call it, a great rock, upon which so many of the standards which made our nation great and which some people still hold dear, are carefully guarded and cosseted. And as Englishmen I think we must thank God for that, and as Australians I'm sure we shall thank God for that too — for cricket.

The rural dean's words were greeted with the tremendous applause one would expect from an audience who has just had their obsession both legitimized and blessed.

Greg watched Ian begin to mould his team. Ian reserved a room at the Waldorf for the team, no friends allowed, just the inmates. 'That was one place the blokes could go and be themselves,' said Greg. 'We made a rule that if you had guests coming you drank with them in the bar.' The hotel bar Ian made his office suite-cum-communications centre. He could always be found there relaxing, accessible, approachable. He was jealous of these hours and refused to sign autographs in the bar. 'Look mate, when we're away from home this is our home,' Ian would say. 'You wouldn't walk into my lounge and ask me to sign autographs.' Greg would wince because one in 10 plaintiffs would persist and a scene would ensue. Said Greg, 'Personally I'd be annoyed by the interruption but 30 seconds to sign was better than a five minute argument.' It was Martin on the front porch all over again. The bar as a confessional was not something Greg altogether approved of, even though he saw Ian use it successfully. Greg, in his cool fashion, thought that if team members had something to say they ought to say it stone cold sober. 'A lot of the time they would only speak their minds when they'd had a few drinks,' he conceded. 'But often it was just argumentative. If they were well and truly pissed invariably it was always to disagree with something.'

More than anything else Greg disagreed with Ian's treatment of county games as practice only. Said Greg, 'Ian would bat for 30 minutes, "Right, that's enough," and throw his wicket away. I can see both sides. Records didn't mean a thing to him. If he finished the tour with an average of 15 in county games, that was irrelevant. He'd say, "The games we have to win are the Test matches. I don't care what happens to the rest, as long as the blokes enjoy it." ' Greg's argument was that when they played for Australia every game was important. To take them lightheartedly and lose was an insult to the baggy green cap. 'Dad insisted we always play every game seriously, even if it was just on the beach,' said Greg. Once more the fundamental and irreconcilable differences between the brothers and their reactions to Martin's tutelage emerged. Except here we may have, in Ian's Tests-only-count philosophy, the unmaking of Australia as a limited-over nation.

Greg received no special treatment from Ian, but that did not prevent him from asserting a fraternal familiarity. In the first Test at Manchester Greg, with his England experience, thought he should have bowled more. In the first innings he bowled 16 overs to John Gleeson's 24. Greg's regular complaint to Ian in Adelaide was that 'You can't get wickets in three over spells.' This was the portion Ian would dole out to him on Adelaide Oval's turning wicket where Ian had Mallett and Jenner ready to spin. At Manchester Rod Marsh gave Ian some advice in sandgroper-speak: 'You're a bloody idiot, you know. This is a seamer's paradise and you've got two spinners on. Get Greg and Graeme Watson on. Anybody that bowls seam is going to have a picnic.' Ian, conscious he was a spin bowling captain, thought, 'Rod's used to Perth, perhaps he's right.'

In the second innings Greg bowled 21 overs to Gleeson's seven. Greg bowled Tony Greig with the second new ball but it was no picnic and did not save the match. Nor did it save Ian from Greg's calculated whinge in the bar that night. Disagreements were second nature to the brothers, almost a coded form of communication. They could spend the best part of a session in slips sniping away, mostly good-heartedly. It was hard only on the nearest outsider, Marsh as 'keeper, and Marsh at the bar, who finally cried, 'For Christ's sake you blokes, come on!'

Losing the first Test set the Australians back. Perhaps they were as bad as was said. Give a dog a bad name. Heading for Lord's, Ian addressed his troops. 'It's not the end of the world, nor of the tour,' he told them. 'We've got a long way to go. Let's just keep applying ourselves.' Manager Ray Steele, a quiet but strong force behind Ian, held up a London newspaper open on a headline which accused: 'Aussies Take Loss Lying Down'. Steele put his glasses down on top of the paper, looked steadily around the players and said thickly, 'Pig's bloody arse we did!' Greg gave signs of good form in the intervening county match against Essex, scoring 181. Of his 28 fours one was a reverse bat sweep through gully, an excursion into unorthodoxy which later delighted West Indian crowds, but is not recommended in any Chappell style book.

Lord's in 1972 belonged to Bob Massie, the 25-year-old, medium-fast swing bowler from Perth who finished his first Test with 16 wickets for 137 runs. Only Jim Laker's 19–90 for England against Australia in 1956 were better post-war figures. Greg stood second slip to Ian and saw a rare equation, magnificent bowling rewarded with equally superlative figures. 'There was no mystery about it,' said Greg. 'They got out going after him. His control of swing both ways was unbelievable.' And yet Massie achieved so much, so soon, it was his undoing. 'It just about ruined his career,' said Greg. 'He was never going to get 16 wickets in a match again. He could have played that match and not got so many wickets. It was the worst thing that ever happened to him I think. From that time on people expected too much from him and he from himself.'

It was a miraculous performance. Martin, Jeanne and Trevor, holidaying in England, saw it all. They were invited by the MCC president, Freddie Brown, to sit in his box and the Chappells were hard put to restrain themselves as Massie's massacre unfolded. 'They weren't too thrilled,' said Jeanne happily. 'Sir Roger Bannister and his wife were there too. At 6.30 p.m. she said, "I thought you said the match finished at 6.30." He explained, "They don't finish in the middle of an over dear." '

The Chappells were on hand the next day for Greg's first innings in a Test at Lord's. The day was overcast, the wicket green, much darker than its normal pale grey. At 2–7 Australia was looking down the barrel. Snow and Co. were poised to run through them as Massie had England. The crowd was quiet and expectant, listening for the trigger to be cocked. Greg walked out, Australian cap, sleeveless sweater, withdrawing into that cocoon which would admit only the primary threats, bowler and ball. He was about to begin the innings which he would describe ever after as his best.

He decided to occupy the crease with Ian as long as he could and hope time would bring docility to the seaming pitch. He settled to his one-on-one contest with the bowler. He did not hear the crowd, the calls flitting between the fieldsmen or the bowler approaching, but he saw everything. His reconnaissance was constant, his tactical intelligence complete. The fieldsmen were pegs in the ground, marks in his mental map of the battle plain. The only face he saw was the bowler's. Their armour was equal, the contest was of wills, the fieldsmen were witnesses. Greg played a little to them, looking authoritative, relaxed, belligerent with the bad ball, portraying his role as, 'This bloke's doing well and he knows it.'

In fact it was the other bloke who was doing well. Ian was demonstrating precisely what a contrast the brothers Chappell could be. He hooked, pulled and slashed his way to an incendiary half century. While Ian swayed onto his back foot, Greg leaned to the front, between them denying the bowlers a comfortable length. It took such a Test, such a crisis, for them to submerge their dangerous individualism in each other's presence to the greater national purpose.

By lunch Ian was gone but Greg was like a painter who had just applied his size. In the dressing-room, alone with his thoughts, he ordered lunch brought down rather than join the team. He wanted to retain his dimension. I once walked in on Greg during such an innings break and backed out as though I had passed through an air lock, so thick was the air with immanence.

Back out again Greg did a stocktake of the fieldsmen: where was Tony Greig, their best? where John Snow and Mike Smith, both athletic? and Geoff Boycott — a ball past him and you could look for two. England captain Ray Illingworth, recalling Perth, feared another Gregory-led recovery. He moved his chess pieces but Greg saw them as just that, moves. It was not like Perth anyway. The pitch did not get easier. Greg essayed no real spells of aggression. It was three hours before he hit his first four and paradoxically it was an off-drive. Since Perth the England bowlers were not allowed to bowl on Greg's leg stump.

Now they were busy improving the quality of his off-side strokes. Not often though. Price, Snow and d'Oliveira mostly bowled just short of a length and the deviation off the seam meant Greg had to delay his stroke to detect the direction. Losing that fraction made it hard to score. So he waited until they overpitched and then he discarded his fetters and drove for four. That, more than anything, impressed the aficionados, to see such grace and poise unleashed, and yet to see it harnessed so long. The greatness of the innings was its understatement.

By tea Greg was dying for the break. He had counted his own score, setting himself targets of 10, and crept up to 50, then 60, each time mentally patting his own back and applauding his concentration. He never looked further. 'Never to 100. I'd have thought, "I'll never get there!"' It was one of the longest days Greg ever put in. 'It seemed to take forever. Physically I was as good as gold but mentally I was tiring,' he said. After tea the pitch seemed to whiten a shade, the ball less red, the stitches less easy to discern. Where the ball landed the soft pitch was marked with tiny indentations and when subsequent balls hit these bruises the ball would seam a little extra.

Greg wrestled with his concentration, not the least because he was now on top. The words hovered insidiously on the periphery of his mind, 'Right, I've got these bastards.' That would be his undoing, to prejudge a stroke, predetermine a ball. He orchestrated his concentration like a conductor, pianissimo between deliveries as he caught a pretty colour or girl in the crowd, andante as the bowler walked measuredly to his mark, allegro as he turned, and concentration fortissimo as he reared for the delivery stride. An instant later, diminuendo.

Listening in Adelaide, in the wee hours of the morning, were Judy and Kay Chappell, Judy making curtains and chair covers, calling, 'Don't run' and 'Run', and slipping away during breaks to make chocolate hedgehog to feed their nerves.

By the end of the day Greg had his century and walked off to a standing ovation, from Lord's, from the England team and from his waiting team-mates. Now, relenting at last on his concentration, the anti-climax set in. 'It was no big deal,' he said. 'It was the focus of my whole attention, all day, my mind, the whole bloody thing. But that's what I was picked in the team for. It was satisfying rather than exciting. It's like the old story about chasing women — half the fun is the chase, so I've been told. Once you get there you wonder what all the excitement was about. Yet you get the chance for a century the next day and you're just as keen for the chase.'

The next day Greg took his score to 131. It had lasted a marathon 6 hours 13 minutes, the longest innings of his career. Though Massie decimated England again he and the team knew half the laurels belonged to Lillee who had begun bowling so fast that the English batsmen preferred losing their wicket to Massie than a limb to Lillee.

The Lord's victory transformed the Australians. Barry Maranta, a future business partner with Greg, was in a little tavern bar next to Lord's that evening. 'There was euphoria,' he said. 'They'd been written off and come back. Absolute ecstasy in the bar.' The Australians team masseur, Dave 'Doc' McErlane, told Martin of his sons, 'Marty, I've got a lot of respect for those gorillas of yours.' McErlane puzzled about their combined skills. And had the answer. 'It must have been their breakfasts,' he told me. 'Breakfast with the Chappells is bananas and mustard on toast, all four of them. Must be good for producing international cricketers.'

A new cheer settled on the tour, with comedy principally led by Ashley Mallett. He bought a deerstalker hat, tweed jacket and hooked meerschaum pipe and at boring receptions where most of the team were huddled together to exclude earbashers, Mallett would declare, 'Hellow, Mallee's the name,' in a murderous Oxford accent. 'From the Antipodes ackchewally, small property in the west, 30,000 acres...' The team fell about. They knew he shared a flat with Terry Jenner in Adelaide.

Rowdy, as he was nicknamed, also took the microphone on the tour bus and made up running descriptions of the grand homes they passed, always at the expense of the English class system. 'It was spontaneous humour,' said Greg. 'It wouldn't translate away from that moment, but it was droll, dry and very funny.' Or else, for a change, he would read aloud an x-rated pulp novel, embellishing it as he proceeded. The Australians all bore nicknames, too numerous to recount, and not necessarily logical. But in the psychology of the small group, nicknames enabled them to relate to each other on a cricket level without having to delve too far into interpersonal depths. Insulting Rowdy or Bacchus (Marsh), FOT (F——ing Old Tart, Lillee), or Fergy (Massey, as in the tractor), was not the same as insulting Ashley, Rod, Dennis or Bob. Nicknames also enabled the team to refer to each other privately in public. And occasionally, it enabled the team to turn its merciless glare upon a player's weakness which the team, in its collective wisdom, thought could cost them a match.

An extension of nicknaming was Greg and Paul Sheahan's made-up team verse, sung to the tune of 'The Quartermaster's Store'. For Keith Stackpole:

There was Stack, Stack, needing saunas front and back,
On the tour, on the tour.
There was Stack, Stack, needing saunas front and back,
On the Aussie–England tour.

There were verses for everyone. David Colley:

There was Fox, Fox, bouncing 'em round their locks . . .

Ross Edwards:

There was Ross, Ross, giving the port a toss . . .

Dennis Lillee:

There was FOT, FOT, giving 'em the V a lot . . .

Mallett:

There was Rowd, Rowd, reading porno books aloud . . .

and so on, verses for all except the composers, Greg and Paul, the team songsters.

In this joyous mood they drew the third Test at Trent Bridge, Nottingham. England had chosen Peter Parfitt to combat Massie's prodigious swing, believing that left handers stood a better chance. For the fourth Test at Headingley, Leeds, no such precautions were necessary. 'I can picture the ground now,' said Greg. 'It was the darkest green you could imagine and then this bare strip, 22 yards by 8 foot, like a bare piece of dirt. You could see all the grass roots showing through the soil.' It was said the wicket had been invaded by a disease, fusarium. To Greg its symptoms were identical with the grass having been mowed, and brushed back and mowed again, until it was burnt down to its roots. It was a dust bowl, took spin from the very first day. Lillee and Massie were blunted, Derek Underwood's 10 wickets won for England. 'The dressing-room at the end of the game was like a morgue,' said Greg. 'We felt we'd been cheated. It was as though the tour had died right at that moment.' Norman Preston in *Wisden* wrote, 'Not for a moment would one suggest that conditions had been deliberately engineered...' thereby leaving that suspicion for posterity.

There was one light moment for Greg, though it took three years to mature. In the second innings he was caught at deep mid-off from Underwood. 'I'd decided before he bowled that the next one he threw up was going back over his head. I mishit it and I was furious with myself.' Greg rarely threw his bat. Once he hurled it into the dressing-room after a disappointing innings at Prince Alfred College but no sooner had the bat stopped rattling off the walls than he became aware Chester Bennett was in the doorway. 'I'd be a bit careful how you treat that bat. You might want to use it again,' said Bennett, and left young Greg to his own humiliation. At Leeds Greg's frustration with his own dismissal was piled upon his anger about the wicket. As he walked past the clothes drying cabinet he drove the handle of his bat into the door and exclaimed, and the words are important to the metre, 'No f—ing justice in this game!' He put his bat in his bag and sat down near Doug Walters. No one said a word. Three years later, on the 1975 Australians' tour, same ground, Walters came in after being dismissed, whacked the same drying cabinet with his bat and said, 'No f—ing justice in this game!' and sat down next to Greg, deadpan.

How Ian reclaimed the broken spirit of his team after Headingley produced Greg's benchmark for exalted captaincy. Ian let the anger and self-pity expire and then began rebuilding at a team dinner before the fifth Test at The Oval. It was a six-day Test, a result was certain. 'It's up to us,' he said. 'If we go home two-all it's been a successful tour. If we go home down 3–1 we'll be looked upon as failures. It will affect the careers of a lot of you who have kicked on out of all recognition on this tour. Now we put Leeds out of our minds and think about how we played at Lord's again.'

The Oval Test has gone into the annals as one of the most exciting of the 1970s decade. Greg and Ian each hit a century, the first brothers to accomplish this in one Test innings. 'It was irrelevant, of no moment to us,' said Greg. They were playing for Australia. The match teetered back and forth for six days until Australia won to square the series. Even though they had not regained the Ashes the nucleus of that team continued through the 1970s. To a man they now knew what it took over five concentrated days of cricket to win a Test match. If one were searching for symbols it could be that Lillee struck Snow such a severe blow he could not bowl in the second innings. *Le roi est mort, vive le roi*! Or that Rod Marsh was at the wicket when the winning runs were posted. He was the second member of the great Aussie trinity. Greg's century made him the third. More important, what Ian had been hoping for had transpired — the rebirth and renewal of Australian cricket. Rod Marsh jumped upon the dressing-room table and gave his famous, joyous, ringing rendition, guaranteed to flush the face, stand hair on end and turn dry eyes brimful:

Under the Southern Cross I stand,
A sprig of wattle in my hand,
A native of my native land,
Australia, you f—ing beauty.

The tour was over except for the Prudential one-day matches against England. Ian told Dennis Lillee, relaxing in a bath at The Oval after taking 10 wickets in that great victory, 'As far as I'm concerned, you've done your job. If you're rooted you can bowl off a short run, or even have a rest. Just let me know.' England won the first easily. On a train back to London Ian grabbed Stackpole and found the tour manager, Ray Steele, and assistant manager, Fred Bennett. 'I'm not the right bloke to captain these one-day matches. I don't give a damn about them. As far as I'm concerned the tour finished when we won at The Oval. It'd be better if Stackie captains the side.' But Stackpole piped back, 'Well, it's no good asking me because I feel exactly the same way as you. Why don't we just go out and have a bit of fun.'

It was agreed. A bit of fun. Australia won the next but lost the last, and the Cup, 2–1. It was extraordinary that at the very moment when Ian Chappell was founding a new epoch of winning cricket with his 1972 Aussie crusaders, he should also sow into its genetic structure such a fatally recessive gene. It handicapped Australian cricket as the traditional game mutated through the 1970s and became a cancer Greg fought to contain during his captaincy just under a decade later. It nearly destroyed him.

10. Windies

The first ball of Greg's first Test match in the West Indies shimmers like a hologram in his memory, a vision of massed colour, bright sun, dark skin and soft grass and, just for a heart beat, absolute hushed silence. It was in Kingston, Jamaica, before 14,000 excited, buzzing cricket fanatics, several hundred of whom were perched in palm trees or high up in light pylons surrounding the oval, hanging by an arm and a leg with a rum bottle in their spare hand. The ground was full but ropes were hauling more over the outside wall despite its jagged broken glass defence. The Australians warmed up on the ground and allowed a little, 50-year-old, barefooted Jamaican, nicknamed Sleepy, to bowl leg-spinners to them. Whenever he beat the bat the ground roared in delight.

Tension climbed as the two captains, Ian Chappell and Rohan Kanhai tossed. Ian won. Stackpole and Redpath padded up. The crowd was dancing and jigging and flapping their arms to din of trumpet blasts, percussion rhythms rapped out on every conceivable object, laughter and the raucous feedback of a thousand transistor radios. The West Indian hope was a young fast bowler, Uton Dowe, their new Wes Hall. He measured his run, turned towards Keith Stackpole and with every step the noise rose to a cacophony until, at Dowe's delivery stride, it suddenly ceased. You can't hear silence but you can hear 14,000 people holding their breath while fate decides which to favour, bat or ball. 'For a split second it was like the whole place had died,' said Greg. Dowe's ball was a bouncer and Stackpole hooked it for four. The coliseum erupted and the noise level stayed there for the rest of the day.

Stackpole hooked Dowe for another four and a six in that opening over and after five overs Kanhai banished Dowe to fine leg. For the new ball Dowe was recalled late in the day with Australia well on top. As Dowe measured his run a voice from the palm trees yelled out, 'Kanhai, haven't you heard the eleventh commandment? Dowe shalt not bowl!'

That was Greg's introduction to Caribbean cricket. It was February

1973. The contrast with England where he had toured only six months earlier was stunning. This was the third great power of world cricket. Greg's expectations ran no further than Harry Belafonte's lyrics about Kingston Town. He was immediately at one with them. They loved cricket and laughter. Their attitude was, 'No point in crying, man, the sun's going to come up tomorrow.' Greg saw their economic deprivation, their huts and lean-to's, their sometimes makeshift cricket facilities, yet shining through it all beamed their knowledge of cricket. That made them and their islands beautiful to Greg.

When the Australians arrived all they heard from the hundreds at the airport was, 'Which one's Lillee, which one's Massie?' Fast bowlers were kings in the Caribbean. But these two became pretenders. Lillee broke down after the first Test and spent the tour visiting back specialists. Massie was in the last throes of his tragically brief Test career. Lord's haunted him. The dry atmosphere and lifeless Caribbean wickets were anathema to his swing. Said Greg, 'We kept saying to him, "When the conditions are like Lord's maybe you can get 16 wickets, but you probably won't. When the conditions are totally against your type of bowling, if you can bowl 30 overs and get 2–50, you've done your job." ' But it was no good. 'Bob kept trying to swing, bowling half volleys and full tosses. He wouldn't bowl straight and be economical.'

In Kingston the team stayed at the Courtleigh Manor Hotel which featured around its pool a resident band of grandfather, father and three sons, the youngest, the drummer, aged only seven. They played the new reggae rhythms that Greg enjoyed so much he bought a collection of cheap reggae tapes, which soon disintegrated. Greg found the traditional steel bands, using steel drums and lids for instruments, often repetitious but their lyrics intrigued. One such song, entitled 'Alec Betsa', has gone into the archives of West Indian folk music. Betsa is Bedser and the song recounts, not a Test in the West Indies, but between England and Australia, the first Test at Trent Bridge, Nottingham, in June 1953. Its key verses go:

It's 1953, has made cricket history,
Australia was leading, while England was struggling,
Then came a sudden disaster, by a medium-paced bowler,
Alec Betsa, who taught you to bowl Australia.

Morris was the saviour, for champion Australia,
Hassett batted pretty, by scoring a century,

Betsa was really superfine, 14 wickets for 99,
Alec Betsa, who taught you to bowl Australia.

He can't be forgotten, this captain Len Hutton,
He made a great attack, he certainly fought back,
Rain came down to save Australia, but ended in England's favour,
Alec Betsa, who taught you to bowl Australia.

Greg pursued his musical odyssey by visiting a studio to watch Cat
Stevens record an album. He and Lillee did not play in the game
against the President's XI in Montego Bay and so toured the set of
the film *Papillon*, which starred Steve McQueen. The ship which
transported Papillon was of balsa on rollers and could be rocked into
the most violent storm by three stage hands. 'It all looked like steel
beams until you tapped it,' said Greg. The Devil's Island gaol was
recreated so well that a Frenchman who had worked there as a gaoler
was overcome by its realism.

Greg and Dennis, who roomed together, also had time for further
mischief. The team's liaison officer was a West Indian woman, a
widow in her forties, named Celia. She told them how much she was
looking forward to a cocktail party and meeting ABC commentator
Alan McGilvray whose descriptions she had listened to for years. The
lads had been teaching Celia some Australian slang and Greg said, 'If
you really want to impress him when you are introduced say, "Pleased
to meet you, why don't you get rooted."' Celia complied enthusiasti-
cally and a shocked McGilvray walked out, averring he had never been
so offended. 'She was absolutely devastated,' said Greg. 'We felt really
bad. We tried to console her and she was great. Then we went and
apologized to Alan but I don't think he's ever forgiven me for it.'

Having drawn the first Test, the Australians moved on to Bridgetown, Barbados, for the second. It was 2,400 kilometres to the east and
they began to understand the administrative problems of the far-flung
West Indian cricket islands. Greg succeeded with 106 in the second
Test, but only after struggling for the first 40 runs. It was the first time
uncertainty interceded since his century at Lord's. Since then he had
averaged 60 in three Tests against Pakistan in the early Australian
summer and began with centuries against both Jamaica and Barbados
in the island matches. It reminded him how fickle form could be. As
this Test too sagged to a draw a giant young West Indian stepped over
the fine leg boundary fence and approached Greg with a dollar note.

'Sign this, man,' he said smiling. 'You play cricket?' asked Greg. 'Yeah man, I'll play against you one day.' Said Greg, 'Well good luck to you.' It was Joel Garner.

Australia's problem was that without Lillee and Massie they could not break through the West Indies batting. Lillee's fear was not that he would not bowl on the tour again, but that he might never bowl again. He kept fit by running each day, and though despondent, maintained his humour. The tour bus drivers were his target. Passing through narrow gates, Dennis would lean out the window and whack the side of the bus with his shoe and enjoy the next few minutes as the perplexed driver searched for the damage. Once, leaving the Governor's grounds after a reception, Lillee noticed the driver had liberally entered into the spirits of the party. Dennis then enacted an elaborate hoax in which he managed by whacks, yelps and crashing about in the dark, to convince the driver he had run over the Governor's dog, no mean crime if the awestruck fellow's face was any guide.

Two months into the tour the show moved south to Port of Spain in Trinidad for the third Test, destined to equal the Oval Test in England as one of the most dramatic in Greg's career. This time it was Doug Walters' turn. On the England tour he had failed, averaging only 7.7 runs per Test innings, eventually being dropped for that famous Oval Test. That hurt the laconic, take-it-as-it-comes soul of the Australian team. 'Outwardly he was just the same, but inside I'm sure it was eating him away,' said Greg. In Port of Spain Walters hit a century between lunch and tea. 'Three times I've seen him do it in Test cricket and each time we've won,' said Greg. 'He was pulling away outside leg stump and almost driving the ball backward of point. He was always a brilliant player of spin, but this was unbelievable batting.' Yet by lunch on the last day the West Indies needed only 66 runs to win with six wickets in hand and Alvin Kallicharan on 91 in full flight.

In Tolstoy's *War and Peace*, before the battle of Borodino, Prince Andre Bolkonsky reflected that in war a battalion was sometimes stronger than a division and yet sometimes weaker than a single company. 'Have we not seen that thanks to some resolute madman, 5,000 men have held their ground against 30,000?' he said. 'Success can depend on one private who shouts hurrah.' As the Australians prepared to file dolefully out from their lunch room to what seemed like certain defeat, Ian stopped at the door, turned and gave that hurrah. He said, 'You've been bowling and fielding like a lot of pricks.

A quick wicket can change everything. We're going out there to win.' A famous speech? Hardly eloquent, or even inspiring, certainly not in Tolstoy's class. But to the loyal assembled it tapped the source of their patriotic power. Ian could do that. And he had some claims to the heroic.

He had sprained his right foot playing tennis two days before the Test. 'He shouldn't have played,' said Greg. 'He fielded at slips so he didn't have to run. He batted down the order and he couldn't leave the crease to play the spinners. That's why in the first innings he was caught and bowled lunging forward.' Yet Ian managed 97 in the second innings when the Australians were decidedly unsteady. So when he spoke it was not what he said, but that he had said it. Said it with that half-lidded glance which made the most honest among them search his conscience. Max Walker opened the attack with a regulation, post-lunch, warm up ball which Kallicharan cut at hugely only to find the gentlest of edges dolly to Marsh. 'You could feel the surge in the team,' said Greg. 'Coming so close on Ian's words. The West Indies just went to water.'

If The Oval victory in England saved Ian's Australians from being branded second rate, Port of Spain raised them to a new plane. Ian Redpath, who did not smoke or drink, always broke his rule after a Test win and he did that evening, champagne and a cigarette. The celebrations continued with a keg in the team room into the early morning. Greg retired to bed, next to the team room and listened to Ian, Doug, Rod and Dennis next door. He heard Dennis announce, 'Come on, we're going to a night club,' though he was in no such fit state. Ian and Doug hustled Lillee into the lift. It descended, then returned and Greg heard Ian and Walters say, 'Righto, across this road, OK, watch the gutter, left turn here,' when in fact they were walking Lillee around and around the old-fashioned internal hotel staircase. Greg twigged, rose and opened his door. 'Here we are, there's a seat over there,' said Ian and walked Lillee through the door and over to his bed. 'You sit there and we'll get you a drink ... Waiter!' said Doug. 'Ahh, you're good blokes taking me out,' slurred Lillee. Greg pushed Dennis gently on the chest and the fast bowler rolled into bed, almost instantly asleep. 'And that was his way of coping with the frustration and disappointment of his back,' said Greg.

Lillee and Massie were two who fell answering Prince Bolkonsky's hurrah. Into their places stepped two bowlers whose hearts swelled to fill the gaps left by their talents — Max 'Tangles' Walker and Jeff

'Bomber' Hammond. Though they may have returned better figures in their careers, they could never surpass their contributions to Ian's call to arms. And not content with sharing that glory they sought to settle who was the better man. The challenge was issued, weapons chosen, a venue agreed — a smorgasbord on one of the small islands. Both ate two full first course plates, and doubled up on desserts. Said Max, 'We may as well top it off with banana splits.' Three bananas, six scoops of icecream. Both nearly expiring, shovelled in the last mouthful, but Max perceiving victory said, 'Oh well, Bomber, I think we could go another one of those, don't you?' Hammond conceded, outclassed! 'They were both pretty good tooth men,' said Greg, 'but Max confessed later he couldn't have gone another mouthful. A dead heat really, though Max claimed a TKO.'

Georgetown, Guyana, on the South American mainland, confirmed the incipient greatness of this Australian team. Victory was working like an amphetamine in their systems. The fourth Test there signalled the emergence of Clive Lloyd, hammering 178 of the West Indies' 366 first innings. But there comes a moment in every contest when self belief ebbs through the very soles of the losers as though the earth is claiming their confidence. That happened in the second innings when a combination of Australian medium pacers and spinners worked their modest magic like voodoo on the West Indians to dismiss them for 109. The Australians waltzed away with the Test and the series.

That evening the Australians celebrated at a nearby disco, the Dog and Bone, about 200 metres from their hotel. They had been warned about night violence. 'Choke-and-rob they called it,' said Greg. 'Mostly on white American tourists. The local police chief told me, "Don't worry. While you're in town the word has gone out: no choke-and-rob. You can't tell an American from an Australian and we don't want any mistakes."' It would have been difficult to mistake an Australian that evening, not the least because they were becoming celebrities on the stage of international cricket.

There were no incidents and Greg's tour memory was of the friendly pat on the back, the wide smile, the gentleness and the jokes, the sun and the music. And their cricket. That was instructive. Ian's captaincy had been the difference between the two teams. 'He was able to inspire victory where there seemed none,' said Greg. 'They'd get into a position to win and then look back over their shoulders to see how they could lose.' To a degree Greg's senior cricket education was

GREG CHAPPELL

complete. On the England tour he had averaged 70 runs an innings, at home against Pakistan 60 runs, and now he had finished the Caribbean tour with 69.3. He was the first Australian to score 1,000 runs on a West Indies tour. He was on the threshold of becoming the most prolific batsman in Australia's champion team. Yet there was more to playing than batting, fielding and spare-time bowling. Captaincy arose before him, a new height to scale in the ever rising fortunes of his cricket career. But Ian blocked his path, in South Australia and therefore, for Australia. Or so it seemed.

DIVINITY (1973–1977)

11. Queensland

By the winter of 1973 Judy Chappell had begun to understand what life with Gregory was going to be. Of the past 13 months he had been overseas for eight. He had played 13 Tests, 10 of them in England and the West Indies. 'Under their contracts players' wives weren't allowed to be in the same hotel or on the same plane,' said Judy. 'I talked with Kay Chappell and she helped me understand that wives really had no place on tour. It made it very difficult for the guys to give their best. It ripped them in two. They wanted to be with their wives, yet with the team.' In Adelaide Judy had begun primary school teaching and at the end of the 1972 tour to England she and Kay had met their husbands in South Africa, a sort of belated honeymoon for Judy and Greg. But Judy did not see her life with Greg as a sacrifice. 'I sensed there was a greatness there,' she said. 'That he was destined... he was a cut above other people in that...' She paused. 'He had a great sense of purpose, yes, a great sense of purpose.'

The executive members of the Queensland Cricket Association agreed. They wrote inviting him to play for Queensland. Was he interested, what would make him interested? Initially Greg was genuinely uninterested. He was a managerial trainee with Coca Cola, time off for cricket, assured of his place in South Australian cricket and society. John Maclean rang and told Greg he would stand down from the Queensland captaincy. They were friends from the 1969 Second XI tour of New Zealand. Queensland had finished last in the Sheffield Shield the previous season, no fault of Maclean's. 'We needed a player of his calibre,' said Maclean. 'To me it was much better being vice-captain of a successful outfit than captain of an unsuccessful one.'

Greg flew to Queensland and met the chairman of the committee formed to attract him to Brisbane, former Test all-rounder, Ron Archer. He had lunch at the Queensland Cricketers' Club with the committee which included Bill Leather, state manager for Friends Provident Insurance. Their offer was a guaranteed company salary plus sales commission, relocation costs and up to six months accommodation, a contract for three years. Greg declined the contract. If he accepted, it would be a trial for 12 months. Adelaide, it seemed, still held some strings, but not for long. The South Australian Cricket Association's response was: we would like you to stay, but if we do something for you it sets a precedent for other players.

The phone rang at Greg's home. Sir Donald Bradman inviting Greg to meet him and co-selector Phil Ridings for lunch. Greg was surprised and apprehensive. He had hardly spoken to Bradman since the changing grip conversation in 1967, six years earlier. He met them at the Stock Exchange Club in King William Street, and ate sandwiches while Bradman, with the air of a successful businessman, talked forcefully about Australian cricket. Greg's feeling was that no special effort had been made to keep him. He heard Bradman compare Queensland cricket unfavourably with South Australian cricket, which Greg should feel it was an honour to play. Years later, in different circumstances and for different reasons, Greg repeated those criticisms in the *Telegraph*, a Brisbane newspaper. On 2 November 1977, he was reported as saying:

> When I first decided to move from South Australia to Queensland, Sir Donald Bradman urged me not to go through with it.
> He said some unbelievable things about some Queensland administrators. He told me cricket here was in a bad state and I shouldn't take on the Queensland side.

Eight days after those comments were published, Bradman wrote to Greg accusing him of inaccuracy and a breach of trust in referring publicly to private and confidential discussions. Further he said he had spent a long time trying to find a proposal sufficiently attractive to keep Greg in South Australia. He said the simple truth was that in the final analysis South Australia was unable to match the Queensland offer. Yet Greg was disappointed his home State made no apparent attempt to help him. 'It made the decision easier,' he said. It is truly extraordinary that two men of such precise natures should meet and part with such utterly opposed impressions of their meeting.

Greg told Coca Cola of Queensland's offer. 'I don't want to horse-trade. I'm just telling you so you hear it from me and not someone else.' In the end the captaincy really decided the issue. Greg had consulted Ian but it was not just a matter of waiting the five years for Ian to step down. For Greg to succeed Ian he needed the experience as captain, otherwise some other State skipper could inherit Ian's crown. The offer by Maclean, 'one of nature's gentlemen', said Greg, tipped the balance.

What did Greg know of Brisbane? 'A big country town, pace not too fast, oppressive summer nights, people spoke a bit slower than elsewhere, plenty of mañana mentality.' He did not know that he was arriving just as Queensland, led by an eccentric, charismatic premier and his conservative Country Party, was shrugging that image and digging into its reserves of mineral wealth. Greg was about to ride this economic wave himself; cometh the awakening, came the man. Three of Greg's first seven Shield centuries were scored at the 'Gabba. It could not be all that bad. Then there was the team. His friend MacLean; Phil Carlson, a talented all-rounder; Geoff Dymock, future Test bowler; and the hugely framed Tony Dell, the only bowler whose bounce worried Barry Richards in the season he opened for South Australia. Judy and Kay, soul-mates through two long tours, shed a tear on each other's shoulder. Martin Chappell was perhaps saddest to see them go. Queensland dollars were breaking up that old gang of his.

From bluestone and brick to weatherboard and stumps. The Chappells cruised Brisbane's new suburbs, Aspley and Sunnybank, aghast at their barren blocks. The trees of upper middle class Kenmore reminded them of Blackwood and Belair in the Adelaide Hills. They bought a two-storey, L-shaped house in Kenmore with a swimming pool, overlooking a natural reserve and a friendly, scrubby creek. Judy moved in while Greg was playing a double-wicket competition in South Africa with Ian. It took a good pair to beat them in the final, Rhodesians Mike Procter and Brian Davison.

I first met Greg in September 1973 at his first club match as captain of South Brisbane, John Maclean's club. About 500 people gathered at picturesque Queensland University Oval, set amid tall gums and squabbling magpies next to the somnolent Brisbane River. Radio and television were linked to broadcast Greg's progress score. The pressure was on. Though pleased to snare a star some Queenslanders were poised to fulminate should the southern smartie fail. South's openers batted well. Greg waited, sentences staccato, laced with swearing. He admitted to verbal diarrhoea as a nervous outlet once he donned the pads. Maclean leaned across to Greg, 'They're going well but you watch, the crowd will start to barrack soon.' Greg smiled and mimicked a barracker, 'Yeah, piss off, we didn't come here to watch you mugs.'

He wore his new club's green cap, hair curling well down to his collar, matching sidelevers, and a tidy, non-Newcombe moustache. When the opening stand was broken he pulled on his gloves and to a chorus of 'Good lucks' left the pavilion, glancing obligingly but unsmilingly at a newspaper photographer. Judy set up a canvas chair beside the pavilion. In a white skirt, green and white top, matching rings and earrings, bare brown legs and platform soles, she made a fetching sight for curious star gazers. Queensland selector Ken Mackay, whom Greg saw defy Wes Hall so mightily in Adelaide in 1961, arrived in old shirt and shorts. 'He told me years later he came to see me captain, not bat,' said Greg, who spent nearly two painstaking hours assembling 30. But then late in the afternoon he scored at a run a minute to reach 100. Yet another, albeit minor, milestone marked with a century. He sat in the darkening dressing-room sipping lemonade and wearily unlaced his boots. He seemed young and vulnerable, too soon to be leading his adopted State. Yet that is what Queensland became, the greening of captain Chappell.

The third match of the Shield season was against South Australia at the 'Gabba. Visiting Adelaide newspapermen were amazed at Greg's high public profile. On suburban bus seats, 'Chappell Plays for Queensland — See Him at the 'Gabba.' Newspaper advertisements proclaimed Chappell wore these clothes and drove that motor car. It was billed as the Battle of the Brothers. Greg had opposed Ian only once before, with Somerset in 1968 when Ian blazed a fast century for the touring Australians. They had never met as captains. Ian, Trevor, father Martin who was South Australian team manager, Ashley Mallett and Terry Jenner, had dinner with Greg at his Kenmore home. Publicly the two teams engaged in mild sabre-rattling. Mallett declared he fancied his chances of bowling out Greg more than he would Ian. Greg replied, 'If I felt there was anyone in the South Australian side we could get out by bowling a few bouncers I would have no hesitation.'

Greg's first ball was from Mallett but only after Greg had wasted time walking down the pitch to tap it pedantically, smiling broadly all the time at the close-in fieldsmen. Queensland overwhelmed the visitors but not without a fight from, and with, Ian. The South Australians were all but beaten when tailender, Barry Hiern, a short, dogged, opening bowler, came to the crease to join Ian, who made 126 in that innings. Greg let Hiern have a bouncer which, even at Greg's pace, slipped off the greenish pitch and hit Hiern in the ribs. Ian turned to Greg, 'If you want to bowl any short stuff, bowl them to me. I'm the batsman, not him.' Greg gave the pro forma reply, 'Why don't you get on with your batting.' Said Ian, 'Have a look at the scoreboard, I am.' At which point Greg lowered the intellectual quality of the ripostes to their familiar backyard script. Back in Adelaide Jeanne asked, 'How's Greg?' Said Ian, 'Oh fine, took us about five minutes to have an argument.' And Jeanne, 'It doesn't surprise me at all.'

On the Australia Day weekend, 1974, after two weeks of cyclonic rain the Brisbane River broke its banks to engulf the city in the second biggest flood on record. Houses floated into the night, 14 people were drowned, the city fell into shock. Creeks feeding the river had nowhere to go but up. That friendly creek below Greg and Judy's house filled the reserve and then rose nearly 6 metres to enter the garage and rumpus room before falling with not much harm done. Next day it came back, almost 4 metres higher and finished the job, hip level through the top floor. On 26 January Greg was batting on the first day of the third Test against New Zealand in Adelaide. He was not out at lunch time and was greeted by Australian Cricket Board member, Norm McMahon, also from Brisbane. 'Got some bad news for you,' said the tall, phlegmatic McMahon. Greg's was one of 14,000 homes flooded.

Judy was in Adelaide with Greg. They had read of the rain but they were only four-month-old Brisbanites. They had no idea. Neighbours floated the Chappells' marital bed out on surf skis. Their car and washing machine bobbed about in the garage. Twelfth man fielded for Greg on the last day of the Test and he flew to Brisbane. Judy was pregnant and with rumours of cholera about she stayed in Sydney. Greg bunked with friends and they patrolled at night with torches and rifles to prevent looting. 'I fired off a few warning shots one night, scared a few blokes off,' said Greg. He hosed the house down and later Judy and her parents scrubbed and disinfected. Insurance eventually repainted, repapered and recarpeted the house but flood damage is a slow rot. Veneer lifts, chipboard swells, materials shred. Like every other flooded family the Chappells suffered trauma. For a year afterwards whenever it rained they were over to the window to watch the creek. They preserved some glasses which, sitting in their glass cabinet, had registered the flood height with a muddy rim. For months Judy kept meeting local residents who told her, 'I saved your bed.'

Under the circumstances it was incredible that Greg was able to lead Queensland to a virtual Shield final against New South Wales in Sydney in the last match of the season. Ashley Woodcock was not surprised. He toured New Zealand with Greg later that year and noticed changes in his Princes College friend. Greg had matured physically, was hitting the ball harder yet making it look easier. 'He had become a more ruthless player too,' said Woodcock. 'He batted with a sort of contempt for the opposition bowling, as if no bowler was good enough to tame him.' The Queensland Premier, Joh Bjelke-Petersen, promised a civic reception for the team if they won the Shield. Queensland, even with Slasher Mackay, Peter Burge, Ray Lindwall and Wally Grout in their team, had never won the Shield. By the time this match was finished Greg had become only the fifth batsman of all time to pass 1,000 runs in Shield matches in a season. He joined Bill Ponsford, Sir Donald Bradman, Norm O'Neill and Barry Richards, finishing with an average of 92 runs per innings. But he did not win the Shield.

Greg and Sam Trimble were cruising in the second innings when a young, powerful, blond-haired New South Wales fast bowler suddenly struck his rhythm. Greg, the 1,000 runs man, was playing and missing at balls which simply flew through him. Bowler's name? Jeff Thomson. 'He was the quickest thing I'd seen,' said Greg. 'Frightening because he was inaccurate. First he hid the ball behind his back with his slinging action. Then he had you off balance because you had to wait that fraction of a second longer to see where it was going, just to make sure it wasn't straight at your head. Then to react with a stroke — he was too quick.' He had Greg caught behind, glancing down the leg-side and Trimble caught cutting. Neither said much back in the dressing-room as an act of mercy towards the incoming batsmen. One was John Maclean. 'His first ball I hardly saw,' said Maclean. 'I had just taken my bat back when it hit me in the shoulder. I thought we were a bit gutless at the time but history proved he was pretty quick.'

Thomson took 7–85, laying waste to Queensland's long cherished Shield hopes. Greg sought out Shiva, their destroyer. He knew him from the previous year when Thomson, in his first Test, bowled with an undiagnosed broken bone in his foot and returned 0–110 against

Pakistan in Melbourne. Thomson had no job, no career. He was unhappy with New South Wales who had not chosen him all year. Thomson suspected New South Wales had played him in the last match just to keep him in their stable. In Brisbane Greg saw Norm McMahon and said, 'I don't want to play against that bloke again. We've got to get him up here.' Greg liaised, Thomson visited in mid-winter and signed on.

Thomson striking his lightning was problem enough for Greg at the SCG, but while batting Greg was further distracted. He and Judy had had a meal at a Randwick club the previous evening and after-wards Judy, pregnant, complained of stomach pains. She returned to her parents' home and Greg to the team hotel. Next morning Greg noticed, while batting, that Judy was not in her normal seat at the SCG. Greg always sensed-saw when Judy arrived in a cricket stand. It was part of his relaxation technique at the crease to look elsewhere than at the pitch. He noticed other friends too but with Judy it verged on telepathy. Separated over 19,000 kilometres Judy would book a call to him and seconds later get through. 'That was quick,' she would say. No, he was calling her. It happened too often for coincidence. This time at the SCG he was not alarmed, but thought her absence strange. When he was dismissed he rang Judy's mother from the dressing-room. Judy had suffered a miscarriage and was under sedation in a private hospital. She had refused to let her parents ring him at the ground because she knew it would disturb him on the field. That was how important cricket loomed in Judy's mind. 'I was totally indoctri-nated at the time,' she said.

The next day Greg left for New Zealand with the Australian team. Judy was in no danger, was in better nursing hands with her mother than with Greg. 'From that point of view she wasn't being left in the lurch,' said Greg. 'But I guess she could have done with a bit of tender loving care.' Greg was keen to fulfil his potential and ambitions on the field. He and Judy had made that choice from the beginning, without discussion, because it was understood. 'As far as I was concerned my destiny, if you like, was on the cricket field,' he said.

His destiny with New Zealand seemed always to be both propitious and controversial. In the first Test at Wellington his two innings aggregate of 247 not out and 133 set a new world Test record. It was the beginning of the records trail which would progress now for the next decade, though it was not until the very end that he really took the slightest notice. 'It was of no big moment,' he said. 'The wicket was unbelievably good, and the outfield fast. But I really don't rate it, other than for the number of runs and for striking the ball.' He was glad to score 200 too, because the odd fool made the carping criticism that 200 was a better test than 100. He was mildly disappointed when Ian declared. 'I was seeing the ball so well, if I was ever going to make 300 that was it. But it was secondary. We'd made 511, there was no point in making more.'

The second Test New Zealand won, their first victory over Australia. The Australians were not new to defeat. But Greg compared New Zealand in victory with the gracious conduct of Ray Illingworth's England team in 1970–71. Ian marched his team into the New Zealand dressing-room as was his habit, to congratulate them, to share a drink and then to withdraw. But they were not allowed to escape unscathed. That victory unleashed various grudges in the New Zealand cricketing psyche. Rain had deprived them of almost certain victory in a Sydney Test only a few weeks earlier. Animosity was also abroad through various on-field incidents which had branded the Australians as 'The Ugly Aussies'. It all came out in a rush. In the Australians' presence a New Zealand official made a jubilant speech — 'It's about time we beat these bastards', and, 'We're every bit as good as them'. Said Greg, 'You just had to bite your tongue, sit there and cop it. A few of their players came up afterwards and apologized.' They wouldn't like their names to be added to the list of supporters of some of those comments, they told Greg. The Australians retreated, the New Zealanders began singing. 'And good luck to them,' said Greg.

That season, a final memory of Greg which endured for the next 18 months, was of his reaching 50 and starting to walk his runs. By 75 he was starting to hunker down to rest at the non-striker's end and if he scored a century that was about his lot. Greg grew up in that generation when medicine decided that even bad tonsils should not be removed. To combat his tonsillitis he was compelled to spend a month on antibiotics and a month off. At season's end, sitting by his Kenmore pool, his father, Martin, said to him, 'It's no good killing yourself for anything. Don't be silly about it.' Establishing himself in Queensland was starting to wear on Greg, just as had his first season with Somerset. Except this time it was work and cricket and the added responsibility of public engagements as Queensland captain. The heat did not help, playing and perspiring, air-conditioning and cooling, leading to sore throats. That made it hard to eat and he followed Dennis Lillee in drinking Sustagen. It also meant on the New Zealand tour that after playing he would retire to his room and have a meal sent up. With no sign of him in the bars or restaurants it was the beginning of his reputation for aloofness. He would learn that the cost of rest, however well deserved or necessary, was that it enabled others to guess at his motives for being absent. The rumour mill had begun to turn.

His absences were added to his natural shyness, to the awe in which younger players were beginning to hold him, to the imperious nature of his batting and he was damned as aloof, bordering on being plain stuck-up. The mills ground away for years at Greg's personality, at his business interests, at his health (condemned forever with cancer) and eventually even his marriage. The Chappells had become public property. He was named Australian Cricketer of the Year. The price of his phenomenal success in a nation which lionized champion sportsmen, was the invasion of his privacy, never to be retrieved until he lay down the instrument of its loss, his Excalibur's bat.

12. *Thommo*

Before Jeff Thomson played his first, eminently forgettable Test against Pakistan in Melbourne in December 1972, Greg had a drink with him in a bar near where the Australians were quartered at the Windsor Hotel. They sat on stools and chatted, an unlikely pair, the controlled ambition of Chappell and the laid back, laissez-faire of Thomson. Greg organized Thomson's move to Queensland and they became mates of a sort, not like Lillee and Marsh, but better than cricket colleagues. Greg was best man at Jeff's wedding and the Chappells entertained the Thomsons at home. Thomson lived on the opposite side of Brisbane and was always up north fishing or swimming so the social contact lapsed. But Greg remembers spending a weekend pig-shooting with him near St George, 400 kilometres west of Brisbane, a hilarious few days in which Thomson's wit, never released on the public, was in full cry.

Thommo intrigued Greg because the fast bowler arrived at his station in life in almost the opposite fashion to Greg. Jeff was a natural, almost totally undisciplined, athletic wonder. 'He was the quickest bowler I've seen by quite a margin,' said Greg. 'Only Michael Holding approached him.' He was as supple as a yogi, could pick both feet up and lock them behind his head, yet rarely stretched or exercised. Greg had never seen a better throwing arm than Jeff's, West

Indians included. 'On the SCG one day he fired a return in from 80 yards out and nearly knocked Rod Marsh off his feet,' said Greg. 'It was so flat it could have gone another 20 yards without dropping.' In team sprints he was the fastest. 'He almost spun the wheels at the start,' said Greg. 'Talk about Daley Thompson, Jeff Thomson could have been an Olympic decathlete if he'd tried.' That was the enigma of the man. He was an imposing 185 centimetres, 88 kilograms, but had none of the fast bowler's usual armoury of narrow-eyed, beetle-browed, flaring-nostrilled looks. He had soft, almost beautiful features, thick lips, a mane of blond hair and a mien which belied the dangerous craft he practised.

'He's a gentle, home-loving fellow,' said Greg. 'Much maligned. He could be a wild bugger, but harmlessly so. The more truthful side of him you can see at his home, like *House and Garden*. He's got a green finger and is obviously very patient.' In contrast to his future Test partner, Lillee, Thomson rarely entered into exchanges with batsmen. If he abused anyone it was himself: 'Slut!' he would curse. 'Dennis was ruthless, he hated batsmen and loved taking wickets,' said Greg. 'Thommo was brutal. He just loved bowling fast.' This he did in a State trial match in the season of the 1974–75 England tour of Australia. 'He bowled the quickest, wildest couple of overs I've ever seen in my life,' said Greg. 'Twice as quick as the year before in Sydney. The batsmen were frightened. Absolutely lethal, 100 miles per hour in any direction.'

Queensland's selectors Peter Burge and Ken Mackay were dubious. How could they pick Thomson when he was so erratic? 'I don't care if he hasn't got a clue where they're going, he'll frighten half these blokes out,' Greg argued. 'They'll be so bloody desperate to get down the other end they'll run themselves out. They'll do anything.' And the poor wicketkeeper? 'John Maclean will handle it.' In Greg's eyes Maclean was not unlike Marsh, not very pretty to watch, but did not miss many once he laid glove on them. To their everlasting credit the selectors deferred to Greg. They told him, 'You've got to take the blokes on to the field, you've got to be satisfied with the team you've got.'

In the first Test in Brisbane, Thomson blitzed the Brits. A photographer should have been commissioned to produce a series of the England batsmen who were dismissed standing on tip-toes, faces turned fearfully to leg, screwed in anticipation, bat held shoulder high by one hand while the ball nicked or popped into safe hands. That was

Thomson's 'throat ball' as Greg put it. 'It would come straight up, like a snake out of the grass at your feet, off a good length,' said Greg. 'It would pitch and cut back in, following your face as you withdrew. So it was very hard to duck, but it wasn't the sort of length you'd be looking to duck. Most bowlers would have to bang it in a yard or so shorter to get it up that high and the ball would be describing a parabola. But his just attacked your throat.'

The only England player to resist was Tony Greig, who backed off and slashed and cut 110 in the first innings. In the second Greg noticed Greig was wearing a new brand of soft rubber-soled boots. He allied that with Greig's high, early backlift and whispered to Thomson, 'Hit him in the sandshoes, that'll slow his footwork down a bit.' Thomson obliged, and yorked Greig for two. Thereafter for Queensland, whenever Greg signalled Jeff by tapping his boot, Thomson would deliver his 'sandshoe crusher'. The throat ball or the sandshoe crusher, you could take your choice with Thommo. During that Test the 'Gabba crowd gave Jeff three cheers, Marsh leapt the stumps and laid an affectionate head on his shoulder when he clean-bowled the last batsman, and the England captain, Mike Denness, was first at the picket gate to congratulate him as he was clapped off.

In the second Test, in Perth, Australia took 13 catches from 14 chances and Greg took seven of them, a new world record for a fieldsman. In fact it was grandfather Vic who had shared the old record with six catches. Greg was not aware of the record, or that he had broken it. Two of them were off Thomson, standing an amazing 36 metres back from the stumps at second slip. 'You didn't have any problems with the ball dropping short off Thommo,' said Greg. 'Your problem was it flying over your head. We were five yards further back than for Dennis, no disrespect to Dennis, who was still quick in those days, but for Jeff we were so far back you couldn't drop them if you tried.'

Of Greg's seven catches, the one which would have made Vic most proud was Chris Old off Ian's leg spin. Ian threw up a wrong 'un which Old, a strong hitter, recognized, and squared his shoulders. Greg was at forward short leg. 'I could see his eyes light up as soon as the ball went up in the air,' Greg said. 'I started hanging back and Old picked it up almost on the half volley and whipped it on a line over mid-wicket. I was about two yards from the bat and I stuck my hand out and it smacked straight into my palm so my fingers snapped on it. It stung a bit, more good luck than good judgement, but it was very satisfying. One of my best catches.'

In Perth Greg was caught off Bob Willis for 62, a lazy, tired shot outside the off stump to Tony Greig at gully. 'Nine times out of 10 I'd smash that ball on that score, but I had no energy,' said Greg. Tonsillitis again. Worst about the dismissal was it occurred an over before tea, sending Doug Walters in for an invidious few minutes. 'It was a sin,' said Greg. 'I felt very bad. He couldn't make runs, all he could do was get out.' Greg never apologized on such occasions. When others did to him he replied, 'Why? Did you try to get out?' But when Walters, not yet having scored, returned minutes later for tea, Greg felt he owed him something. 'I thought I'd just give you a hit before tea so you could get your eye in for 100 in the session.'

On the last ball of the next session Walters was 96. The team was egging him on, 'Do it, c'mon!' and five and ten dollar notes were flying on 'Yes, he will' and 'No, he won't'. Willis bowled a bouncer. 'I can still picture the shot now,' said Greg. 'Straight over square leg, cleared the fence by 10 yards.' The dressing-room went beserk. Walters was so popular. Then realization. Walters was also known to possess the fastest, funniest and most merciless one-line quip in Australian cricket. It was Walters who told both Greg and Marsh, after they had dropped catches in their first Tests, 'Don't worry, mate, you're due to catch one soon.' It was Walters who left the slips helpless when he said, as he saw Mike Denness — who suffered a poor series at the hands of Lillee and Thomson — coming out, 'Oh, wouldn't it bugger you!' The rest of the cordon looked questioningly. 'Bloody Mike Denness is coming in. Don't tell me we're going to have to put up with this bloke for another two or three balls!'

Thus the collective thought: it would be too excruciating to wait for Walters to enter, expecting to be cheered and clapped about the back. They cleared out, into the shower and toilet cubicles, and Doug, in his moment of triumph, entered — an empty dressing-room. When they all then trooped out to shake his hand they were rewarded with Doug's slow smile, acknowledgement that just this once, they had got in ahead of the master marksman.

By Sydney, the fourth Test, Thomson and Lillee were making their mark, literally. Lloyd, Amiss, Edrich and Titmus had all been wounded at the front. Also suffering was Rod Marsh whose sucked breath and winces Greg could hear from second slip. Jeff's and Dennis's new ball attack was like gloving iron shotputs. A physiotherapist developed a protection of elastic bandage. 'Every morning he cut strips and stuck them on the wall in front of Rod's locker,' said Greg. 'It was quite intricate, short strips between the fingers and long across the knuckle pads. That's where it hurt, like a stone bruise on your foot. Never heals until you rest it.' Greg knew. Three times in his career he suffered finger fractures or dislocations in slips and two of them were off Thomson. John Maclean differed. He enjoyed keeping to Thomson for Queensland. 'I always put it down to superior technique,' he said, with a grin meant just for Marshy.

Greg had passed 50 runs in five of his previous six Test innings, succumbing as his health waned with each course of antibiotics to combat the toxins from his tonsils. In Sydney he enjoyed a remission and seized the moment to score 144 to seal Australia's victory and regain the Ashes, lost on that same ground four years earlier to Ray Illingworth's crack team. Three Tests up with two to play, Ian led the celebrations from the Koala Motel, where the team stayed, to a restaurant called The Different Drummer in Kings Cross. The name comes from the early nineteenth century American naturalist author Henry Thoreau whose words were framed above the downstairs bar:

If a man does not keep pace with his companions, perhaps it is because he hears a different drummer; let him step to the music he hears, however measured or far away.

Greg did not keep pace with his companions. By early morning most of the team would be over the top but Greg would have retired to his hotel room. Said Ian, 'He'd have half a dozen and then pull the rein.' Ian always compared them: Rodney Marsh was like Ian, Greg was like Rod's brother, Graham, the Australian golfer. The latter were always in control of themselves. The music the Aussies heard was rock from a juke box and the bleeps from an electronic video games machine with which they tomfooled. The bar was in a cellar of sandstone block walls, low ceiling of massive beams and antique furniture. With its subdued lights and bunkered aspect it was not unlike many cricket dressing-rooms. It was natural that after the glare of public adoration and individual exposure on the sun-blasted SCG the players should retreat to such a shadowy shelter to relax. Ian ordered a wiener schnitzel with egg on top, drank Carlton draught because he was not fond of Sydney beer, and propped himself at the bar with Rod. The conservative element in the bar soon vacated but the manager, David Edmondson, welcomed the revellers. 'We knew they'd won and they were very popular,' he said. Dennis Lillee wandered about with the silver tray from a sweet dispenser on his head like one of the Kaiser's soldiers, signed serviettes and even a girl's stomach — she proudly returning the next week with the autograph intact.

Early in March after England had departed, *sans* Ashes, Greg had his tonsils removed. One tonsil was nearly eroded and the other was a mass of scar tissue. Greg haemorrhaged at midnight, filling bowl after bowl with blood. His surgeon removed a clot the size of a golf ball from his throat and an injection staunched the bleeding.

After that trauma it seemed impossible that within weeks Greg was enlisting for the 1975 World Cup tour to England. He had lost nearly a stone and was flying to England's dank climes. If he needed any further disincentive Judy was pregnant. Their first baby was due two weeks before the World Cup final. Yet there was no question of Greg not going. Judy was as firm about it as anyone. 'No. Oh no. Absolutely not. I wouldn't have thought to ask him not to go,' she said. 'We didn't even question it in our minds, to ask each other or ourselves. It just seemed natural for him to tour and I would stay home and mind the baby.' She was not at all distressed, but here she gave a clue. 'It's funny because it almost meant more to me to have my mother and father here than having Greg because I'd just got so used to him being away and being independent,' she said. She and Greg were developing a cricketer's marriage, a strange half-life of unity and separation, similar to that of mariners, workable only through unquestioning trust and acceptance of clearly defined roles by both partners. The Chappells had that. During the last three months of pregnancy, when harassed fathers-to-be are hustled along to share ante-natal classes beside their corpulent wives, Greg would be gone. The moments of physical and emotional anxiety, normally shared with a husband, Judy bore alone.

Nor was it in contention in Greg's mind. Cricket was his vocation, his career, not well paid ... yet. 'All my life had been designed to get where I was,' he said. 'It seemed almost expected of me.' In those days two tours of England was all most players could expect. The best, like Ian, made three. If Greg withdrew he would have missed 50 per cent of his possibilities of going to England. And if further argument was required, he was appointed tour vice-captain.

The World Cup was a cricket innovation, two weeks of one-day cricket at which England, because of their Gillette Cup and John Player League experience, and the West Indies because many of their team were county players, were favourites. Ian Chappell was sanguine. 'The one game we wanted was to beat the Poms,' he said. 'We used to get so pissed off with them saying how we couldn't play one-day cricket. How you had to play different cricketers. We all just said, "Bull. A good cricketer is a good cricketer. We'll adjust." '

Headingley, Leeds, 18 June 1975, dustbowl scene of Australia's 1972 shafting by Derek Underwood, was this day a green, seamer's delight. Newcastle all-rounder Gary Gilmour bent the ball like a safety pin, in the air, off the pitch, finishing with 6-14. England was all out for 93 with only 36 of 60 scheduled overs bowled. Gilmour baffled Greg. 'Nobody had more talent than that bloke, as much as Gary Sobers — maybe that's a big statement — but not many blokes had his natural ball skills. Brilliant fielder, strong upper body, but very poor legs, ankles not really strong enough for his weight.' Gilmour's problem was his self confidence. He was billed from his early career as the new Alan Davidson and that albatross often made it hard for him to start in case he should fail. How to elicit his genius when it was needed? They mollycoddled him or abused him, tried everything, but Gilmour's talent, like an incandescent star, pursued its own orbit. It appeared in that semi-final. Having dismissed England cheaply, Australia then slid to 6–39, Ian (2) and Greg (4) falling to John Snow. At 34, and after two years out of Test cricket, Snow was invited back to combat Thomson and Lillee, to fight fire with Snow as it were. But then along came Gilmour. 'If it was up Gary hit through it, if it was short he smashed it,' said Greg. Gilmour top-scored with 28 not out and he and Walters steered Australia to victory. 'That was as good an innings as I saw him play,' said Greg. 'Sometimes 28 is worth a century.'

To Ian that win was almost as good as winning the final. He was happy to be playing the West Indies in the final because he knew it would be a game of cricket. 'If you played the Poms there'd be six blokes on the boundary and all on the on-side,' said Ian. 'That would always beat us because we'd say, "You can't play cricket like this," and our blokes would start getting out.'

That final at Lord's on 21 June, began at 11 a.m. and finished at 8.43 p.m. 'It was one of the most exciting day's cricket I've ever put in,' said Greg. 'We were at the ground for over 12 hours. It was a huge crowd (26,000) and the West Indian spectators made the atmosphere exhilarating.' Australia opened with a substantial slips cordon. 'With the experience we've had since then the field placings would be different,' said Greg. More conservative? 'No doubt about that. But we were working on the theory we were an aggressive side. We had no experience bowling to defensive fields. If we could get early wickets that was the key to it.' And so they did, 3–50 until a Kanhai and Lloyd rescue saw the final score 291 from 60 overs.

Australia then suffered five run-outs in finishing all out for 274. Two of them were the Chappells. *Wisden* described Ian's as setting off for an 'impossible third run'. Greg's was not so ill advised. Ian was on strike, Viv Richards just in front of point. Ian drove it off the back foot very square, well to Richards' left hand. Ian called, Greg responded. 'We knew he was a good fielder but in one-day cricket you pushed the odds to the fullest,' said Greg. Richards pounced, fumbled the ball from left to right hand and, still off balance, falling away from the wicket, threw a return. It landed, bounced again, and hit the stumps. Said Greg, 'He was virtually dead side-on, 15 to 20 yards from the wicket. The reason it bounced twice was because he couldn't generate any power in the throw. In two bounces it might have changed direction. The odds of him doing it, if he picked it up 100 times, even Viv wouldn't have hit it 10 times.'

Ian fancied Australia's chances of getting those runs — still thinks they would have if Gary Gilmour had hit a six off a Keith Boyce bouncer instead of being caught 10 metres inside the boundary by Kanhai. 'He hits that for six and he's away,' said Ian. Greg was not so certain. 'Without having much knowledge of one-day cricket — we'd only played half a dozen serious games — we felt we had a chance of getting them,' he said. 'Now, with hindsight, and bearing in mind the game's a lot more sophisticated than it was then, I don't reckon we'd have got them at any stage.'

The Australians had so much to learn about one-day cricket. About running diagonally forward to cut off balls rather than around the boundary, about bowling defensively, about negative field placings. Their whole attitude was so reluctant it took years for them to adapt, years in which they were humiliated by lesser cricketing nations. To Ian's Aussies the Tests were the test. But one-day cricket was on the march.

Four Tests, defending the Ashes, were very much a postscript to the World Cup for Greg. On 10 June, ten days before the cup final, Judy gave birth to their first child, a son, Stephen, Greg's second name. The Chappell–Richardsons are given to such dynastic tendencies. Greg had been calling home every three or four days. Judy's father, Harry Donaldson, rang Greg with the news at the team's quarters in the Kensington Close Hotel in London. 'From that time onwards I found it very difficult to keep my mind on cricket,' said Greg. 'I was really looking forward to going home. From 10 June, if we could have gone home the next day, I'd have been happy.'

Now for the first time since Somerset he had time to stand cricket against the other developing priorities in his life and once more some of the sheen chipped from the glorious face of his sport. First the need for a business career and now fatherhood. But not yet, note, the singular pressure of marriage. It was parenthood which plucked at his heart, not his role as husband. At home Judy and her parents were marvelling over their priceless possession. 'Every time he moved or woke we'd say, "Oh, isn't he gorgeous",' said Judy. In England Greg prepared for four Tests against a country which he had already played 15 times in six years. His heart was not in it.

Nor was his health. Ian's memory in those Tests was of Greg coming up with a towel round his neck or wearing extra sweaters and saying, 'I'm having a bit of trouble with my throat.' Ian would say, 'Oh yeah, bad luck,' but he knew Greg would play. 'That was the amazing thing,' said Ian. 'Physically he wasn't strong, nowhere near as strong as I was, but the concentration and effort was still there. It was a tremendous performance for him to drag that out.' How he performed is in the eye of the beholder. Tony Greig wrote in *Cricket, The Men and The Game*, published in 1976:

> *Chappell really had a terrible tour. Take away the one score he did get and he'd averaged under 10 which, for a player of his class, was unbelievable.*

In fact he averaged 44.8 in all matches, fourth behind Walters, McCosker and Ian, and 21.2 in Tests, eighth. Greg's interpretation is that he scored well in the minor matches where there was less pressure and he played his shots. Against Glamorgan he scored a century in 66 minutes, the second fastest of the summer, and according to Ray Robinson, faster than Bradman ever scored an English century. He hit another against Sussex opposed to Tony Greig who had just replaced Mike Denness as England captain for the second Test.

Ian was wearying of the captaincy. By the time his disenchantment reached Martin Chappell in Adelaide, it had swelled to Ian's imminent retirement from first class cricket. Martin laughed it off as the stretched rumour it was. But there was a tinge of concern too. He hated the idea of Ian's cricket career cresting. Fortunately there was Greg

119

to follow. That was beginning to be understood by other players as well.

Assuming the captaincy against Sussex, at Hove, Greg pulled two senior Australians into line for lackadaisical on-field behaviour. It might be acceptable to Ian, who did not give a fig about county games, but not to Greg. The two he chose could scarcely have been closer to him. He reminded Doug Walters, 'You're wearing the baggy green cap.' Ashley Mallett pre-empted a similar rebuke when he apologized, 'Yes, I know, I'm playing for Australia.' It seems cruelly ironic that two years later in that same seaside town, news would break which would place Greg's loyalty to that cap under far greater question than Doug and Ashley's mild skylarking.

If Greg was starting to be quite homesick he was not the only one. Newly married Jeff Thomson was like a transplanted native with too little sun. He shopped for toys for the children he hoped to have one day, gazed around at the rain, the steadfast completeness of the architecture, the in-turned gaze of the Britons and told an interviewer, 'I'd rather be home than over in this joint.' Not that he had a poor tour. Only Lillee took more Test wickets. But the England players had neatly indoctrinated English umpires with the thesis that Thomson's action decreased his chances of getting lbw's.

Thomson cannot get in close to the stumps with his action. Where Lillee could flick the stumps with his ball hand Thomson would kick the stumps down with his left foot because of his exaggerated coil stride. Equally he can't bowl around the wicket for fear of knocking the stumps over with his right hand when he loads up behind his back. Said Greg, 'I think with a few of the umpires it didn't matter where he hit, he'd never get an lbw decision. They just crucified him. Not that it was his or their fault. They just reckoned if you couldn't bowl stump to stump you didn't get too many lbw's, unless you pitched it full.'

To compensate for that, and for England's less than flint-hard wickets, he searched for extra pace and spent a summer of no-balls. In the second Test he was no-balled 22 times for overstepping the front crease and added four wides for good measure. 'Thommo was always bowling bloody no-balls,' said Ian succinctly. Greg knew why. In the nets Thomson bowled off 18 yards as often as he bowled off 22. 'He just practised his rhythm,' said Greg. 'Never his run-up. It was a terrible habit to get into. The number of times we spoke to him about it and the number of times he didn't do anything was unbelievable.

Unfortunately that's the way Thommo was.' He was still doing it 10 years later.

Greg's sequence was a duck in the first Test, which Australia won, and 73 not out in the second, which was a draw. The third was the famous Headingley Test sabotaged by the Chappells' namesake, Peter Chappell, with a gallon of crude oil poured in knifed holes near the popping crease. Could Australia have won? Set 445, they were 3–220, both Chappells gone. Ian had psyched Walters up to emulate the victory by Bradman's 1948 team which, on the same ground, scored 3–404 in the last innings for what is considered the ultimate cricket victory. 'To be realistic I think the odds were in England's favour,' said Greg. Pouring rain that day rendered the question superfluous.

Before that, in England's second innings, Greg took three successive, stunning catches in second slip off Gilmour, Lillee and Thomson. In Perth he stood 36 metres back for Thommo, but at Leeds only 10 metres because of the slow wicket. John Hampshire slashed at Thomson, caught the ball with the bottom of the bat and it accelerated at Greg. 'I saw it in front of my face,' said Greg. 'Just a matter of protection. You had to catch it or be dead. Bloody dangerous. Thommo's edges never came low. The ball was on its way up when they hit it, which is good because I'd rather take it from waist high upwards. Anything down is harder because it's below your eyeline.' Greg scored 24 Test centuries, each one a full cloth of weft and warp, some colourful, some dun, but all able to be followed and judged as their final pattern emerged. He took a world record number of Test catches, most of them in slips where the action is a blur. I have seen him fall and rise with catches so magical he could be a sideshow alley showman rising with a bullet between his teeth. The pity is they are almost as swift in the telling as in the executing.

Greg returned to London from Leeds with Alan Turner and Thommo in a British racing green Jaguar XJ12 courtesy of the Jaguar company. With one Test up and one Test to play the Ashes were safe, if not the series, so the trio were in a jovial mood. Greg dozed in the front seat until after half an hour he heard Thommo ask, 'What do you reckon I should do?'. 'About what?' asked Greg. 'That blue light flashing in the rear vision mirror,' said Thommo. How long had it been there? 'Oh, about 20 minutes.' Then he had better slow down and let it catch up. Thomson moved into the second lane and a police Range Rover pulled them over in pouring rain.

Police:	*Do you know the speed limit on the motorway is 70 mph?*
Thommo:	*Yeah.*
Police:	*Do you realize I've been following you for the past 15 minutes at 120 mph and couldn't gain on you?*
Thommo:	*Yeah, that'd be right.*
Police:	*Do you realize that when the road's wet if you hit the brakes you're aquaplaning, your wheels aren't actually touching the surface of the road?*
Thommo:	*Yeah, I've done that three times already.*
Police:	*Bloody hell! I don't mind if you kill yourself but I've nearly killed myself twice trying to catch you!*

After identifying their culprits the police radioed base and relayed their instructions: our jurisdiction runs out five miles down the motorway, be a bit sensible and get going.

The fourth Test at The Oval was memorable. Ian scored 192 and at Test's end retired as captain. Greg scored a duck. Opener Alan Turner was out for two at 11.20 a.m. on the first day and Greg sat padded up, psychologically, for 24 hours until Rick McCosker was out for 127 at 11.20 a.m. the next day. 'I had just sat there all day concentrating for Rick and Ian,' said Greg. 'I was absolutely exhausted. I walked out like I was in a dream.' The Oval has a terraced sight screen, called the shooting gallery, where spectators sit with just their heads above the white painted desk-like seats. First ball from Chris Old a spectator rose and walked across the gallery. 'I knew I shouldn't be distracted but I couldn't help wondering whether he would be right behind Old's arm as he bowled,' said Greg. 'That was the sort of thing I was thinking about, which I would never normally do.' Greg got the faintest touch and Alan Knott caught it, first ball. In his mind Greg was already flying home. When he did, a few days later, he was handed his son Stephen, now three months old. 'How do I hold it?' he enquired. He had a firmer grasp on the Australian captaincy.

13. Captain

The passing of the sceptre of captaincy from brother to brother was accompanied by no fanfare of heavenward horns. Greg, as Napoleon advised, merely wielded the baton he had long carried in his Adidas knapsack. As Greg put it himself, 'The side was running itself. Even if Billy the Goose had taken over he'd have to try to bugger it up to ruin Ian's good work quickly.' At 27 Greg had entered that zone of intense activity and responsibility that is Australia's gift to its young men. A wife, a child, house mortgage and car loan, and a relatively new job which would reward the ambitious, in a State where the genre was admired. Now he was also physical and spiritual leader of his nation's most popular sport.

Several observers, including Dennis Lillee and the late Jack Fingleton, subsequently wrote that Greg's captaincy was marked by a schoolmasterish quality. That implies he treated his players as students, as inferiors. It would be foolish to expect that given his ascension to the pinnacle of Australian cricket he would remain some humble altruist. His whole approach differed from Ian's. Australian masseur Doc McErlane described it superbly. 'Ian grabbed the bull by the horns. He said, "He's going to rip me up the guts if I let go so I'll hang on," and sometimes the bull gave in and Ian would win. But Greg was ever devious, his mind watching, a great thinker, he premeditated his dismissals.'

Greg did not favour the kind of inspiring address Ian delivered at the dressing-room doorway in that famous Port of Spain victory in 1973. 'Walker may have taken that wicket after lunch whether Ian spoke to the team or not,' Greg conjectured. He dismissed the analogy between cricket and football where a coach could rant at his team and have them running white hot through brick walls for 80 minutes. Cricket was a slow burn all day and required what he so clearly possessed, a black determination, bordering on the obsessional, that was unsheathed with the first ball of the day and returned with the last.

Ian accomplished his transition smoothly. 'You know where I am if you want any help. Just sing out,' he told Greg. Only one incident came to mind in the ensuing few seasons that he played under Greg. A tailender had taken the long handle to Dennis Lillee, who was becoming irritable at being belted down the ground. Greg persisted with four slips and a gully. Afterwards Ian went to him. 'A word of advice, because I've made the same mistake myself. When a tailender's slogging you tend to think, "He can't get away with this for very long," and nine times out of ten you're right. They mishit and that's it. But sometimes they do get away with it and you should give yourself a bit of protection. Have three slips, but drop gully and push cover, mid-off and mid-on back a bit. Otherwise they'll get 20, get confident and think they can bat properly.' Greg agreed. 'I do have a tendency to over-attack the tailenders,' he said.

But the two brothers remained essentially their own masters. That year Terry Jenner, who used to excite the emotions of drunken crowds, was being abused while bowling in a Shield match. Said Ian, 'Leave them to me.' When next they began baying Ian gave them the two fingers up signal and they went for him like hounds to a lure. That was Ian's captaincy style, to cop the crap. Greg would prefer that cool prevail and that all odium dissipate for lack of a victim.

At State level friend John Maclean noticed two lamentable manifestations of Greg's presence. If Greg made a large score other players felt less responsibility to score themselves. If Greg failed, it either put the fear of God into those to follow or gave them an excuse to fail too. Indeed, one of Greg's nomenclatures, among the faithful of the Queensland Cricketers' Club, was God. BC was Before Chappell and He had arrived to raise them from the bottom of the Shield. In an early match that season Greg very nearly gave credibility to that title with an innings of breathtaking dimensions.

27 October 1975, the 'Gabba, Brisbane. New South Wales captain Doug Walters appeared to have sealed off any chance of a Queensland outright win by setting them the impossible target of 165 runs in 18 overs — an average of nine runs per over. In modern one-day cricket six runs is considered a certain winning run rate. Nine runs per over is difficult to achieve even during the last few slogging overs. A run rate of nine maintained for 50 overs would return a one-day score of 450, some 200 runs more than normal. Walters could be confident of his draw.

But Greg was annoyed with his Aussie team-mate for not having declared at tea and set Queensland a reasonably risky target. As he walked off after expelling the last New South Wales batsman, Greg caught up with 41-year-old veteran Sam Trimble and said, 'Come on mate, we'll give this a go.' Greg did not normally open. He simply strapped on his pads in the dressing-room and everyone knew the fight was on. Several factors weighed in his favour. The chances of Queensland being bowled out in so few overs were remote, so any mad dash was failsafe. They could be sure, too, that Walters would attack them at first and so give them a shot at free scoring. By now Greg had come to terms with the fact that Brisbane had twice the rainfall of his hometown Adelaide and most of it fell in January and February. Unless Queensland achieved outright victories before Christmas they might as well not enter the Shield.

New South Wales had a near Test attack — Gary Gilmour, Len Pascoe, David Colley and Walters. Greg took 22 runs off Gilmour's second over. 'Five fours he hit,' said Trimble. 'They weren't bad balls, but Greg hit them to all different parts of the field. I thought, "Cripes, if he does that I'll put my two-bob's worth in here and we'll get them."' Sam whacked and missed. His captain proffered wise words to the old head. 'Settle down, take the singles and the fours will come.' Greg danced down the wicket and struck Pascoe back over the fast bowler's head for four and smacked Walters for six over mid-wicket. About 5,000 hopeful souls, of whom I was one, straightened in our chairs to just . . . wonder. Gilmour and Pascoe were rattled. 'Lenny tried to knock our heads off,' said Greg. They raced to 50 in five overs. 'Chapp-ell, Chapp-ell,' the small crowd chanted. Walters curbed his attack. The bowlers pitched short of a length to stop Greg's driving, but by now Sam was oiled and running. He plays in the vee-square, so short was fine for his glances, cuts and pulls. The 100 came up in 9.7 overs. When they bowled full to Sam he dabbed a single and if they did not immediately adjust their length for Greg, whack, another driven four. Sam was the perfect foil to a batsman who at that moment was playing like the world's number one he was rated.

They cut the run rate to 8, to 7. Both Martin Kent and Jeff Thomson were padded up. 'Every shot, the boys were jumping up and thrusting their fists into the air and shouting "C'mon",' said Kent. After 86 runs in a mere 33 hits — eleven fours and one six — Greg broke his bat. 'It just stopped his momentum,' said Trimble, because Greg was then caught. When Greg left, Trimble was on 60, and the run rate required was a sedate 4.7 runs per over. Greg motioned with his arm for the bowler to come in and Kent nudged Thomson with his toe, 'Away you go, Two-up.' But Thommo went for a duck and it was left to Kent and Trimble to cruise home with nine balls to spare. Afterwards New South Wales was shell-shocked. Walters for once was speechless. 'What could you do?' he asked. Greg called it his proudest innings for Queensland.

With those sorts of feats and others — he was Sportsman of the Year in Queensland at the start of the season — Greg had become a much courted marketing commodity. John Maclean took Greg to a barbecue at the Tarragindi home of a friend, Barry Maranta, a history lecturer turned property developer. During the evening, Greg idly passed the comment to Maranta and another Brisbane businessman,

Kev Norris, both cricketophiles, how difficult it was to put a price on his appearances and speeches at functions, especially at night when it was an imposition on Judy and Stephen. Now he was Australian captain, yet no wiser. The next day Maranta asked Norris, who had experience in sporting investments and management, 'Why don't you help Greg?' Norris replied, 'Why don't you?' So Maranta became Greg's friendly factotum, a third party to ward off the merely onerous and to ask $150 for invitations Greg had previously performed for nix.

'At first there was resistance, even resentment,' said Maranta. 'But I'd explain that if someone wanted three hours of their time every night of the week wouldn't they eventually feel put upon? And they'd say, "Yeah, you're right."' Between them Greg and Maranta learned to draft or discourage sensation seekers by imposing a very high fee. But they still had no real benchmarks, until matters took a quantum leap.

Maranta was negotiating with an advertising agency to do a television commercial which Greg and he agreed was worth about $1,000. How much did Greg want? the agency asked. A small portion of the total budget, would not that be fair? said Maranta. What was their budget? Crossed wires. The agency man thought Maranta was asking what would be Greg's share. '$3,000,' he said. Maranta, believing it was the total budget, said in shocked tones, '$3,000!' The agency man saw his fish fleeing. 'Well, we'll offer him $5,000 if you like.' Maranta's shock was now pleasantly genuine. Done! And that was how the fast and clever world of marketing and commerce arrived at a felicitous floor price for the services of Greg Chappell, captain of Australia. It equalled in one stroke the amount he was being paid each year by the Queensland Cricket Association to lead the State.

A brief peep into the domestic scene at this stage sees Greg not providing quite the same value. Gallivanting cricket tourists are mollycoddled breakfast-time to bed-time. Theirs is a world of idolatry where every whim is treated as an imperative, meals, accommodation and transport are signed and delivered. Their one duty is to play cricket. Greg had been touring, it seemed, almost every winter since his marriage and now he was spending a summer at home with an extra, Stephen, who did not yet know he should fit in with cricket practice. Judy had become friendly with Helen and Ashley Cooper, of Wimbledon fame, and accepted their invitation, when Greg returned from the World Cup, to use the Coopers' weekender at Moffatt Beach, Caloundra. 'Stephen was not feeding well and crying a lot and after four days it really got on Greg's nerves,' said Judy. 'He didn't cope at all well, it was very new and very strange to him. I got into such a state we ended up having test feeds at the local Caloundra Hospital.' At the time Judy felt resentful that Greg was making such a fuss about this screaming baby. With time she saw how unreally cricket had isolated Greg from the common irritations and exasperations of this everyday housewife who had given up her previous life for him.

Having beaten Australia in the World Cup the West Indies arrived that season to complete the lesson. Clive Lloyd was only moderately more experienced than Greg as captain. Each side packed pace firepower and explosive scorers. Lloyd, Richards, Greenidge, Holding, Roberts — names that would take the Windies to the top, but not yet. The first Test, in Brisbane, Greg tossed with his 1932 king's head penny, won, as he did five times out of six that series, and sent the West Indies in. Greg opened up with five slips, a gully, a bat-pad, fine leg, third man, and 'keeper. It took two or three balls before he realized he did not have a cover. 'There were times Ian must have bitten his tongue and thought, "He's got to find out for himself,"' said Greg. 'Nothing monumental, just errors.'

By the end of the first day the pitch surface began to craze. Bowlers and batsmen were leaving large marks and indentations. The wicket would be a spinning minefield by the fourth day when Australia was batting. Second morning Greg inspected the wicket. Not a mark on it. No spikemarks, no indentations. Greg collected Lloyd. 'I thought he might not notice the difference,' said Greg, 'but I knew he would. I thought he would explode.' Lloyd looked and nodded. 'There's no point in making too much of a fuss. We wouldn't have got much of a game if it was left the way it was.' They stared at it together. 'The wicket's been remade,' said Greg. 'Yeah, I know,' replied Lloyd, who could have made an international incident out of it if he wished. But did not.

Greg scored a century in the first innings and he joined Ian in the second when the West Indies were threatening alarums and excursions over Australia's relatively simple task of 219 runs. Lloyd brought on greying off-spinner Lance Gibbs, who had nabbed Greg several times in the Caribbean in 1973. When Gibbs was bowling well he seemed perpetual motion; bowl, quick pick up, few strides, turn, bowl. Could finish an over in two minutes. 'He mesmerized you,' said Greg. 'You seemed to be facing a never-ending succession of balls with no time to breathe. You started thinking, "I'd better face up because he'll be bowling in a second," and hurrying destroys your concentration.' So Greg broke the cycle. Walk down the pitch and delay Gibbs, turn away and make him check, until the over was at Greg's pace, not Gibbs'. In the end Gibbs became frustrated because he knew the conditions suited him but he could not break through. Losing that small battle, Gibbs faded as a force in the series. Between them Greg, 109 and Ian 74, both not out, guided their ship to safety.

Which century to talk about. 'Beautiful, wasn't it?' said Clive Lloyd dolefully afterwards. 'He's just a great player. My only consolation is that he can't possibly do better than that on this tour.' English cricket writer Pat Gibson wrote:

If he could spare the time — and assuming the Governor-General was agreeable — Greg Chappell could become the Prime Minister of Australia in the forthcoming election.

With his first innings century Greg joined two other Australians who scored centuries in their first Tests as captain, Alf Noble (1903), and Lindsay Hassett (1949). With his second innings century Greg discarded those two worthies and every other captain in cricket history. No one had ever done that before. Jack Fingleton wrote of Greg's first innings:

I have seen all his big innings, and there has been none better than this...

Until the second perhaps. Of this Ian, who ought to know, wrote in his newspaper column:

I thought the one in the second innings showed a new high in an already illustrious career.
He has made all sorts of scores on all wickets and against all bowlers but I have always thought him to be less at home on a turning wicket.
On Tuesday he showed this is no longer so and he did it in his usual batting style — dominating the bowling.

There was a further aspect to that innings. Greg had arrived in a tight situation against Gibbs, yet he scored his century in a serene and peaceful display, as though it was predestined to happen. 'Nothing else existed,' said Greg. 'It was almost total relaxation. The only thing in the world was what was going on out there. Any other problem I had I didn't think about. It just seemed so easy.' Greg experienced that feeling only twice again in his career, during centuries against England in Adelaide, and New Zealand in Christchurch, both years later, in 1982. It is probably significant that the intervening years were filled with turmoil not conducive to such a psychological state. But on those three occasions he was overcome with a sense of timelessness where he was so at one with himself that the ball was rendered venomless, the crowd a-madding in the distance.

Canadian sports sociologist Mihaly Czikszentmihalyi identified this holistic state as 'flow', usually experienced in such activities as rock climbing, running, dance and music composition. He defined it as being able to concentrate on a limited field of stimuli, using skills to meet clear demands, thereby forgetting other problems and even one's own separate identity. It was the total immersion in *ludus*, Latin for play, the alternative to interlude. That Greg could achieve it, however rarely, in such an adversary sport as cricket, says everything about his performance on those days.

Australia lost the second Test in Perth. 'The West Indies went bozo and we put in one of the worst bowling performances I can recall by an Australian side,' said Greg. 'They were just incapable of bowling to instructions. It was bouncer, yorker, bouncer, yorker. I couldn't set a field to it.' The Australians could not forget how they had snuffed England, but here all they murdered was Greg's sleep.

One Test all. The next match was a one-day game in Adelaide, the danger game in Greg's eyes. Before the match Greg addressed the players from the head of a long team table in their private dining room. Perth had been diabolical but he did not dwell on the past. 'This is the key game of the tour. If we win it gives us the psychological edge for the rest. If we lose they're on the crest of a wave.'

Australia won that one-day international against the West Indies by five wickets, which led, as Greg predicted, to a victory in the Melbourne Test, to go to Sydney 2–1 up. Greg exerted his captaincy. After Perth, where Australia succumbed to Roberts and Holding, Greg proposed a third opener to bat number three to ensure the run-scorers, Ian and himself, did not face a newish ball. Ian was reluctant. 'I've batted three all my career, I'd prefer to stay there.' Team masseur Doc McErlane knew why. 'Ian loved the situation when an opener failed,' he said. 'He used to turn around and say, "What, again!" but you knew it was a challenge.'

McCosker filled the role in Melbourne but was replaced by Victorian left hander Graeme Yallop in Sydney. Greg had explained his theory to two selectors, Phil Ridings and Sam Loxton, and so tacked the Sydney batting order on the notice board. Yallop, in his first Test, was number three. Loxton, also from Victoria, stormed into the dressing-room where Greg sat alone.

'What are you doing to the young fellow?' said Loxton.

'If you're referring to Graeme Yallop, Sam, I'm batting him number three.'

'You can't do it to him.'

'Where does he bat for Victoria, Sam?'

'At number three, but that's got nothing to do with it.'

'Listen, I explained in Adelaide what my thinking was. I wanted someone who could bat high in the order. You picked this bloke.'

'He should bat at five or six.'

'Sam, you pick the team, I pick the order. That's the end of the story.'

Apart from his strategy, Greg did not want Yallop and Gary Cosier, playing their first and second Tests respectively, matched at five and six in the order. By the sixth Test, Cosier was gone, McCosker back and Yallop back down at six. 'The selectors finally relented, to please Yallop I'd say, not me,' said Greg.

When Australia fielded in Sydney Greg sought to undo any tension that might have built between Yallop and himself. Where did Graeme normally field? 'Covers,' said Yallop. 'But I prefer slips.' Well then, covers it would be, said Greg. 'But I prefer slips,' replied Yallop. Said Greg, 'Then you've got a bit of bad luck, Graeme, because we've got Ian at first, I'm at second, Redders is third and Ashley's at gully. So you've got a few blokes in the queue ahead of you. You'll field in covers.' Greg was taken aback. In his own first Test if he'd been told to field in the members' stand he'd have been happy to obey. At the ripe age of 27 Greg had struck the new generation.

In Sydney Greg observed the Napoleonic dictum concerning a preference for lucky generals. Chasing a large West Indies first innings Australia was in trouble. Greg faced a fiery spell from Andy Roberts. As malevolent as was his bowling he looked even more dangerous. 'He had real mean eyes,' said Greg. 'Subsequently I found him a hell of nice bloke, but bowling he did a good job of making you think he was a Black Power man.' On 11 Greg was dropped by Keith Boyce from Roberts. And there the series ended for the West Indies. Greg went on to make a grateful 182 not out. Tony Greig wrote the next day:

> *That 182 not out was the finest innings I have seen by a captain when his side was in crisis with possible defeat hanging on his success...*
>
> *He proved once again that the reins of captaincy are not weighing too heavily on his shoulders. He seems to be thriving on it.*

Greg then demonstrated just how much he was enjoying the tactical battle. The West Indies second innings began with just an hour of the day left. 'They were tired after nearly two days in the field. They'd gone from a good position to where they were losing their grip on the game,' said Greg. 'I planned to bowl as tight as we could, make them think about bouncers, but not give them any. Then give just three in the right place.' Fredericks, Kallicharran and Richards, all keyed up, hooked joyfully at bouncers and were caught on the fence. 'It's a mental thing, the essence of Test cricket,' said Greg.

Setting fields for Lillee and Thomson required the fine touch of a master cracksman. Thomson would let Greg set the field. Dennis occasionally demanded what Greg and Ian called Melville fields. It was a joke at the expense of Lillee's captaincy of his Perth club, Melville, after he hurt his back in the Caribbean in 1973. In the 1974–75 series against England, fourth Test in Sydney, Lillee insisted on a very fine, very short, leg slip to England opener David Lloyd. He stood Thomson nine suicidal metres from the bat when Marsh himself was back 20. Lillee basically wanted to intimidate Lloyd. To the Chappells' eternal misery Lloyd tucked Lillee off his hips straight at Thomson who, being the superb athlete he was, caught it. 'You couldn't bloody shut Dennis up after that,' said Greg.

The major differences in fields for the two great pace men were a bat-pad for Thomson because his speed often caught the batsmen on the glove. Thomson would have a leg gully whereas for Lillee it was a packed off-side. Lillee, with his Exocet accuracy, could bowl without a third man, but Thomson gave batsmen more chances to slash. Nor did Thomson really care about the new ball. Again Doc McErlane had his theory. 'Thommo wanted the old ball, not because he liked it, but because he didn't want anyone to argue about the new ball.'

Jack Fingleton observed at the tour's end that Greg's biggest problem had been who to toss the new ball to, Thomson, Lillee or Gilmour. As far as Dennis was concerned it was Lillee first over, Thommo second. But Lillee missed the Sydney Test with pleurisy and when he returned for the fifth Test in Adelaide, Greg flicked the cherry to Gary Gilmour who had just hit 95 and whose talents were making their characteristically unschedulable, brilliant, appearance. When Lillee came on an hour later as first change he deliberately bowled poorly. On his own admission, in his book, *Lillee, Over and Out*, published in 1985, Lillee said Marsh roused at him that his wayward bowling would be the perfect justification for Greg not opening with him. Whereupon Lillee turned serious and took two quick wickets.

However difficult organizing his fast bowlers was, it did not compare with the extra-curricular captaincy burdens that were beginning to weigh on Greg. The captaincy on field was exciting. For someone with Greg's knowledge of the game it was not difficult. But off the field he found himself the spokesperson for Australian cricket. Who would win tomorrow, from half a dozen different cricket writers. Whatever happened around the vast domain of international cricket, if the South African question blew up, get a statement from the Australian cricket captain. Greg quickly tired of answering the same inane questions over and over.

'You could just guarantee that every time we sat down for breakfast or dinner the phone would ring,' said Greg. He saw how Ian, by being available, had made a rod for his own back, yet he followed suit. He quickly found the more helpful he was the more demands were put upon him. In the end he obtained a silent number only to discover it was common knowledge within a few weeks. When some harassed sports writers rounded up the number and did get through they offered their reprimand: the Australian captain should be available. That would set Greg off. He was on the cricket ground 10 hours a day during the season, and eight hours a day in his office between games. He deserved some privacy at home. In later years, unless it was one of the major writers, Greg would say, 'I'll be in the office in half an hour's time, ring me there.' Occasionally the caller would become pompous: You can't cut me off, I'm from the so-and-so newspaper. And Greg would say, 'What do you mean, I *am* cutting you off.'

Fortunately Greg's health had at last responded to the removal of his tonsils. He put on weight that season, grew stronger and scored runs. He finished the six Tests with an average of 117. Consider the achievement. There is no single point in tennis, no single stroke in golf from which recovery is not possible. There is no equivalent, nothing which quite undoes the player as does the error in cricket which brings instant dismissal. That is the standard beside which Greg's batting may be laid. It was a first class season approaching perfection — 1,547 runs at an average of 85.94, including six centuries, the best season of his career. Only Sir Donald Bradman (1,690, 1,586, and 1,552) and Neil Harvey (1,659) had ever scored more. Fortunately, Greg had the ability to go home after his exertions, switch off and relax. 'A lot of people need a drink or television to unwind,' said Judy. 'He could just put his head on the pillow, take a few deep breaths and he was off.'

Proof that he was well came when he extended his season to captain the Richie Benaud-managed International Wanderers' Tour to South Africa. The brief tour cemented various opinions in Greg's mind. No thinking person could agree with apartheid. It was a mistake for the white government not to be more generous in offering education and other opportunities to the black people. 'I felt sorry for the players,' said Greg. 'They really fought hard to make the concessions required by the International Cricket Conference and copped a lot of flak at home over it. But a hell of a lot that was done to integrate cricket didn't flow through to everyday life.' He thought South Africa ought to be re-admitted so that the progress made by the Springbok cricketers at home would not be lost.

International ostracism intruded into the Wanderers' matches as well. 'It wasn't expected that South Africa would win, it was demanded of them,' said Greg. 'It put the umpires under so much pressure.' In Durban Greg was caught off a ball he declares bounced twice. 'It went low the whole way, bounced once and the fielder dived forward and caught it on the half volley on the second bounce,' he said. The umpire who gave him out Greg subsequently accused of using two sets of rules, one for the home side and one for the Wanderers. The umpire replied, 'I take a dim view of those remarks, Mr Chappell.' To which Greg replied, 'Well, that makes us even because I take a dim view of your umpiring.'

Greg was summoned with Benaud before the tour organizers and charged with accusing the umpire of cheating. 'No, far from it,' defended Greg in his best bush lawyer manner. 'I would say that from time to time his patriotism gets in the way of his decisions, but I've never accused him of cheating.' In 1976 it meant so much to South Africa to show the rest of the world their standards had not fallen in the six years since being banned, visiting sides were on a hiding to nothing. 'Really, we couldn't get a wicket unless we knocked the stumps over,' said Greg.

As Australian captain he underwent substantial pressure to return to Australia and speak up for South African cricket. He heard their arguments, accepted some of them, but never returned to South Africa. He had no intention of becoming a guinea pig to prove their cause. Fortunately the Commonwealth Gleneagles agreement on sporting contacts with South Africa was signed in 1977, after that visit, a timing which fell happily for Greg in later contacts with West Indies teams. In 1981–82 Greg was offered $650,000, any bank account in the world, to play two seasons in South Africa. But Greg did not have a price. Four years later when a team of Australians defied the ACB and the Australian Government to join a rebel tour of South Africa for far less than Greg declined, Greg understood their motivation.

'Only a few of us were silly enough to play cricket for so long for so little,' he said. 'Everyone thinks the honour of playing Test cricket for your country is great. And so it is. You'd sacrifice anything for the first 10 Tests. But the longer you play the more you need real financial compensation.' Greg was sympathetic to those who wanted to go to South Africa and see for themselves — that was their right as individuals. But he also recognized the danger South African tours presented to Australian cricket. A team of 15 South African tourists from the 70–odd Shield players in Australia was a large proportion compared with 15 English players from the 200 or more who comprised England county teams. Australia could ill afford to lose the equivalent of a first class team from its ranks.

While on that Wanderers' tour Greg saw a half century in Pretoria by a 16-year-old named Kepler Wessels. Greg had already negotiated with Viv Richards to return to play for Queensland after the West Indies tour. When Wessels came to Australia Greg convinced him to migrate north, as he did Allan Border too. Being the best himself, Greg surrounded himself with the best.

The season ended peculiarly. Ian Chappell called the entire South Australian cricket team out on strike with him over the selectors' failure to consult him on the make-up of the squad for the eastern States' tour. I wrote in the *National Times*, 15–20 March 1976:

This was Chappell, cricket's reluctant radical, taking issue, alone initially, with the game's administrators, over matters which will eventually shape the future of cricket in Australia.

This will affect nearly every other player in Australia more than Chappell, whose first-class career is ending, if not over. His skirmishes are the forerunners of player action...

But he's not out to bust the system which has produced the world champion cricket team, he seeks to improve it and make it more equitable.

Innocently prophetic words. What struck me at the time was that Ian, as popular as he was, could command a unanimous vote. Was there some unspoken disaffection abroad in the ranks of Australian cricket? Greg heard of, but was not involved in, the strike. He looked forward to a few years of peaceful captaincy, perhaps retiring around 1979 or 1980, hopefully leaving behind the legacy he inherited, a powerful, united, winning Australian team. He got just two years.

REVOLUTION (1977-1979)

14. Conspiracy

When I bought an insurance policy from Friends Provident covering a home loan in 1975 the salesman was Greg Chappell. I was surprised. Already he seemed beyond mortal needs, but in fact his key sources of income then were the business over that desk, cricket, and various personal advertising endorsements, primarily Metropolitan Permanent, Queensland's largest building society. He was wont to get calls after lunch from his friend, Barry Maranta, asking, 'Listen, we're down at Tatt's playing snooker, how about coming down?'. To which he said, 'No, I've got to earn a bloody living. It's all right for you semi-retired blokes, I've got a job to do.' Maranta learned never to invoke Greg's fierce concentration — a challenge or a bet and a 3.5 metre golf putt became a gimme. 'Once he got that haughty look I knew I'd lost,' said Barry. But he respected Greg's business intellect as others admired his cricket. He once introduced Greg to Ray Seashore, general manager of Utah, the giant coal mining company, to discuss an incentive by Utah based on runs scored by Greg. Seashore was an American who thought cricket was an insect. Greg's encyclopedic knowledge of American baseball, gleaned from that childhood tome *The Fireside Book of Baseball*, soon won Seashore over. Once Greg had made that initial breakthrough, as grandmother Peg Lester has already said, 'Greg knew how to please people.'

One day that winter Greg did join his friends at Tatt's, but not for snooker. He arrived with a South Australian acquaintance who was offering Greg the rights to market a revolutionary insurance policy in Queensland under the name of Living Insurance. The policy overturned the century old reversionary policy which paid pre-inflation interest rate bonuses of 3 and 4 per cent. Living Insurance, by separating the death cover from the investment portion of the policy, was able to offer bonuses at a contemporary 7 and 8 per cent interest. The more Maranta spoke to contacts in the industry who said it would not work, but could not say why, the more interested he became. Greg roped in an experienced insurance friend, Barry Martin from Friends Provident, who not only thought it would work but accepted Greg's invitation to help set it up. Maranta needed little coaxing.

The partners moved into a new building in St Paul's Terrace, just out of Brisbane city proper, and while they waited for office partitions and furniture, sat on boxes and dialled on telephones on the carpet making appointments. The winter of 1976 Judy probably saw less of Greg than during the cricket season. He had half-hourly appointments, 8.30 to 5.30 and lunch was a business conversation. By June 1976, Greg won Living Insurance's national trophy as top marketing director for that month. In his first year Greg sold a million dollars worth of insurance. But the partners took no wages, they pumped it straight back into the company. They had an added incentive to succeed.

'The major insurance companies bagged us around town,' said Greg. 'They said we were charlatans, fly-by-nighters and wouldn't be there next year.' Living Insurance was barred from the Life Underwriters Association of Queensland, and Maranta recalled some rude events, one at a function at Ballymore, headquarters of Rugby Union football in Queensland. Greg crossed to Maranta in an agitated state, 'Got a pen, got a pen?' He wanted to write this man's name down. He had said to Greg in a group, 'Well, Greg, you're going to be out of a job in a couple of months, so when you are, come over and I'll give you one.' Some six months later the speaker himself was out of work and Maranta and Chappell were able to ring him and magnanimously offer him a job.

Greg's prime expertise was in being well known, but Maranta was adamant Greg be seen as more than just a sportsman. He organized conventions for salesmen at which Greg would master the ceremonies and deliver a motivational speech. Over business lunches Greg would provide insights about cricket and cricketers for the first 15 minutes, over entrées perhaps. 'He would pay them the respect of telling it all honestly, not just superficially,' said Maranta. 'But then he would discipline himself and enquire back, "How many employees have you got? What's your superannuation fund like?".' Over these lunches Maranta was privy to some of the most detailed and impressive dissections of cricket and cricketers he ever heard. 'I thought how it was wasted on me,' he said. 'It was meant for young cricketers.'

Greg's cricket obligations often distanced him from the day-to-day growth of Living Insurance. But he brought his cricket skills of analysis and synthesis to business conferences. 'I've sat at round tables and Greg has not said anything for 20 minutes,' said Maranta. 'Then he will say, "Why don't we do this and this," and sum everything up. That doesn't mean the rest of us pale into insignificance, but after it happened a dozen times I just thought, "Well, he's done it again."'

That was no more than Australian masseur Doc McErlane would have expected. 'In dressing-rooms you could be doing a puzzle and he'd come along and stand talking to you and say, "What are you up to?" And he'd look down and say, "Put that one there and that there," and walk away and he'd have solved it. A brilliant young man, believe me.'

Living Insurance became the largest independent insurance marketing group in Australia. In the process Greg detached himself from the cricket clique in which he had gladly mingled for so long and ventured into the high climes of commerce. He broke the pure cricket mould in which his father Martin had so carefully cast him.

All of which made him receptive to the tentative approaches by potential intruders into the Australian Cricket Board's monopoly of the sport. First there came Sydney entrepreneur Jack Neary looking at end of season promotions, then an Indian group made contact promising English pounds, not rupees, for exhibition matches. Most serious was an approach in February 1976 by the D. J. Foynes Organization, from Perth. They envisaged five days' cricket at the MCG, Australia versus the World, $100,000 prize money to players, 10 per cent net gate receipts to the Australian Cricket Board. Foynes drafted a calculated note to ACB secretary, Alan Barnes: 'Whilst we are keen to remunerate the players more than adequately, we are acutely aware of the need not to set precedents which could prove embarrassing to any present cricket authority.'

Foynes offered Greg a 12.5 per cent interest in the promotion company, the same as offered Tony Greig. He said Richie Benaud had agreed to act as a consultant. Greg directed Foynes, as he had all previous approaches, to the ACB, where history records the promotions vanished without trace. A less formal approach came in January 1976 during the Test in Sydney against the West Indies. Greg met television entrepreneur, John Cornell — 'Strop' of Paul Hogan fame — for drinks with Rod Marsh, Dennis Lillee and Ian in the Koala

Oxford Hotel. Cornell sounded out reactions to an international cricket series outside the ACB. Greg thought he would hear no more about it. Cornell told Greg years later that the idea went a little flat after that initial meeting.

Meanwhile the season had begun anew. On 12 December 1976, Greg took the Queenslanders to Perth for the Gillette Cup one-day final. On a WACA wicket seaming as treacherously as when Lillee took 8-29 against the Rest of the World in 1971, Queensland dismissed Rod Marsh's sandgropers for just 77 runs. In Brisbane, when that score was broadcast on the radio news, cricket fans began rejoicing in offices all over the city. Queensland versus Western Australia, Chappell versus Marsh and Lillee, had become the contest we all enjoyed. The previous year Greg had taken 3-38, including the last vital wickets, to defeat Western Australia by just four runs in the cup final at the 'Gabba. It looked like a repeat win. But Greg knew the match was not over. When six Western Australians, including Kim Hughes, Rod Marsh and Craig Serjeant all scored ducks, it meant the pitch was near unplayable. 'They had arguably the best seam attack in Australia,' said Greg. 'Dennis, the best in the world, Wayne Clark and Mick Malone. We weren't overconfident.'

Nor were the Western Australians according to Ian Brayshaw, who was run out for five of those 77 runs. In *Caught Marsh Bowled Lillee*, published in 1983, he recounted how even Rod Marsh looked a little resigned as he led his players out of the dressing-room. Then Lillee burst towards the door, shouting fiercely, 'Let's get 'em ... we can do it.' Viv Richards, who had joined Queensland that season, and Greg, were the main hopes. Lillee bowled three consecutive bouncers at opener Richards and clean-bowled him with the fourth, pitched well up. Greg scored 2 before Lillee at the top of his mark noticed Marsh standing well to leg-side and motioning for a high ball. He bowled that line, Greg touched it faintly with his glove, and there was Marsh, ludicrously wide on the leg-side, taking the catch. They were ecstatic and have modestly said so in their books. With Greg gone the Western Australians seamed through the Queenslanders to win by a comfortable 15 runs.

'Yeah, good bowling, good combination,' conceded Greg of his carefully conceived dismissal. 'A fair chance of coming off. A fair chance if they'd bowled at the stumps too that day. To say I was astonished is probably taking it a little too far.' And then Greg let fire a few good-humoured broadsides at his cocky mates. 'You always remember your good days. Dennis and Rod obviously enjoyed that. A couple of times we humiliated WA but we haven't gloated over it. The number of times I've got Rod out, and what's more I've got him bowling medium pace, off-spinners and leg-spinners. As I've told him many times, "It's only a matter of running up and bowling, mate. Doesn't matter what I bowl!" '

Marsh showed less aggression and imagination two weeks later in the first Test against Pakistan in Adelaide. On the last day Australia, six wickets down, required 57 runs to win in 70 minutes. Marsh and Gary Cosier finished 23 runs short. Marsh stonewalled to end not out on 13. He received a lashing from the Australian press for not 'having a go'. Marsh's argument was that Pakistan played ultra-defensively. To attack would have risked defeat and played into Pakistan's hands. But Australia had dominated the Test and was the only team with a realistic chance of winning. Greg did not give Marsh any instructions. Rod was, after all, vice-captain. 'Had he been a less experienced player I might have been inclined to impose my will,' said Greg. 'But I didn't want a situation where I was saying one thing with him feeling another, and having that upset his concentration.' And what was Greg's will? 'I thought they were just waiting until we were safe and then have a go for the runs,' he said. 'I thought we had a chance to win it.'

Marsh had shown similar extraordinary caution under Ian Chappell in the 1974–75 series against England. In the third Test in Melbourne he and Max Walker, requiring 55 runs in the last hour, managed seven runs off seven overs from Titmus and Underwood to effectively settle for a draw. Admittedly those two spinners would daunt any batsmen but Australia were 2–0 up in that series. Batting at seven Marsh was always going to be left with some challenging decisions for Australia. Posterity records he declined those two.

Australia drew that summer's Test series against Pakistan but by then the Australian team was only a shadow of the world champion team of 1974–76. Ian Chappell, Ian Redpath, Ashley Mallett and Terry Jenner had retired and Thomson had dislocated his shoulder in a horrific collision with Alan Turner in the Adelaide Test against Pakistan. Nearly half a team lost. In January 1977, Greg was made ABC Sportsman of the Year for 1976. It was for deeds past and gone. Greg set about the long haul of rebuilding Australia's strength.

To this end he enlisted the support of team seniors Rod Marsh and Doug Walters in introducing early morning fitness runs at the start of their tour of New Zealand in February 1977. First morning at the Avon Motor Lodge in Christchurch Walters was last to rise and joined in wearing three-tone boxer swimming trunks and a singlet emblazoned with Dukes, a new brand of cigarette. Walters soon dropped off the back of the pack and was not seen until he rejoined the squad 200 metres from home whereupon he sprinted home first, ran straight into his room and collapsed. The next morning he arrived with a new Playboy T-shirt with the message on the back, 'Jogging Can Kill'. Walters usually had the last laugh and he did in the first Test. He scored 250 which provoked from Greg in *The 100th Summer*:

> *It is difficult to convey the magnitude of such an innings ... What makes Doug Walters so unique is that he doesn't do things just once. He repeats outstanding feats such as Test double centuries just to show that it is he, not the performance, that is a measure apart.*

In that first drawn Test Greg had a run-in with New Zealand's world-class batsman, Glenn Turner. Greg knew him as a quiet, introverted man from their county days. An Anglified New Zealander, Turner had the reputation that if he was sure he was caught, he would walk. Rick McCosker caught him off Lillee, centimetres from the ground. Neither umpire was sure whether the ball had carried and so gave Turner the benefit of their doubt. Both Greg and McCosker assured Turner it had not bounced. Turner stood his ground. Greg is cynical about walkers. 'They walk when it suits them, when it is clear to the umpires they are out. Then, when it is unclear, they stand their ground and their reputation as walkers weighs in the umpire's mind. I reckon that's hypocrisy. If everybody left it to the umpires you'd have fewer problems.' Greg was angry Turner would not accept his or McCosker's word. Turner, they decided, was only a part-time walker.

The second Test, in Auckland, Australia won and with it the series. It was notable for Greg's encounter with a streaker, off whose white backside he bounced a couple of forehand bats. The very next ball Greg was run out, missing McCosker's call in the din of the streaker being escorted off the field. The local police chief took a statement from Greg on the matter and told him not to worry. But Greg did worry, right up until Terry Alderman was badly injured in a spectator incident five years later.

During the Test John Cornell asked to meet Greg again. Lillee,

Cornell, and ex-footballer-writer Austin Robertson visited Greg at 7 p.m. in his hotel room. Cornell, in his quiet, persuasive way set out the facts. Since they had last spoken, a year ago, Cornell had obtained the backing of media magnate, Kerry Packer, in a new international cricket promotion. Cornell and Robertson had flown around the world and had written or verbal agreements with some 40 players. The ACB was not being informed until the whole scheme was organized. They told Greg, 'We want to tie up a lot of other Australian players but there's probably not much point in talking to them here if you're not interested.' They did not want an immediate answer. They were there for the Test. Greg told them he would think it over, what it meant to cricket, himself and his family.

In the whispering air-conditioned dark of his hotel room, where cricket travel compelled Greg to spend so many hours, he pondered yet one more vital decision. He thought it could not work. He did not even get as far as thinking it would end up in suspensions all round. 'I just thought the ACB would tell them to go jump in the lake,' he said. Next morning in the bus on the way to the ground he sat behind Doug Walters. He wondered if Doug knew. Rod and Dennis, up the front of the bus, were in on it. Cornell had said he was not approaching any others until he had Greg's answer. Greg asked casually, 'Have you had a chat to Austin and John?' Walters nodded. Greg expressed his doubts about it getting off the ground. 'They've got to. It's got to work,' said Walters vehemently. Greg sat back.

That night Greg thought it through again. He was captain, a Board-appointed position. He felt some fidelity to the Board, but equally knew that the Board was really a giant cartel monopolizing all cricket employment. In that way he felt a loyalty to the players who were being exploited. He could inform the ACB, thereby dobbing in his mates, a decidedly un-Australian act. He could join the revolution and therefore be accused of treason by the Board. Or he could neither inform nor join, in which case he would be seen to be a weak-kneed muddler not worthy of leading either army. He realized what a risk Cornell had taken in coming to him. He could scuttle them with one phone call. He felt uncomfortable with such electricity at his finger-tips. Cornell was counting partly on kinship. Ian was deeply impli-cated in the conspiracy. If Greg elected to stay with the ACB it would almost certainly be Greg's ACB Australians against Ian's rebel Aus-tralians. Brother against brother in a cricket civil war which would cause irrevocable schisms within a family in whose veins the game's blood coursed.

But these were mere rambling thoughts. He was a player first, a captain second. If indeed a large number of players had signed, it meant they were all of the same mind. Things were not good. Cornell had said he would approach the ACB in the long run so it was not as if Greg would be agreeing to fatally undermine the Board. Anyway, he was clear that his greater loyalty was to the players before the Board. 'I felt that if I was in trouble the players would stand up for me,' said Greg. 'I was not so sure about the Board.' On the evening before the last day of the Auckland Test he told Cornell, 'I'm in favour, but I'm not prepared to sign at this stage. As Australian captain I don't want to have it seen you're running off me as an organizer to sign up other players.' If other players wanted to consult Greg he would explain that he was in favour of the concept. Cornell was satisfied.

Greg contemplated his future confrère in cricket's revolution. Cornell was an entrepreneur, planner and thinker. 'My first impression was that he was smart, straight and well organized,' said Greg. 'He knew entertainment more than cricket and had no hang-ups about tradition. He did not think it sacrilegious to tamper with the game. Probably just what was needed.' Greg promised a final decision by the Centenary Test in Melbourne two weeks hence.

Back home he discussed it with Judy, who was pregnant. On the surface it seemed Greg would have more time at home, with fewer tours, if any. Since their marriage in 1971 Greg had spent three winters overseas in major tours, half their married winters. If Greg needed any convincing of the prima facie case to join, Judy had the figures. 'Greg went to England in 1972 for over five months, for $2,000 taxable,' said Judy. 'In 1948 Don Bradman's side went to England on £1,000 taxfree.' Judy had met the New South Wales Premier, Neville Wran, at a function and Wran had told her his parents bought a house in Balmain around that 1948 period for £846. 'In 1972 after you'd taken tax out of $2,000 you couldn't even put a deposit on a house,' said Judy.

Greg made a note to himself at the time in his small, concise, legible handwriting, of the argument for joining. 'Shorter seasons — shorter tours — more money — less reliant on commercialism of self — more security.' He wrote: 'If accepted by establishment minimal disruption to existing system — in fact complementing it … J.P. Sport (Cornell) were offering an alternative to what I believe to be a tyrannous regime.'

Late in 1976, and far too late to save itself, the Australian Cricket

Board set up a sub-committee of State captains to co-ordinate sponsorship for the Australian team. Previously the players had promoted themselves in a damaging, topsy-turvy fashion, sometimes pumping petrol for promotional photographs only hours before a Test match. Benson and Hedges picked up the sponsorship, $350,000 for three years, a song, as Kerry Packer was about to prove. When that captains' committee met early in 1977 under the auspices of the ACB most of its members — Walters, Marsh, Richie Robinson and Greg, all except Ashley Woodcock for South Australia — were already, or would be, Kerry Packer signees. Greg had no qualms. 'We all felt it was going to be presented to the ACB and we hoped to walk into the gathering twilight arm in arm,' he said. 'I thought the ACB would have no alternative.' A correct assessment that would cost millions of dollars — Packer's and the ACB's — to be upheld in the law courts of the British Commonwealth.

Before signing Greg mentioned it to his business partner, Barry Maranta, who, like Greg, was alarmed until he thought it through and glimpsed the future. After the Centenary Test Greg also told his father. He was surprised how easily Martin, whom Greg thought of as a traditionalist, accepted the idea. But by then Greg had physically signed a Packer contract. This he did when he met Cornell again just before the start of the Centenary Test in Melbourne in March 1977. He then gave peripheral advice on what other players to sign. 'Yes, he's pretty good,' and, 'Bit early for him.'

So at the moment when hundreds of cricketers, past and present, gathered in Melbourne to celebrate 100 years of matches between the Old Foes, Greg was contributing towards its fracture and reformation. He was aware of the paradox of the timing as he signed his name — the G and S initials almost identical, the two P's sitting as high above the line as the two L's — to a document of excommunication from the game he had practised so faithfully at Lynn Fuller's Sunday morning services. But people are only fully aware of history in retrospect. At the time Greg was studying his contract for five years, which was his career expectancy, beginning on $50,000 a year and escalating to $70,000 by the last. Greg's was the only five-year contract of the 50 or more then on offer. The best were three years like brother Ian's which, according to Christopher Forsyth's book, *The Great Cricket Hijack*, published in 1978, was worth $10,000 signing on and $30,000 a year. The same book gave Greg's contract as substantially less than Greg told me. This brings into question other figures quoted by

Forsyth, who worked for World Series Cricket, as the show had become known. But even Forsyth's figures were twice the $20,000 being returned by the Benson and Hedges sponsorship through the ACB to Greg annually.

With all this commotion behind hotel doors it seems impossible that the Test itself should be memorable. Yet it was, third only to The Oval, 1972 and Port of Spain, 1975, in Greg's list of the best. First there were the functions. 'Almost too many people,' said Greg. 'You didn't have time to talk to anyone. But it made me conscious of the depth of the game. When you walked into the MCG they had all the old scoreboard name-plates stuck up along the corridors and under the stand. There was a fair build-up and a sense of excitement.' England came to the MCG with a 3-1 win record over India, against Australia's 2 wins, 2 draws and 1 loss against Pakistan and New Zealand. England's captain was South African born Tony Greig. Greg thought him an average Test cricketer, made good by his sheer competitiveness. 'He wouldn't have made it as a bowler or batsman, but his determination made him a top all-rounder. And he had great hands, a great catcher.'

The MCG wicket for the first two days was a desperate combination of seam and spin with first Underwood and then Lillee reducing batsmen to ill-controlled puppets. Greg scored 40. Low as it was he was easily the top scorer in the first innings. In fact only one other player passed 20 on both sides, Rod Marsh, who registered 28. Greg battled out another epic contest with Derek Underwood. 'He was accurate and gripping and holding up,' said Greg. 'You just had to wait and wait. Unless he gave you room it was hard to score.' It was this Test that caused Mike Brearley, when he replaced Tony Greig as England captain, to remark to himself that 'Underwood to Chappell was a good thing'. It was a fatuous generalization. Underwood bowled 94 balls for 16 runs that day and took three wickets. 'Under those conditions I'd back him to bog a lot of blokes down,' said Greg. 'Or else he'd get them out trying to force it along.' Which is what Greg did, clean-bowled going down the wicket as he ran out of partners. 'It was a sacrifice,' said Greg. 'I rate that 40 as one of the better innings I've played.'

As wickets tumbled commentators began predicting the match would be over in three or four days. That irritated Greg. It was plain to him that the occasion, as much as the pitch, was bringing good batsmen undone, and that such nerves would not apply in the second innings. 'These commentators, you'd think they had never played a game of cricket to carry on like that,' he said. It was his first inkling that the small walk from the wicket to the commentary box produced giant brain changes in formerly rational cricketers.

As the game proceeded Greg, who hated losing any Test match, became determined he was not going to be listed as the Aussie captain who lost the 100th Year Test. By the fifth day the tension was such that minor incidents became unforgettable. Greg introduced the Queen to his team and winced as Lillee asked for her autograph. He could have expected it. In 1972 at Buckingham Palace he flanked Lillee and where everybody else had muttered 'Your Highness' or 'Ma'am,' Dennis gave her a very broad Aussie 'G'day'. As the official party trooped onto the MCG, to Greg's astonishment there was a solicitor acquaintance, Ian Harris, from Brisbane among them with his camera. 'What are you doing here?,' Greg asked sotto voce. 'I wanted a close shot,' said Harris. As the Royal party came down the passageway Harris saw a gap, jumped in and walked out. It was too zany but large and small events were registering clearly in Greg's consciousness.

Other memories flash through Greg's mind about that Test — Rick McCosker offering through clenched teeth and the swathes of bandages of his broken jaw, 'I want to bat again,' and he did; Greg's words to Kerry O'Keeffe who was brought up the batting list to open, 'I want you to play the bloody innings of your life,' and he did; David Hookes, his heart ruling his head, smashing five consecutive fours off Tony Greig to sway fortunes Australia's way; Marsh's Australian wicket-keeping record, and his century, the first by an Australian 'keeper against England.

Then the Derek Randall incident. Greg was bowling, intent on slowing the run-rate from one end to husband his tiring attack. He saw a straight forward deviation off Randall's bat and Marsh diving forward to catch it. Randall was on 161. It was a crucial catch approved by umpire Tom Brookes. As Greg ran down the wicket Marsh got up shaking his head. Marsh told Greg, 'He didn't hit it.' To which Greg said, 'It's nothing to do with you,' following his policy that he always played the umpire's decision. But Marsh added, 'Anyway, it didn't carry.' Greg was deflated, but immediately turned towards Randall who was trudging off 20 metres away, called out and signalled him to come back. Though Greg normally fielded at slip he then went down to fine leg at the end of the over and fielded there for four overs.

Dennis Lillee in his latest book, *Over and Out*, wrote:

Greg was brimming with emotion and took himself down to fine leg shortly afterwards. He didn't stay there long, but I thought it significant that he wanted to be alone in our hour of need.

Greg listened to that and shook his head. 'That's Dennis' assumption. It had nothing to do with it.' Greg had bowled almost through that session, a superb display of accurate seaming which dried up the runs at his end, 16 overs at less than two runs an over. 'I was finding it hard to concentrate in slips,' he said. 'Having done all that hard work I didn't want to undo it all and drop a catch. Nor did I want to make an error of judgement in my bowling changes.' The odds were in England's favour at that stage and Greg was fighting to keep control of the game. He turned to Marsh and said, 'I need a break. I'm going down to fine leg to relax in between overs.' When even close friends on the field misinterpret the action simply because they are out of earshot, it is no wonder that spectators and commentators are so often astray. 'That's what I said to Rod, that's the way it was,' said Greg.

Well, 'twas a famous victory for Greg, the Centenary Test, if an emotionally and mentally exhausting one. But as the nineteenth century poet Robert Southey asked in his poem, *The Battle of Blenheim*: 'What good came of it at last?' Did he really have to draw with Pakistan, and then defeat New Zealand and England all in one season to wear his captain's hat with pride? The rewards came from strange quarters. First a letter from Walter Hadlee, father of Richard and Dayle and president of the New Zealand Cricket Association. He wrote:

Since I returned from the wonderful occasion of the Centenary Test, I have several times thought I would like to write to you and to Rod Marsh to congratulate you both on your action in asking the umpire to reverse his decision that Randall was caught behind the wicket.
I do heartily commend this approach to the game ...
Neither you nor Rod will have any regrets for you have placed the game above the winning and that in itself will give you lifelong satisfaction.

Then there came the McNair-Anderson report that the Centenary Test reached 56 per cent of all television homes, a fillip to the World Series Cricket organizers, their secret only months from breaking over an astonished cricket world. And finally Greg realized that if Australia could only just best England on the MCG, the Ashes were in jeopardy on the five month tour of England in just a few weeks' time.

In those few hectic weeks he and Judy managed to share in their second adventure of parenthood. Greg was present for the birth of Belinda. Judy was not sure whether she had prepared Greg for the experience adequately. 'I think he was a bit frightened by it all.' Not so, said Greg. He enjoyed it. And there we leave them as Greg left for his third, but not yet his last, tour of England. Belinda was a week old. When he next saw her she would be five months.

15. Revolution

In the Palm Court lounge of the Waldorf Hotel, London, several Australian cricketers idled at a table overlooking the sunken floor where guests read and wrote. The Palm Court was a scene of anachronistic splendour, a massive expanse of white marble floors, covered with runner carpets in wine red and gold floral design. Brass abounded in ornate rams' heads supporting the fluted columns of lanterns, in elbow height ashtray stands and in dully shining stairway hand rails. The lounge *maître* in tails, white bow-tie and flyaway starched collar hovered near the players. Across the lounge a pianist at a Steinway bent caressingly to a muted rendition of Beethoven's 'Moonlight Sonata'.

The Australians, in their tracksuit tops and casual clothes were like actors on the wrong set. It was rest day during the first Test, the Jubilee Test, at Lord's, 19 June 1977. David Hookes read aloud Ted Dexter's Sunday newspaper column accusing Len Pascoe of being a chucker. Early that morning Greg, in a brief press conference, branded the charge as pure manure, or words to that effect. If only his problems were so small. Some five weeks earlier, on 9 May, the Packer professional cricket news was broken. Word had leaked after a party under a huge marquee in Tony Greig's backyard on the outskirts of Hove, Sussex. The day the story hit the streets in Australia pandemonium reigned in the Australian team's hotel.

Greg confronted the tour managers, Norm McMahon, the Queenslander who in 1974 had borne the bad news to Greg that his house was flooded, and Len Maddocks, a Test player of the 1950s. 'They accused me of all sorts of things,' said Greg. 'Sheep in wolf's clothing, betrayed trust, deceived the board.' He thanked them for their opinion and said he would speak to the chairman of the Australian Cricket

Board, Bob Parish, when the opportunity arose. Greg immediately sent off handwritten air letters to both Parish and Sir Donald Bradman, the latter because he was a senior member of the board who would have some say in any punishment meted out to the Packer signees.

The letters briefly outlined the reasons the players signed. Greg feared some penalty would be decided without the players ever being asked for their side of the story. He wrote that the players signed with the intention that they play with permission from the board. He never heard from Bradman. Not that he specifically expected to, but he was hopeful. The Vic Richardson factor notwithstanding, Greg respected Bradman's efficient, businessman's brain. It was just possible that in this matter of cricket commerce Bradman would see clearly where less shrewd board members would be blinded by prejudice. Parish was arriving for a meeting of the International Cricket Conference in June. Sure enough, one morning Greg rounded a corner in the Waldorf foyer and Parish walked in towards the lifts. Greg called out, 'Excuse me Bob, I'd like to have a chat with you at some stage.' Parish replied, 'I don't think we've got anything to discuss,' and turned on his heel.

If Greg was in doubt of his fate with the ACB the English establishment provided the answer by swiftly sacking Tony Greig from the England captaincy for his part in the Packer coup. The ACB could scarcely sack Greg, although rumours constantly swept the team in the early days that the team would be flown home. Greg's relations with McMahon and Maddocks froze. He was distressed, though not for himself and the other senior players. 'If they wanted to ban us for life, that was fine,' said Greg. 'But I felt for the younger blokes with their careers ahead of them.'

Greg's predicament was eminently predictable. If he had examined his heart carefully he would have known that the challenge to the bureaucracy of the ACB, the conspiracy of silence against it, the moral ambiguity of his own role, would have been burdensome enough at home. To have left Australia knowing that the news would break sometime on tour, left him like a Roman general, in action abroad, whose name has been found on a list seeking to overthrow the emperor. He may as well stay in Gaul.

The leader of that cricket coup, Kerry Packer, flew into London in late May to bring comfort and aid to his players. Greg joined a collection of the cricket contractors in cabs to the Dorchester Hotel where Packer had his private suite. Greg had not met him before. He was a big man, an imposing figure, who talked bluntly, with a few bloodys and fewer frills and whose love of cricket exceeded a reasonable knowledge of the game. John Cornell introduced the players, poured beer and looked reassuring. The younger players, nervous at rumours they would be banned for life, asked questions. Where would they play, what sort of games? Packer told them he still hoped it would be all done with co-operation from the ACB, but no matter what, their contracts would be honoured. After an hour everyone suddenly realized the enormity of their commitment. They had signed on a concept, with hardly a detail in sight. 'There had to be a hell of a lot of trust on both sides,' said Greg, 'I suppose the players had more to lose than Packer. But from day one whatever he promised was forthcoming, and then some.'

When I met Greg at the Waldorf during the Jubilee Test he was in an altered state. As courteous as ever but with an air of having jammed his thumb in the dyke, still valiantly shielding the tour and the Tests to come from corrosive controversy. Yet sitting with the younger players it was clear they were undergoing a crisis of conscience, confused at being led by Greg into an apparent dead-end. It was demeaning also to see Greg reduced to merely a Packer signee at the Dorchester, instead of the detached figurehead to whom they should all defer, Packer included. The nature of cricketers was beginning to tell on them as well. Footballers could never have kept the Packer secret so long. They are too gregarious and open in their type. Cricket isolates players, turns them into solitary, independent individuals. The admirable characteristic which saved the secret now left them without a group communality to lean on. Each day new Packer headlines haunted them as they boarded their long summer's bus journey into uncertainty.

To make it worse there was disunity on this mutinous voyage. Four tourists, Gary Cosier, Geoff Dymock, Craig Serjeant and Kim Hughes, had not been offered contracts. Cornell or whoever should have been branded for that piece of ineptitude. It handed the tour management the wedge to split the team. One evening at the Waldorf, Serjeant and Hughes jokingly barracked each other over which of them would captain Australia. All good fun but if the captaincy was losing its mythical inviolability, where did that leave the team?

It left them ill-prepared for the Jubilee Test but, at that stage, as much from rain as rumour. They had played the equivalent of only four full matches out of 10 scheduled. Greg had arrived without Lillee, withdrawn with an injured back — o' lucky man — and with Thommo only 80 per cent fit from his collision with Alan Turner. Greg and Rodney Marsh met the selectors Phil Ridings, Neil Harvey and Sam Loxton, before the tour and asked for an experienced player to offset the likely content of youth — Hughes, Serjeant and Hookes. They wanted Ian Brayshaw, the cool-headed, competent all rounder from Western Australia. He would have been perfect. 'They ignored us,' said Greg. 'We were left high and dry in the batting. I felt I'd been let down by the selectors.' I looked at Greg incredulously. He felt let down? He laughed. Eight years after the events he was still dividing the cricket from the politics, a manoeuvre he now knows to be impossible.

Greg's own form could not be faulted. He scored three centuries in county matches and 125 not out in a Prudential one-day match against England. He had eschewed the sheet anchor role he had experimented with in New Zealand and the Centenary Test to steady his inexperienced team. Better to adhere to Richie Benaud's words of 1969 after his century in Perth — play his shots. To that end he was enjoying the tour. After the match at Bath against his old county, Somerset, Joel Garner approached and asked Greg if he remembered him. 'Sure, I just played you,' joked Greg. 'No, man, in the West Indies,' said Garner. Greg was stumped. Garner then produced the paper Barbados dollar with Greg's autograph on it, scribbled that day in 1973 when Greg toured the West Indies under Ian. That tour cemented Garner's ambition to play Test cricket. He kept that dollar note as a symbol of his goal and he took it to show Greg in Bath. Greg would see enough of the giant fast bowler in years to come to wish he had never inspired the man.

Before the third one-day match Greg called a team meeting and declared his displeasure with the team's general application. They had been outfielded by England. Greg had begun a sheepdog role, nipping at their heels. He maintained this watch even at parties, shepherding players around arguments, calling for music if the action became too boisterous. I could see how the schoolmasterly metaphor came about.

And he also embarked upon long, chess-like manoeuvres against England's new captain, the likeable Mike Brearley. In their respective books covering that 1977 tour it was conceded Greg checked Brearley with a legal technicality at Lord's. At the start of the Australian innings rain interrupted play. Greg refused to let the groundsmen cover the bowlers' follow-throughs. That way, however dry the follow-throughs were when play re-started, he could be sure the wicket would be drier. He was ever conscious of Underwood's ability on a wet pitch. Brearley objected, but later wrote, 'I looked it up in the rules. Chappell was right.'

During the Australian innings Greg batted with Serjeant who was pinned like a butterfly to his crease by Underwood. It took him 39 minutes to hit his first Test single. Greg roamed constantly down the pitch to exhort him to concentrate, or to stay calm. Serjeant made an admirable 81 but another youngster, David Hookes, went for only 11 and was heard later to ask manager McMahon, 'You'll have to show me where that shop is in the morning, Norm.' What shop was that? 'Rent-a-run,' joked Hookes self deprecatingly. Yet it was Hookes who succeeded on the tour, while Serjeant's form slumped. Greg had several long chats with Serjeant, how important it was, if he made a start, not to throw his wicket away. It was Chester Bennett's old advice to Greg at Princes — 60 was not enough. Hookes was popularly thought to have failed to live up to his Centenary Test promise on the tour, but Greg disputed that. Hookes averaged over 30 in the Tests. 'If he'd been allowed to be one of the young players on his first tour, people would have judged him differently,' said Greg. 'Instead of batting at six we had him at four. He was thrust into the role of one of our main batsmen.'

Lord's was drawn. Greg thought if Australia had won that, the tour's complexion may have changed. My impression was that the Englishmen comprehended with every passing day how weak was their adversary. Before the second Test at Old Trafford, Manchester, Brearley contemplated where lay Greg's weakness. At Lord's Willis got Greg soon after bowling him a bouncer. Someone else thought Greg liked to take a single between mid-off and extra cover. A run-out perhaps? Greg laughed. 'If that's how they thought of getting me out I was obviously playing all right.'

And never better than at Old Trafford. In the second innings Greg was batting in vain to save the match. The wicket was dusty, cracking and Derek Underwood bowled with his usual maddening accuracy. Greg took only 68 balls for his first 50, but 128 for his second. It was a royal battle. Underwood was too quick for Greg to get down the pitch to turn his spin into a half volley. 'He never gave you that luxury,' said Greg. 'His line and length were so good you could have placed a handkerchief on the wicket and he'd have hit it every bloody time.' Underwood invited batsmen to take risks. He tied them down until they started manufacturing shots to score. He always left straight hit open because Greg liked to hit his slower ball back over the bowler's head. It was a matter of who would weary first on the day and both were supremely patient men, Underwood more naturally so, Greg because he had taught himself to be.

England captains regularly summoned Underwood to his mark whenever Greg walked to the crease, but in a way, what else could they do? A myth was better than nothing. Greg chatted with Derek over the years, reliving their tussles. There was mutual respect. 'He was delighted whenever he got me out and I when I made runs against him,' said Greg. 'You could argue whether he was a genuine spinner or a medium pacer, but on dusty or damp pitches Underwood was the best I played.' Underwood responded once on television:

> There have been some stupid Pommies who have said that Greg's a bit my bunny and I always answer by saying, 'Well, if all the runs were totted up and worked out according to the number of times I got him out, it would give a much truer picture of how great a player he was.'

On this occasion at Old Trafford Greg came in first wicket down with the score still nil and was finally out with the score on 202 and two tailenders left. He scored 112, most of them against Underwood, who eventually bowled him. Even then Greg's concentration was intact. 'He only bowled one bad ball all day, wide and short and it hit a crack and didn't bounce,' said Greg. 'I'd gone to give it the big one and when it stayed down it hit the bottom inside edge and back onto the stumps. Amazing.' Brearley subsequently wrote, 'His was a memorable performance, one of the best I've ever seen.' He added that the way England handled Greg at Old Trafford represented a tactical and psychological victory, because Greg did not score another 50 in the series.

It certainly was a turning point, but not for Brearley's optimistic reasons. At tea on the second day of that Test Greg again had to dress down the team for poor ground fielding. He wrote in his book with David Frith, *The Ashes '77*:

> Everybody seemed to have their bums dragging along the ground and the fielding was so slovenly that I simply had to demand an immediate and marked improvement.

But the students continued to stare out the window. Greg felt the tour go dead after Old Trafford, just as it had in 1972 at Headingley. But whereas Ian had only to grapple with Deadly Derek and the youth of his team, Greg had to cope with Packer as well who was making headlines wherever he went. Late in June Packer had made it clear that his main, if not sole, aim was to gain exclusive rights to televise Australian cricket. From that moment until World Series Cricket played its first match, Packer lost some ground in the fight for the hearts and minds of his contracted players. They respected his power but his philosophy of helping the players' cause was now suspect. Greg had no illusions about Packer's altruism. 'He saw himself as a white knight in shining armour, but he also knew if he did this, the end product was that,' said Greg.

At Leicester at the end of July Greg called another team meeting. Several players wanted to talk about Packer but Greg said Packer was irrelevant. 'That's something in the future,' he said. 'Our object is to remain united and defend the Ashes.' Reports emerged of a rift, bordering on violence, between Marsh and Maddocks. In fact Marsh told the meeting that the green cap meant as much to him as it ever had and he would punch the nose of the man who disputed it. Needless to say, Marsh was the other player, with Ian Redpath, who Greg said would not only die for the green cap, but would kill for it. Greg then issued a statement:

> There have been a number of rumours floating around recently which would lead people to believe that the Australian players who have signed with Kerry Packer are getting cold feet. In view of the fact that this is untrue I have been asked by those who have signed to make a statement to this effect.

The Australian Cricket Board subsequently wrote to Greg informing him it would withhold $500 from him for making the statement, a breach of tour agreements. Greg replied that he, Marsh and Walters had approached Maddocks about poor team discipline. Greg wrote:

> One point we made strongly, and which Mr Maddocks did not dispute, was that we were aware that he and Mr McMahon were responsible for many of the rumours circulating about unrest amongst the Packer signees...
> Happily no more rumours were spread from within and team morale improved rapidly from that time.

The letter was an indication of Greg's difficulty in keeping a true perspective on the maelstrom of action about him. It became impossible for him to separate the two, the tour and the troubles. Ever since the revelations at Hove a schizophrenia had enveloped Greg's role. He preferred to be the Australian Cricket Board's captain on tour, but increasingly he was being tarred as the quisling within, who for months had intrigued against cricket's friends and followers. In the first few weeks in England Ian arrived on his own business and when he was seen drinking with Greg the word spread that he was influencing Greg on team selections. The Chappell name was inducing as much hate as it once had hope. Ian was at the root of it all right, from right back when he led the South Australian team on strike. 'It has all come to pass,' he told me. But not as he would have preferred.

Still the cricket persisted. At Trent Bridge two memorable names graced the scoreboard, Geoff Boycott returning to Test cricket after three years' self-imposed absence, and Ian Botham, in his first Test. Boycott ran out the local Nottingham hero, Derek Randall, and looked shattered. 'The crowd went right off,' said Greg. 'When Alan Knott came in later he figuratively shook Boycott by the scruff of the neck. I couldn't hear what Knotty was saying but I knew what was going on. "Listen, forget that, the way to make it up is make runs for the team." I felt like telling Knott to stay down his own end and mind his own business.' Knott and Brearley were two of the few players who had a rapport with the difficult Yorkshireman. Said Greg, 'Boycott, I reckon, would have been quite happy to have got out and off the ground and away from the heckling and feel sorry for himself.' Instead Boycott stayed, and stayed, the whole tour long. In the next Test, at Headingley, Leeds, Greg had the dubious distinction of bowling the ball off which Boycott struck a four to reach his one hundredth 100 in first-class cricket.

Then there was boisterous Botham. When Boycott was finally dismissed for 107 at Trent Bridge, in came Botham, edged the third ball from Thomson straight to Greg at slip, who ... dropped it. Never mind, son, Walters should have said. The signs were there, the stress was beginning to show. When Greg batted the England bowlers ganged up on him as usual. Chappell was Australia. He took 90 minutes to eke 19 runs before Botham was introduced. First ball, short and wide, Greg gratefully launched himself at it, a sure smashed four ... and didn't move his feet. He got an inside edge and deflected it into his stumps. And that was how Greg helped Ian Botham begin a great Test career.

Before Trent Bridge, news of the International Cricket Conference ban on all Packer players reached the Australians. Greg's phone rang non-stop, interrupted his sleep, his thoughts. After Trent Bridge, contrary to Greg's letter to the ACB, morale deteriorated. Greg and Marsh rested from the next match at Sunderland, 4 August, and Doug Walters became the centre of a shellacking from certain players over selections. Greg heard of it in a roundabout fashion and Walters assured him it was over. Greg described it as a hate session with the bitterness of the frustrating tour spilling into personal criticism.

At Leeds, before the fourth Test, Kim Hughes boldly confronted Marsh, not Greg, and told him the team needed a technician who would go in and make runs. There were too many shotmakers in the side. Kim modestly declared he had the best technique in the side. He was the man. Marsh relayed the news to Greg. 'He's got confidence in himself, but at this stage I don't agree,' said Greg. Hughes had not been invited to join World Series Cricket. Four players had marked the card against him. Greg, Ian, Marsh and Lillee. 'There was no vendetta. He hadn't been around long enough to upset anyone. It was an independent assessment that the guy was too immature,' said Greg.

The team was staying at the Post House Hotel outside Leeds. One evening Greg, returning from a meal, walked into the bar only to be nearly charged down by Rod Marsh, barrelling out with tears in his eyes. Greg headed for an alcove where Gary Cosier, Mick Malone, Richie Robinson and Kerry O'Keeffe were sitting. Robinson volunteered there had been an argument, but it was all right now. 'Well, it's obviously not because Rod's just burst out of here in tears, so who's going to tell me what's going on?' It emerged the argument was that Richie Robinson had been chosen in the Tests because he was Marsh's and Greg's mate rather than on his cricket ability. Marsh was so hurt by the allegations he offered to fight them over it. One of the quartet sought to soothe Greg by suggesting it was not the time to talk about it. 'That's bloody interesting. It seemed to be the right time just a while ago,' said Greg. He was ropable by then. 'Your first comment was right. Now's not the time. If you've got any complaints about selections my door is open 24 hours a day.'

In this frame of mind the Australians were crushed in the fourth Test and so relinquished the Ashes. For the record Robinson ranked third in run aggregate for that Test, equal with Greg. The gloom in the Australian dressing-room may be imagined by reversing the joy evident at the Different Drummer restaurant in 1974–75 when Ian's crew won the Ashes. Greg gallantly sipped champagne on the balcony and like the good loser Brearley said he was, made a small congratulatory speech. Headingley remained a sadness for Greg. He was the first Australian captain to lose the Ashes single-handed since Ian Johnson in 1954–55. If victories like The Oval and Port of Spain were to be remembered with pleasure, then Headingley was a low. Greg saw it as a microcosm of life. He had played through Australia's triumphant years and now the circle was completed. After the fifth Test was drawn Greg said: 'We've been beaten by a better side and we're quite happy to admit it. It doesn't do any harm to see the other side of the fence. It puts the game into true perspective.'

Brearley later wrote of Greg on that tour, 'He has superb bearing on the field; whatever he does he looks graceful. I cannot remember him playing an ungainly shot.' But by the end of the summer Brearley noticed Greg yawning frequently on the field. 'He seemed less engaged, less exacting, more resigned.' Brearley also wrote that he was irritated by frequent and facile suggestions that Kerry Packer's spectral presence contributed to Australia's defeat. He argued that Greg's tourists would have been bonded by a 'last fling' mentality. This ignores the obvious fact that four of the players could not be bonded. The key error in Brearley's normal generous assessments of Greg was the word 'contributed'. Greg agreed that Packer did not cause Australia's defeat but the unhappy evidence is there that he contributed to it. Greg denied it for four months to maintain team morale but once the Ashes were lost he conceded external events had created an air of unreality. His more methodical analysis of the tour was that most of the Australians were stroke players and English conditions did not favour them. 'In Australia we might have got away with it,' he said. 'There, we just weren't good enough.'

Greg then had in his mind a letter he would soon write to the ACB. It said simply: 'I would like to officially advise the Board of my retirement from Test cricket following the 1977 tour of the UK.' ACB secretary, Alan Barnes, wrote back, '...I feel sure that your written decision will be received with regret.' Strange as that remark might seem it rings true. John Arlott observed in his 1979 book, *An Eye for Cricket*:

> *...more than anyone else who joined World Series Cricket, Greg Chappell did so with dignity and with courtesy towards the Establishment game which had produced him. He will surely return.*

Perhaps, but at the time there were no signs of leniency. Greg, then 29, professed to be ready to finish his formal career anyway. But he had given himself 10 years and taken only eight. The shame of it was that the Packer intervention denied Greg a chance to test his captaincy skills in ordinary conditions of adversity, as Ian had experienced in 1972. Nor was Greg given the opportunity to take Australian cricket and mould a new body around the strong frame of a restored Lillee, a strengthened Thomson, Marsh as ever, and himself. They were the natural challenges in the trajectory of his career. Packer simply took him off the graph.

Back home Judy had been practising her usual routine during Greg's absences, tennis and barbecues at the Marantas' on Sunday morning, closing up house for a few weeks and taking off for Sydney and her parents and then back again before Greg returned. This time, before the last Test at The Oval, Judy, aided by good Samaritan neighbours Jim and Joan Sokoll who looked after Stephen and Belinda, flew over to meet Greg. Say it quickly and it sounds simple. In five days she weaned five-months-old Belinda, obtained a new passport with the help of friend and future State Liberal leader, Dr Llew Edwards, and jumped on the flight with her previously ample bosom retreating at a ludicrously lopsided rate. Still she was a sight for sore eyes for Greg at the end of his beleaguered tour and they joined Rod and Ros Marsh for 10 days' holiday in Sardinia. Chaos accompanied their flight to a tiny beach resort on the island. When confusion reigned Greg and Rod would step aside and start talking loudly and Ockerly in English while Judy struggled with her first year university Italian.

At the resort Greg slept and read, usually a Harold Robbins, something with a bit of sex and violence. And he and Rod sampled the local beer sitting under Cinzano umbrellas while Mafia style Citroens skidded about unloading locals for fun and festivities. They also practised their Italian: *due birra*, because two beers was all they needed to know. Except one morning when Judy and Ros went shopping, the likely lads wandered over to the beach which happened to be a nude beach, which gave them a variation on their theme: due booba! When the moment arrived to prove they had the gift of tongues they accosted the bartender and, to an accompaniment of hand flourishes and raised eyebrows, requested: *due birra*. To which the bartender replied: 'You want two beers mate?' The linguists stared at each other and laughed. Somehow their separation from the Australian Cricket Board could not make them sad.

16. WSC

Dennis Lillee and Jeff Thomson were caught in almost identical poses, glaring down the pitch over their right shoulders having just let fly with the ball. Lillee adorned the glossy covered World Series Cricket season programme and Thomson the Australian Cricket Board's. An ACB marketing consultant predicted: within six months Australian cricket will have new heroes to replace the champions of the Packer series. WSC consultant Richie Benaud responded that he would wait until 1980 to judge the success of WSC's multi-million dollar operation. Any other perspective was crazy.

In the summer of 1977 Greg retreated from the crossfire. Offered the captaincy of WSC Australia he deferred to Ian. 'In my opinion he's a better captain and I'm just as happy to take a back seat,' he said. It was with profound relief Greg shed the onerous duties of leadership. The Australian and English summers had seemed seasons without end. If Greg had continued he risked a psychological burn-out wherein his form would suffer, his enjoyment of cricket diminish and his final retirement hasten. Faced with that prognosis he chose prophylaxis. Now Ian's unsmiling visage began to dominate Martin Chappell's newspaper cutting scrapbook. Those pasted pages were unshakeable testimony to the stress of the Australian captaincy. Ian was unsmiling because what general smiles before a war. Greg retired to gladly take orders.

But evading the national spotlight did not save him from repercussions in Queensland. Even while in England he was voted off the State selection panel. Subsequently he was not chosen for Queensland though his Packer contract made him available. The QCA paid out his contract, $15,000, a high price just to stand on their high horse. John Maclean attended a Queensland Cricket Association meeting while Greg was away. 'I think I was the only guy that got up and spoke in Greg's favour,' said Maclean. 'A bloke that everybody had given a great deal of respect to. Suddenly nobody had a good word to say about him. What amazed me was that hearing things from England they should change their opinion of the guy.' Sam Trimble, by then retired, wished WSC had come in his time. Cricket had used him up but not set him up, as golf or tennis would have. 'It never made any difference to our relationships, Greg and I. Players are players, aren't they?'

And administrators are administrators. Greg attended the 'Gabba at the start of the season. People he had known for four years either looked the other way or said 'Hello' and hurried on. Conversations stopped when he entered rooms. Once, in the press box, a QCA official greeted Greg with, 'Pleased to see you, hope everything goes well,' and departed. The journalists burst out laughing. 'You should have heard what he was saying about you before you walked in,' they said. Greg was Queensland Sportsman of the Year in 1976, but during World Series Cricket he was never invited back, even though past winners are invited every year. When WSC finished the invitations reappeared but Greg has declined ever since. 'It was just too bloody pathetic,' he said.

Greg was not entirely blameless. In an interview with Brisbane journalist Peter Hall in the *Telegraph* on 2 November 1977, he struck back at Queensland administrators who cold-shouldered him. He repeated criticisms of the Queensland administration that Sir Donald Bradman had made over lunch in 1973 when Greg was deciding whether to move to Queensland. He was quoted in the story as saying:

I didn't take Sir Donald's word for it. I came to judge people for myself and I was happy with what I found.

I'm just sorry that after all the work I put in for Queensland the authorities aren't prepared to come to me for my side of the story.

However much these words stung Queensland sensitivities it could have been nothing to the ire it aroused in Bradman. Eight days after the story was printed Greg received a letter from Bradman taking the strongest possible exception to his remarks. Sir Donald wrote:

... you have blatantly distorted the comparative context to try and present a picture which bears no relationship to the problem you were then trying to work out.

Your article is clearly designed to stimulate sympathy for your-self in a completely new situation which subsequently developed and which has nothing to do with me or with any discussions we ever had.

Sir Donald concluded:

May I remind you of the truth of an old Chinese proverb — 'HE WHO THROWS MUD LOSES GROUND'.

That Greg had used Bradman's remarks out of context was true and Greg acknowledged as much in a reply to Sir Donald on 16 January 1978, in which he apologized. In that letter Greg took the opportunity to raise other areas of misunderstanding, such as Sir Donald's failure to respond to Greg's air letter sent to Bradman from England when the Packer story first broke. Bradman took up the correspondence. He believed Greg's letter from England had been purely informative, seeking no guidance or reply. He wrote:

> *As you made it clear that you had written in a similar vein to the Chairman of the Board, I believed you had placed the matter on at least a semi-official basis and that it should properly therefore be left in the hands of the chairman.*

Sir Donald appreciated that Greg had been under pressure, albeit some of it confessedly self-inflicted, but assured Greg he, Sir Donald, was in no way to blame for any arguments between Greg and the tour management. Sir Donald concluded:

> *Your own experience should make you realize that because of my prominence as an ex-player and administrator, the press some-times tend to attribute matters to me when in fact I am in no way responsible and I am grossly misrepresented.*
>
> *This is a cross which unfortunately I've had to bear longer than you have been on this earth. It should obtain your understanding and not be used as a stick to beat me with.*

Sir Donald was in his seventieth year when those letters were exchanged. Greg had no desire to take further issue with the legend of Australian, and world, cricket. It was extraordinary how the paths of Australia's greatest and second greatest batsmen crossed through-out Greg's career. They would once more before Greg put aside his bat, when Sir Donald would claim to be grossly misrepresented in the press concerning Greg, and, true to Sir Donald's plea, Greg declined to use the occasion as a stick with which to beat his revered predecessor.

But all this faded as cricket prepared for the greatest experiment in its long history. Because he did not have to organize, Greg watched and talked. To David Hill, the enigmatic guru of Channel Nine's sports department. His camera crews were more used to covering a chorus line than a slips cordon. Television crews and players stayed in the same hotels and Greg chatted with Hill in the evenings. 'A real hyped up character,' said Greg. 'The only people I'd run into like him were in the advertising game,' which the humorous Hill may take any way he wishes. Being involved in insurance marketing himself Greg could tune in to the television marketing ideas that competed with cricket conversation at night. The more he heard the more Greg knew that was one of the reasons he had joined WSC — to see the game leap pell-mell from the nineteenth to the twentieth century.

Some of Hill's ideas were stillborn. Microphones on the captains to hear their field placings, mikes on umpires to hear appeal decisions or no-ball explanations. Some were modified, like the mikes in the ground to hear the batsman's voice. 'It was pretty hard after you'd been whacked on the finger by Joel Garner to just say, "Oh gee whiz, that hurt",' said Greg. But he fought hardest to retain the Hill innovation of live interviews at the gate with dismissed batsmen. It was an intrusion into one of the great private moments in a sportsman's experience. 'But that was the beauty of it,' said Greg. 'If we were going to attract people, in competition with tradition, we had to try it.' The majority of players rejected it. Why did they have to put up with that crap? Consequently Greg always copped the questions. There were times when he wished he did not have to, but he consoled himself. 'As long as they stayed out of the dressing-room,' he said. 'That was my privacy. If I'd stood up there with a smile on my face and given a sensible answer, that was their business. If I walked 50 paces and broke the dressing-room up, that was mine.'

It hardly applied to Greg but Ian warned his cohorts that the Mates Act no longer applied with the media. Ian was not unaware that Packer had his competitors among newspaper proprietors. General writers might lurk to see who was chatting up the birds and who was falling around drunk. Greg had already experienced how the media was biased. His Brisbane agent, Judy, told Greg by phone during the ill-fated 1977 tour in England, that whatever ABC doyen Alan McGilvray was saying there, his radio reports were decidedly anti-Packer.

Greg saw little of curator whiz, John Maley, but he soon had a first hand knowledge of his product. In the first Supertest at VFL Park on 2 December 1977, Michael Holding quickly discovered the join half-way down the pitch in the pre-fabricated wicket. 'He hit it twice in three deliveries,' said Greg. 'The first flew past my nose, the second I just raised my hands in front of my face. It hit my gloves and went straight to Roy Fredericks in gully.' Out for a duck, an inauspicious start to the New Cricket. Maley's pitch at the Sydney Showground was simply the fastest Greg ever played on. The WACA at its worst did not compare. On the Showground Greg, for the first and probably only time in his career, beat a Test batsman, and not just any Test batsman, Viv Richards, off the pitch with sheer pace. 'If you ever needed any proof of how quick it was, that was it,' said Greg. He hit Richards square between the eyes hooking. 'He got the staggers,' said Greg. 'The old knees went, but he fought back. I told him, "Well, I've made my point. You won't have to worry about me bowling any more of those."' Greg was not anxious to provoke any more bouncers from the West Indians than he was already collecting.

The Showground suited the West Indies. In the second Supertest there they just ambled up and everything bounced eye high. In the second innings David Hookes decided to take on his oppressors, took 17 off one Garner over and 22 from Holding. Then Roberts smashed Hookes' jaw. Greg felt a flood of sympathy for him. He had not been able to nurse Hookes in England and here Hookes had been billed as a Supertest superstar. When Kerry Packer occasionally wandered through the Australian dressing-room Hookes would call out, 'Righto boys, here comes the big capitalist!' One day Packer turned to him and said, 'Hooksey, I've worked you out. What do you get off me, thirty grand a year? Yet every time I walk through here you have a shot at me. Now I see why you're a university drop-out.' But Dave McErlane, who had transferred his masseuring loyalties from ACB to WSC, knew Hookes was only joking. 'Hooksey was a boy on a man's errand,' he said. 'It was too much for anyone.'

When Hookes went down Packer brushed aside the calls for an ambulance. It would take too long. He raced Hookes to hospital in his Jaguar. Ironically Hookes' martyrdom was the greatest service he could render WSC. Any suggestions of sham disappeared. Greg was in no doubt of the standard. 'In Test and Shield cricket I'd operated at about 60 per cent efficiency. At WSC, from the start, I was working at 90 per cent. That's how tough it was in comparison.' Martin Kent, who later played Tests for Australia, was adamant. 'WSC was the hardest cricket anyone could play. There was a lot of good fellowship right throughout,' he said. 'But it didn't matter if you'd had a few beers with Michael Holding the night before. He was still trying to knock your block off the next day.' Good fellowship except of course between Ian Chappell and Tony Greig. If he lost Ian was always first into the opposition dressing room for a shake hands and 'Well done'. To Greig Ian would say, 'Just as well your team played well.'

Having lost the first two Supertests the Chappell brothers commandeered the third in Adelaide for an Australian win, before the smallest crowd to date. Packer was said to have stood in the carpark forlornly counting the few cars arriving. 'It made no difference,' said Greg. 'At that stage the crowd was secondary. It would have been nice to see 20,000, but we were still proving ourselves. All we could do was play our bums off and wait.' For the time being the players generated their own excitement, 50 players with one aim, to play their very best. That was a singular pursuit which was its own pleasure. The fact that the ACB put obstacles in their way made them all the more determined. If after two or three years the crowds stayed away then ... 'the blokes would know that no matter how well they played, no one wanted to watch. Then the teams would have dropped off,' said Greg. That was the war of attrition in which the ACB and WSC were engaged. The players saw little of their supreme commander, but what they saw, they liked. The younger players reverently referred to him as 'The Boss' and were delighted when Packer turned up at the nets occasionally to throw a few balls or pick up a bat. 'I think he loved it,' said Greg. 'As much as he was after the television rights, he loved being around top sportsmen.'

The fourth and fifth Supertests against a World XI, comprising the best of the West Indians and the Rest of the World, were masterpieces of mismatching. In the fifth, in Perth, the World XI's first three batsmen, Gordon Greenidge, Barry Richards and Viv Richards topped 500 runs alone. It would have required a team from Mars to resist them. To cap it all Andy Roberts broke Ian's little finger. It slowly dawned on the WSC organizers that they were decimating their drawcards. 'It was a bit unfair,' said Greg. 'We didn't mind losing a few games. But the Rest of the World didn't have a bad attack without adding the best of the West Indies. We were becoming shellshocked from the barrage of fast bowling.' At that stage the Australians had won only one of the five Supertests and lost Hookes and Ian Chappell injured. Jeff Thomson was with the ACB and a depressed Lillee was slow in finding form. Amid this crisis Greg, as he had consistently throughout his career, rose to the challenge. Taking over the captaincy from injured Ian for the last match in Melbourne, he scored a superb 246 not out to notch Australia's second Supertest victory, and the first over the World XI.

In that marathon first innings Joel Garner jagged the ball back so fast and so often he eventually shattered the shin cane inside Greg's left pad. The jarring and jamming left Greg with fingertip indentations in his left shin for years afterwards. In the second innings Garner's first ball nipped back and struck Greg on that battered shin. Greg hopped about in pain and shouted up the pitch, 'You big bastard, if you hit me on the shin again I'm going to come down and hit you with my bat.' Garner smiled and had Greg caught down the leg side soon after for just six runs. 'I reckon I was just making sure I didn't get my shin in the way again,' said Greg. Bruce Laird eventually had two cysts cut from his thigh from the battering he received as an opener in World Series Cricket.

Greg rated Garner as accurate as Underwood. High praise. But Joel's degree of difficulty was increased by his height. 'Your brain picks up the length of a ball by the angle it leaves the bowler's hand,' said Greg. 'Everything from Joel looked like it was going to be short yet he kept hitting me on the foot.' Greg could detect the short-pitched ball from some bowlers from their actions. Tony Greig tended to give an extra whirl of his arms. 'I could read Tony before he left home,' said Greg. Andy Roberts gathered himself noticeably for his short ball. Colin Croft and Bernard Julien too. Dennis Lillee gathered himself and ... bowled something else! Greg could pick a change of pace from Derek Underwood and Lance Gibbs' quicker ball. Later, Pakistani spinner Abdul Qadir almost smiled before he bowled his wrong 'un. 'There were days — some — when I could almost read Richard Hadlee's mind,' said Greg. 'And I could read Michael Holding's short one, but not reliably,' a case of a little knowledge being a dangerous thing. Bowlers who hid the ball, like Jeff Thomson, or bowled off the wrong foot, like Max Walker and Mike Procter, Greg could not read. But from Joel Garner Greg got nothing except deceit, a sore shin and very occasionally a slow smile across that large, impassive face.

As Ian Chappell's WSC Australians fought and lost their tough Supertests on strange grounds against a background of barren stands, Bob Simpson's ACB Australians were blessed with a dream 3–2 Test series victory over the touring Indians, with the result in doubt until the final day. Greg saw some of it on television but never ran into any of the ACB team members. J. N. Rutnagur in *Wisden* offered the opinion that the Indian spinners would have had just as good a tour had they to contend with all the batsmen removed from circulation by Packer. Greg blanched at such temerity. 'The fact that Simpson had reasonable success against them at his advanced age suggests to me that Ian and Doug might have succeeded too,' he said. Not to mention himself. Greg finished with a Supertest average of 60, fourth behind Viv Richards 86, Barry Richards 77 and Hookes, who played only three matches, 63. They were the cream of the world's batsmen and they were WSC.

The first day–night match of limited–over cricket at VFL Park on 14 December 1977, shone brightly for the WSC camp. Ian Chappell sensed the change. 'There were about 7,000 there and they left thinking, "There's something in this night cricket." ' More than they could possibly have imagined.

But night cricket also had its problems. Greg, for one, thought the white ball harder to see than the red. Max Walker at nets one evening bowled an old red ball at Greg. 'Where'd you get that from?' Greg asked, astonished. 'I haven't seen a ball that well for ages.' Maybe it was the cricket mind trained to pick out red rather than white, but more evidence accrued. Whenever Greg was beaten by a good ball his habit was to reach out and, within a radius of a few centimetres, tap the spot where the ball pitched. With the white ball he would blink and wonder, 'Where did that land?' He noticed that under lights the ball cast as many shadows as there were light stanchions, yet the ball, for having less shaded area itself, appeared smaller. Greg also argued the white balls behaved differently to the red balls. It took years before ACB executive, David Richards, discovered Greg was right. Inferior leather had been used, compensated for with extra coats of lacquer. Not much escaped the kestrel eye of G. S. Chappell. He once said, 'As the koala is attuned to the eucalypt, so I am attuned to the cricket field.' That was his natural habitat. They might just as well have tried to rope in a piece of cactus on this cricket koala as give him an inferior cricket ball.

As an afterthought in that first season there was an interesting one-day match at VFL Park on 24 January 1978 before a crowd of 24,000, the largest then for a WSC match. The West Indies needed 20 runs as Greg began bowling the second last over. 'There were a couple of mis-fields at deep mid-off, I won't accuse anyone,' said Greg. 'And there were a couple of fours hit off my over, but there was nothing I could do about it.' Down to the last over and with two balls to go Western Australian medium pacer Mick Malone was bowling to Wayne Daniels. The West Indies needed six runs to win. Daniels, though the number eleven batsman, was quite capable of a wild village yahoo. Ian, fielding at cover, walked up to Malone. 'Any thoughts?' said Malone. Ian replied, 'Well, bounce the first one over the top of his head and if we get away with that, I'll think of something for the next one.' In those early limited over days bouncers were not as strictly ruled wides, likewise balls shunted wide down the leg-side. But Malone was not confident. 'There's not enough bounce in it. I can't get it over his head,' he said. For want of anything better, Ian opted for the leg-side.

Malone did the right thing. But Daniels started to charge and Malone banged the ball in faster, shorter. 'He just dragged it down a bit and it finished right in the slot for Daniels,' said Greg. 'He picked it up and boom, hit it 20 yards over the boundary ropes.' The Australians were devastated. They had played well, deserved to win and had it snatched from them. 'We just sat in the dressing-room afterwards stunned,' said Greg. 'Just couldn't believe it. How did it happen?' Ian and Greg discussed it over a drink later. Then at practice Greg experimented.

The key to it was ensuring the ball had no bounce so the batsman could not get under it to lift it. Greg tried bowling from a 30 yard mark and landing the ball halfway down the pitch or less to reduce the angle and height of the delivery. But that was hard to do. 'Hard to control,' said Greg. 'Once it hit the ground it could go anywhere. Could run off to be a wide.' They both came up with the yorker on the stumps. If the bowler erred it became a full toss. 'But a full toss, when the ball's coming down, is very hard to hit for six,' said Ian. So that was the theory. But Greg had one other idea which he idly threw up. Ian demonstrated to me. 'He thought of just rolling his arm over and letting the ball go dadum, dadum, dadum along the ground.' In the highly unlikely event of ever having to foil a last ditch six again.

17. Victory

The executive room in the members' stand at the Sydney Cricket Ground was normally occupied by five-star generals of the Australian Cricket Board. On 28 November 1978, two colonial floors high and behind a guarded grey door, the heresiarch Kerry Packer had cuckolded the generals in their own eyrie. WSC executives and their ladies and top echelon Channel Nine and Consolidated Press employees lolled with charged glasses to admire their handiwork — 50,000 fans taking up their orgiastic cry of 'Lill-llee' against the West Indians. In a small room abutting the executive view an assortment of media and entertainment personalities gyred and gimbled about a bar and a National television projection screen showing the match taking place at their backs.

Greg popped in briefly, just another famous name among the famous. Paul Hogan, John Cornell, Harry Miller, Bruce Gyngell, Delvene Delaney, Tony Greig, Gary Sobers and the Marilyn Monroe look-alike model, Linda Kerridge. Dennis Lillee, the man with the machismo moustache and counter-tenor voice-box, uttered in wonder, 'I never made it up here when I was with the cricket board.' An air of unreality infused the two rooms, fuelled by the head lightening euphoria of the crowd that grew and grew. On the walls sepia people in frames looked on amazed — Don Bradman scoring his hundredth hundred.

Greg and the players strolled out at tea to stare at their popularity and listen to that maddening piece of doggerel, 'C'mon Aussie, c'mon, c'mon.' Returning to the field Rod Marsh skipped past Ian Chappell, snapped up the ball and cried jubilantly, 'We're f—g back.' It was WSC's first match on an official cricket ground. After Australia won Greg invited me into the dressing-room where Packer, Clive Lloyd and Rod Marsh were exchanging pleasantries.

'Got you at last, you old bastard,' said Kerry to Clive. 'It's been a long wait.'

Lloyd, full of bespectacled, dark dignity, replied, 'We thought we'd do the right thing by World Series Cricket.'

Marsh gave that lie the blasphemous poesy of which only wicket-keepers are masters.

'Pleased?' asked Lloyd.

'Of course, what do you think I am, a sadist?' said Packer.

'I expected 60,000,' said Rod, disappointed. They all laughed.

'I'll see you in Barbados,' said Kerry to Clive.

'Thommo should be playing by then, that'll be a fabulous series,' said Marsh.

'Will he?' frowned Lloyd. 'I may not be available.'

When it was all over, the oval bathed in a soft, apple green light, Packer stood, arms akimbo, presiding fondly over the sea of humanity seeping reluctantly from that enthralling scene. He reminded me of the Great Gatsby gazing over Long Island Sound towards the shimmering lights, and at Daisy, gazing at the mistress cricket he had courted, and won. The incongruity was that Packer at that moment, so removed from the hoi polloi below, should have tapped the Australian egalitarian myth and achieved the proletarianization of cricket. He had enticed sports fans out of the pubs, away from drive-in cinemas, away from their television. It was a stunning salient into the establishment's lines and the ACB was in retreat thereafter.

That match was played three weeks into the WSC's second season. I was astonished when I walked into the Press box mid-way through the match to find only two cricket writers present, an agency reporter and Phil Wilkins from the *Australian*. A week later at the ACB's first Test against Mike Brearley's tourists in Brisbane, I counted 39 English and Australian journalists. 'I think Phil Wilkins was a bit dirty he had to cover us and not the Test,' said Greg. 'But in his defence he was always very fair, very evenhanded. He was a professional who acted like one.'

With a WSC season to play Greg began experimenting with helmets. The WSC injury toll: 13 batsmen struck in the head. He did not like the full face mask. 'It was eerie. The wind seemed to whistle through the openings,' he said. The grill guards did not appeal. He settled for the Lawrence Rowe temple guard, named after Rowe who especially requested it. In the West Indies later that season, Greg was at slip when Thomson smashed a ball into Rowe's temple. 'It looked and sounded terrible,' said Greg. 'I thought even with the helmet he was dead.' In fact it broke the temple guard and fractured Rowe's cheek. And saved his life. Mike Brearley watched amused as more and more Australians slowly adopted helmets. When he had first worn one in the Jubilee Test at Lord's in 1977 a few Aussies had condemned him. 'Weak bastard,' they whispered. But Greg knew better. Helmets saved the careers of batsmen like Rick McCosker and David Hookes after their severe injuries.

Before the season began Greg flew to Sydney for a golf and business trip with Barry Maranta. They dined one night at a Paddington restaurant and mid-way through overheard a diner at an adjacent table talking cricket. The diner in question later introduced himself to Greg, 'Andrew Caro from WSC'. Greg was polite, but had never heard of Caro. After Caro departed Greg said, 'I think I've upset that bloke. I hope he's not signing the cheques.' The next day Caro's appointment as managing director of WSC was announced in the news.

Caro fought a running battle to keep Kerry Packer's sense of occasion from interfering with the cricket. It was an unequal battle culminating in the fourth one-day final between Australia and the

West Indies at VFL Park on 30 January 1979. Australia was behind time bowling its 50 overs, but Packer did not like matches to be won on run rates. He pressed Caro to ensure there was a full finish. Caro sent out a message via the Australian twelfth man that the ground lights would remain on until Australia had bowled their 50 overs. The message reached Ian Chappell but not the umpires or the West Indies. At 10.30 p.m., the original match finishing time, the West Indies were 12 runs behind, with two wickets and nine overs still to be bowled. Ian believed he had a chance of bowling out the two tailenders inside 12 runs. But the West Indies were fractionally ahead on run rate and the umpires declared them the winners, of the match and the finals 3–1. 'Ian went off his brain,' said Greg. 'He demanded Packer cancel the result or award the points to us.' Packer's compromise was that the Australians would receive the same prize money as if they had won. 'Stick your money,' said Ian. 'It's the principle of the thing.'

It was a measure of Packer's growing confidence in WSC's eventual defeat of the ACB that he told the team, 'The offer remains until tomorrow. If you tell me then you don't want the money, that's fine, but the result stands and we promise it won't happen again.' Greg was appalled. It was the first sign that Packer, like the ACB, had warts. 'It was damaging to our reputations as much as WSC,' said Greg. The incident triggered Andrew Caro's resignation a week later. 'Kerry bawled me out, bullied really,' said Caro. 'He used to say, "Fix it," and expected me to devise the means to his ends.'

Nevertheless Packer remained on good terms with the teams and threw an end of the season thank-you party for the lot at his home in Bellevue Hill, Sydney. They had a steel band and black entertainer, Delilah, did a floor show. Clive Lloyd, whose nickname is Groover, got up and danced with her. 'He did a fairly good job too,' said Greg. 'He's a big bloke, had back injuries, knee not too good, but he could still dance pretty well.'

Australia lost the Supertest grand final to the World XI and the one-day series grand final to the West Indies. Though the siege mentality bred a special camaraderie the competition was fierce. In Greg's mind WSC was the making of the West Indies. 'They had always been good front runners,' he said. 'Their only weakness had been that they were a bit impetuous, they couldn't pull out of a dive. But living together for two years made them believe in themselves. WSC matured them.'

If the West Indies flourished, Greg's form faltered. Though he finished third in the Australian Supertest batting averages, it was only 26.8, half the average he had been regularly posting for years. From third in the overall WSC international averages in 1977–78, he fell to thirteenth in 1978–79. The incessant hail of bouncers had forced Greg, a natural front foot player, to hesitate and make his first move backwards. 'I decided if they weren't going to pitch the ball up, getting on to the back foot was more sensible,' said Greg. 'I thought I could increase my scoring opportunities.' Instead he became uncertain. Richie Benaud showed him television tapes which pin-pointed his poor footwork. 'I was shuffling around getting nowhere, lbw twice in the Supertests to Colin Croft,' he said. He decided to return to the technique which had served him well for nearly a decade of Tests. But his decision to revert was interrupted by another more serious development.

He was lunching with Judy in Kings Cross, Sydney, one day when he began blinking and trying to focus on his image in a reflecting window. His throat had been sore for several days. One side of his tongue felt strange. He asked Judy, 'Is there something wrong with my right eye?' No, but his left eye was not closing, she said. He ducked into a doctor's surgery, was oblivious to the pins the doctor stuck in one side of his face and tongue and went to hospital for tests. Without raising Greg's suspicions the staff did a brain scan for blood clots before diagnosing the numbness as Bell's Palsy, a viral infection of a nerve canal which paralysed one side of his face. Kerry Packer collected Greg from the hospital. 'I've had it myself,' he said. 'I've got my own neurosurgeon. I'll pick you up tomorrow to see him.'

It was a mild case, but sufficient to put him out of the Supertest grand final. He could not close his eye and there was a danger of foreign particles damaging it, the specialist told him. It should clear up in two weeks, the day the WSC Australians left for the Caribbean. Greg told the doctor, 'I want to go.' The doctor said, 'I would advise you not to go.' Judy said, 'Don't go.' Greg was desperate to prove he was still good enough to make runs against the West Indies' attack. The doctor told him, 'If there's no sign of improvement I'll just tell Kerry you're not to go and that's that.' The departure day Greg felt pins and needles in his face, the first signs of recovery. But he still could not blink. Greg mounted a full scale attack on the specialist. The team would be travelling for two days with two days rest upon arrival, he would not play for a week, he would buy welder's goggles (he bought safety glasses) to practise in.

What was it that pushed Greg to take even a minor risk with his eyesight? In WSC's second season Greg's form suffered a decline. From 1975, when he had led Australia to master the West Indies, here he was, a relatively failing batsman about to forego the opportunity to redeem himself. It would be six months to the next Australian season, six months before he could test his front foot theory. And there was this: as successful as he had become as a businessman, he judged himself, and believed others judged him, as a cricketer. That was the foundation of his confidence, his self image. If he missed the Caribbean he would not be a full-time businessman, he would be an out of form, out of work, cricketer. He decided. 'Bugger it. I want to make a lot of runs, I'm going.' The specialist relented. After a week in the West Indies Greg could close the eye, and after that the discomfort disappeared.

But the disease had not helped his form. In the first Supertest he scored 6 and 20 as the West Indies crushed Australia. Ian must have felt a sense of *déjà vu*. 'Righto,' he told the team. 'You just lay down and let them walk all over us. There's an air-ticket here for anyone who is not prepared to give 100 per cent from here on.' Clive Lloyd scored 197 in that match but Andy Roberts turned the knife with 89. Greg placed Roberts high in his respect for West Indian players. 'If they were diving, he got up their shirts,' said Greg. 'He hated losing. He could bat and won a couple of games with really pugnacious innings. I think behind the scenes he would be standing a few up in the corner and asking them to have a look in the mirror.'

A riotous tension accompanied the Australians on their tour. In Kingston during the first Supertest, Martin Kent was fielding at long-on in front of chicken wire enclosed stands. 'Hey, Kent, you been to South Africa?' a deep voice boomed. Kent took four paces in from the fence, turned and nodded. He was with Greg's 1976 Wanderers. 'You going again?' Kent turned again and said, 'No, no, not me,' and the crowd cheered.

The next Supertest, in Bridgetown, Barbados, was abandoned after lunch on the last day because of bottle-throwing provoked by West Indies batsmen disputing umpiring decisions. 'We had the feeling that any time we got into a position to win there would be a riot,' said Greg. Greg struggled for 45 runs in the first innings there, and then, like a thoroughbred released from the barrier, struck his stride. 'I've never batted better than I did in the next three weeks,' he said. It began with 90 in the second innings at Barbados, 7 and 150 at Port of Spain, 113 at Georgetown and 104 and 85 at St Johns, Antigua. He made them against The Force in world pace bowling, Roberts, Holding, Croft and Garner and finished with an average of 68. It gave him a final Supertest average for the combined Australian and West Indies season of a run or so under 48, once more restoring the axiom that whenever he walked to the crease in Test cricket he was worth 50 runs.

The third Supertest at Port of Spain was also disrupted by bottle-throwing. Trevor Chappell, who had joined his brothers on the international scene, was fielding at fine leg when the first shower fell. He disregarded Ian's call to come to the wicket, turned and shouted to the crowd, 'Righto, if you throw them at me they're coming back at you.' Despite Greg's 150, it was not his century which won Australia the match. It was Bruce 'Stumpy' Laird's 122 in the first innings. 'On a wet pitch he was hit all morning, bruised from the soles of his feet to the roof of his mouth,' said Greg. 'He stood there and copped it. We were 3–18 at drinks and 5–32 at lunch. For anyone to survive that first session was unbelievable.' When Laird was finally out Greg went over, shook his hand and said, 'That's one of the best innings I've ever seen.' After the match Viv Richards followed suit. 'I would be proud to have played an innings like that,' he told the diminutive opener. Unfortunately it would never be recognized because as Greg said, a Supertest was not a 'real' game of cricket. Yet Laird inspired Australia to one of the best comebacks in modern Australian cricket history. From that disastrous start Laird's and Greg's centuries set up a target which Lloyd's men failed to reach by 24 runs. 'It was a better win than when Max Walker took that wicket after lunch at the same oval in 1973,' said Greg. Yet he too omits the match when he recalls his great moments, conditioned not to compare it with 'real' cricket.

The crowd at the fourth Supertest decided to wreck the ground at Georgetown, Guyana at 3.10 p.m. on 25 March, before a ball had been bowled. That is when the first bottle sailed through the stand clock and stopped it. The crowd was furious because play had not started. The day was glorious but the night before rain had saturated the field. Greg said, 'We told the WSC organizer, Bruce McDonald, to get to the ground early to keep the gates shut or else we'd be in trouble. Bruce went down at 7 a.m. and the gates had been open since 5 a.m.' By the time the players arrived at 10 a.m. the ground was full. The crowd drank and waited, amused by a spectator who brilliantly mimed an entire match by himself, bowling, batting, appealing and umpiring with exaggeration and insight. Greg, as an erstwhile one-man cricket team himself in his childhood, appreciated the display. Then a spectator grabbed a ground microphone and yelled, 'There's nothing wrong with the pitch, I've just inspected it, play should start immediately.' Restlessness became anger. 'The wicket was OK, but the outfield was hopeless,' said Greg. 'The fielders could not have stood up. The bowlers could not have run up. It was never going to be right that day and the crowd should not have been let in.'

The crowd was no longer interested in cricket. With a roar they broke through the wire fences, stormed the pavilion and smashed the bar and administrative office separating the West Indian and Australian dressing-rooms. The Australians barricaded themselves, grabbed helmets, wrapped towels around their arms and wielded their bats. 'Not one of them came in our room,' said Greg. 'The only time I jumped was when I heard a gun go off. It was tear gas fired by the riot squad.' Trevor Chappell recalled an armed guard, meant to protect the tourists, closing french doors onto a players' balcony only to have them smashed instantly by rocks. Martin Kent has an image of the same guard sitting white-knuckled with fear by the door. 'Well, he's not going to save us,' thought Kent. Armed guards eventually led the Australians across the ground to their bus and they were escorted front and rear by two mini-buses bristling with guards carrying automatic weapons. 'We weren't in any danger at all,' said Greg. 'But the driver of the mini-bus behind us started to overtake and the blokes all yelled at him to stay behind.'

That evening the majority of the team wanted to go home. Greg argued the Australians were not the target. 'If we go back and play cricket they won't riot.' Some players wanted armed guards in the dressing-rooms. 'In that case count me out,' said Greg. 'Because if some silly bugger starts shooting some other silly bugger will shoot back and then we will be in trouble.' In the end Ian, just as he used to cop the bad result in the backyard with Greg as kids, and took the heat off Terry Jenner in the field in Shield cricket, managed to become the focus of a West Indian administration looking for a scapegoat. 'It was a harrowing couple of days,' said Greg.

Yet he enjoyed that visit to the West Indies almost as much as the 1973 visit. They drew the Supertest series one-all and Greg rediscovered his best form. But a certain sadness had pervaded the tour after Guyana, at the end of March 1979. The previous month the ACB had quietly backed down and accepted the concept of a commercial station televising Tests instead of the ABC. The ABC's contract expired on

31 March. The television rights were to be re-sold and there was never a doubt that Packer's Nine would succeed. On tour there were meetings, phone calls and telexes. 'The young blokes were happy,' said Greg. 'They had tasted WSC and now they wanted to try Test cricket.' The older players were apprehensive. Packer kept asking: what did they require out of the peace? The Australians were too far away. They felt they were the meat in the sandwich. They could not ram home the gains made under WSC. Greg could see the benefits of the compromise. Despite what he and the rebels were accused of, he had no wish for the ACB to be so brought to its knees that the game was damaged irreparably. 'Packer could have owned cricket lock, stock and barrel,' said Greg. 'But he could see the infrastructure was too big. He didn't want it.' Instead he paid out the player's contracts on a discounted basis.

Beyond that the Australians felt a sense of loss. 'We'd been a great big family for a couple of years,' said Greg. 'Now we were splitting the group. There had been a tremendous spirit in all the teams, between the players. I'm not sure international cricketers will ever feel as united again.' It was hard to determine the champion nation. It may even have been South Africa with Barry Richards, Clive Rice, Kepler Wessels (who played for Australia) and Mike Procter in the top eight Supertest batting averages of the Australian season, and Garth Le Roux first and Mike Procter third in the bowling. 'They would have given us a run for our money,' said Greg. 'We'd have beaten them in Australia and vice versa.' Greg felt a special sympathy for Barry Richards. WSC was Richards' last chance to play international class cricket. 'He only played four Tests before South Africa was banned,' said Greg. 'He never said much, but deep down I knew it hurt him.'

The war was over and reconstruction would begin. Greg's two years of grace had ended. Mid-way through the season he had been made a Member of the Order of the British Empire, an MBE, for his contribution to the sport of cricket. The award stated:

> *His outstanding cricketing ability and his gentlemanly approach to the sport are recognized throughout cricketing nations of the world.*

Greg was about to be restored once more as the figurehead of Australian cricket. What he or Packer or the ACB didn't fully comprehend was the nature of the chimera the war had forged and with which Greg was about to do battle.

RECONSTRUCTION (1979–1980)

18. Peace

In the spring of 1979 I asked Greg to name a compromise ACB–WSC Australian team. Sure, he said, and leaned back in his office armchair. Laird, Wood, Darling and Hilditch for openers. Kent or Border first wicket down. Ian should bat at six to stop the chronic collapse of Australian tails. He named 17 players in all. But when I saw Ian that same week in Sydney he still preferred batting three, thanks brother. Kim Hughes or Rick Darling could bat six. And the captaincy? 'If they give me the job I'll do my best,' said Ian. 'But I'm not going to buy a box of tissues if they don't.'

A WSC lobby had been pushing for Ian as captain. They persuaded him to play one more season to protect the young WSC players against ACB discrimination. Ian suspected his patience had run out and this was confirmed after an unnecessary clash with an umpire in the first Shield match of the season in Devonport, Tasmania. He rang his supporters from the dressing-room, 'I'm not in the right frame of mind. It would be the worst thing for me and for Australia.' Especially when he was subsequently suspended.

If the captaincy was clear-cut, and the team selection slightly confused, the playing schedule was utter chaos. Up to the end of 1977, when Australia lost the Ashes in England, Greg was able to apply almost total recall to any series, Test, innings and even strokes. In those ordered days only one country toured Australia per season and perhaps, but not always, Australia toured overseas in the off-season. Greg could sing the psalms — '72 drew in the UK, '72–73 won in the West Indies and so on. World Series Cricket interfered with the clarity of his recall. But the year which shorted out his mental computer was 1979–80, the Year of the Peace. The ACB, prompted by Channel Nine and PBL Marketing, which had swallowed World Series Cricket, produced an itinerary of madness.

England and the West Indies toured, playing three Tests each against Australia, which was unfair from the start, because it meant Australia played six. Nor were the Tests played in succession. They alternated, first Test Windies, first Test England. To add to the confusion a dozen or so one-day internationals were squeezed in between the Tests. In the first Australia–West Indies Test in Brisbane, Greg declared 45 minutes before stumps on the last day to give Lillee, Thomson and Rodney Hogg a psychological shot at the West Indies openers. They took 3–40, but by the time they played the second Test the West Indies had played umpteen other matches. 'Any psychological advantage we gained was lost,' said Greg. 'The itinerary was impossible. Gave us no hope.'

Greg, supported by the ACB, had knocked over PBL's move to play the one-day matches before the Tests, thus saving the Tests from relegation to second-class cricket. The more Greg, as putative compromise captain, heard, the more he realized Packer had won the commercial war and the players had lost the peace. 'I think we were forgotten in the race,' said Greg. One concession obtained was for the Test selection committee to be increased from three to five, one of whom was the captain. But this became a two-edged blade. Greg found it hard to dissociate his emotions from objective selection decisions. Just one more stress for the captain.

Greg began the peace tentatively. At the first captain's committee meeting with the ACB he met the chairman, Bob Parish, for the first time since Parish had ignored him in the foyer of the Waldorf two years earlier. The meeting proceeded as though nothing had ever happened. Greg shook his head in disbelief at the memory. But he was not surprised. 'That's how they got into trouble in the first place,' he said. 'Just pretended things that were happening, weren't happening.' But attitudes had mellowed somewhat. Greg wrote a newspaper article headlined, '8 Certs in Test Team,' on 6 November 1979. A week later he received a letter from Parish that Greg had broken the player-writer rule. Parish's letter was mildly admonishing but conciliatory. For an offence of similar gravity in England in 1977 the ACB had threatened to fine Greg $500.

Greg coped with the stressful season to come by defining his goals. Tests were more important than limited over cricket. As much as he respected the West Indies, England was the true enemy, led by Mike

Brearley who had lifted the Ashes in 1977. In Brearley Greg was pitted against a captain as different from himself as English wickets from Australian. Greg, tall, lean and hard, with an axeman's gaze; Brearley shorter and softer with the eyes of a Richmond Park fawn. Brearley read and relaxed with the classics, Tolstoy's *Anna Karenina*, and Beethoven's 'Rasumovsky' string quartets. Greg's culture was popular, airport novels and Pink Floyd rock arias. John Arlott once remarked to Brearley, 'Mike, you're the only England captain who knows it doesn't really matter'. The same could never be said of Greg.

Greg liked Brearley, 'a quiet, delightful bloke'. He recognized that Brearley was a wonderful leader of men, saw how he harnessed Botham, nurtured Boycott, and read the game exactly. 'So he should,' Ian Chappell once said unforgivingly. 'He spends most of his time in the dressing-room with nothing else to do but watch it,' being Ian's comment on Brearley's batting. It was said of Brearley he had a degree in people, the very instinct Greg admired in Ian. But for Brearley's batting Greg would pick him to captain a best-ever England team in the 15 years Greg played them.

The first Test in Perth against England was marred by the aluminium bat incident, the start of four consecutive seasons where controversy was to add to the stress of captaincy. Two of them involved Greg's friend, Dennis. In his years standing beside Ian, and then as captain, Greg had developed a fine understanding with, and of, Lillee. 'From a shy, gullible bloke when I first met him, he developed an unbelievably supreme ego,' said Greg. 'It's not a criticism. Most of us were the same.' Lillee had become a shining emblem for fast bowlers of the world, fighting off injury, substituting every inch of speed he lost with a breadth of guile. More importantly, the fire still consumed him. New Zealand's Richard Hadlee once said, 'When things are going badly I often think, "What would Lillee do?" And the answer is: "He would not give up." '

Greg learned to treat Lillee with kid gloves, with just an occasional charge or damper depending on the fast bowler's mood. 'He was such a strong-willed bugger and such a good bowler you had to accept that occasionally he was going to be pig-headed,' said Greg. 'The adrenalin would pump so fast he'd go over the top.' Such as when Lillee set extraordinary fields. Rather than argue, Greg would set the field and as Dennis' anger died, gradually return the field to normal. 'Usually he was angry with himself or the batsman,' said Greg. 'When he was that intense he became irrational. The trick was to have him channel that anger towards the batsman. If I got it wrong he would divert the anger to me.'

That happened in the first Test against the West Indies in Brisbane in December that year. Lillee was bowling badly, no-balling, and in the middle of an over shortened his run to three paces, turned and bowled an off-spinner. Greg was surprised. Back three paces, turn, but this time Greg called from slips, 'Hey, hey hang on. Are you bowling fast or spin?' Lillee glared back. He was bowling spin. 'Right,' said Greg. He would set a field for it, one slip and so on. Marsh stood up to the stumps. Lillee off three paces then bowled a lightning bouncer. The batsman Alvin Kallicharan, ducked, Marsh gloved it in astonishment and Greg took action. He ran up. 'Either bowl quick or spin, make up your bloody mind.' Lillee returned to his long run. At tea Greg caught Lillee alone.

'What's going on?'

'You can't tell me what to bowl.'

'I've never tried to tell you what to bowl.'

'You did out there.'

No, Greg said. He had set a field for what Dennis said he would bowl. 'You could have killed Marshy. If you'd broken his hand what's that doing for the team?' Therefore would Dennis mind behaving in a reasonable fashion and not carry on like a bloody schoolboy!

In 1976 against Pakistan in Melbourne, umpire Tom Brooks began wagging his finger at Lillee for bowling bouncers. Lillee returned like for like. Greg intervened. They could not afford to upset the umpire. 'He can't treat me like that,' said Lillee. Fair enough, said Greg. 'But we might get decisions going against us. In the long run we'll be losers.' Just then a balloon blew across the ground. Lillee caught it, ran in and bowled it, the perfect riposte.

The other side of the coin is that Lillee was often not his own worst enemy. Sometimes, it was the captain. Greg stands indicted of deliberately provoking Lillee to get him steamed up and snorting at the opposition. The day before the first Test against England in Perth in December 1979, Lillee practised in the nets with an experimental aluminium bat in which he had a vested interest. Greg picked it up for a trial. 'It was a real tinny thing, hollow, just didn't go,' said Greg. 'It went BOINGG, BOINGG, jarred and you couldn't hit the ball off the square with it.' Greg had a mild shot at Lillee. He wasn't going to use that, was he? Lillee whipped around, 'What do you mean?' Greg's evil mind chimed: here was a way to get the boy stirred up.

In retrospect Greg believed that had he told Lillee that in the interests of the team he should use a normal bat, Lillee may, or may not, have used his favourite Duncan Fearnley. Greg did not know that bat was cracked. Greg did know that Dennis, batting at nine, would be bowling soon. He intended to let Lillee bat for an over, take the bat off him and fire Lillee to fury when bowling. Events went awry. Rodney Hogg took the cracked bat out to Lillee who rejected it. Lillee came in for a new one and Greg sat like a sphinx knowing that one blink would set Lillee off. Rodney Marsh saved him the trouble. 'It's not like you to let people tell you what bat you can use,' he said deadpan. Lillee stopped. Marsh was bloody right. Out he went with the metal bat again. 'Thanks for your help, Bacchus,' said Greg, exasperated. He looked around for Hogg to take another bat out, but Hogg would not have a bar of it. He told Greg later, 'I could see myself, on national television, before a packed ground, and Dennis hitting me between the eyes with his aluminium bat.' Greg then had the tiger firmly by the tail himself. Fortunately Brearley had involved himself at the crease. When Greg arrived with a new bat Lillee heave-hoed the aluminium and to Greg's relief the Poms became the cause of it all. The furore that followed, the interviews and explanations, all fielded by Greg as captain, was a high price to pay to steam up a nice fast bowler like Dennis. Despite one more incident in seasons to come, Greg had little but praise for Lillee. 'We're very similar in a way,' he said. 'We're both keen to have the last say. Usually he was as good as gold,' a metal more precious than aluminium.

The second Test, in Sydney, demonstrated Brearley's opportunism. Greg told him he thought the wicket was too wet to play. Brearley disagreed. It was up to the umpires and they decided to play. In August 1984, four years later, Greg met Brearley at a charity match in Newcastle, north England. There was something Greg wanted to ask him. 'Yes,' said Brearley. 'It was a fair gamble. We were one down in a three match series. If I'd won the toss Derek Underwood would have bowled you out. Win the toss, win the game.' Greg won the toss, and the game.

In the last Test, in Melbourne, Australia were left 103 runs in the second innings to win. Greg came in at 2–42 and told Ian, 'I've got a plane to catch, let's get this over and done with.' Greg struck 40 in 54 minutes and was on the 5.30 plane home to Brisbane. He had been away for three months. He did not worry about after-match press conferences or sipping bubbly drinks. 'I'd had a gutful of it and I was going home,' he said. He had fulfilled his priorities. He led Australia to a 3–0 series win over England, but was not rewarded with the Ashes because England had argued that three Tests did not a series constitute. Greg's view was that his 3–0 victory over Brearley in 1979 was no more a true reflection of the strengths of the two teams than his 3–0 loss in 1977. It was a more magnanimous, and probably more accurate, assessment than that presented by Brearley after Greg's Packer-plagued loss in 1977. Greg also attacked the West Indies so determinedly in the limited over series Australia beat them 3–1. But losing to England 4–0 Australia failed to make the limited over final.

Remarkably the man who denied Australia the one-day wins was Geoff Boycott. 'He was almost at the peak of his form on that tour,' said Greg. 'He played some magnificent innings in the one-day games. He showed just how much talent he did have. If he could have relaxed enough to play some of those shots in Test cricket he'd have been one of the greats. As it is his record suggests he's one of the top players but no one will ever admit that because he bored them. But in those one-day games, even as opposing captain, I really enjoyed some of his batting. Real virtuoso stuff.' The West Indies also defeated Australia 2–0 in their Tests of which West Indies commentator, Tony Cozier later wrote in *Wisden*: 'Few individuals have so dominated a season as (Viv) Richards did this one.' Richards averaged 96.5 runs against Australia in three Tests but the innings which took Greg's eye was Richards' 76 in the first innings of the third Test in Adelaide. Said Greg, 'We sent them in on a pretty green pitch and he decided that attack was the best method of defence. Under conditions which favoured the bowlers he mauled us and swung the game around.' Though Clive Lloyd's 121 on paper seems the highlight, Greg said, 'Viv made it possible. He was magnificent.' Greg's impression of Richards was of a delightfully arrogant man, no backward step, no casual laugh with the opposition bowlers, just a steely glare. 'Viv didn't need conditions tailormade for him. There are plenty of batsmen who can tear an attack apart on a perfect pitch but put them on a strip doing something and they don't want to know. Viv was great in any conditions. The best I saw in all my years in Test cricket.'

It was a mixed bag of results for Greg in a thoroughly exhausting season yet, despite his pleas of weariness, two weeks after the domestic season ended Greg was in Pakistan leading Australia on a three Test tour, thus making it nine Tests, against the three major cricket nations, in one season. Various forces played on him. He was tired and Judy was pregnant again, though he would be back from Pakistan in time. But having just been made compromise captain he did not feel he could immediately pull out of the first tour of the peace. Former Test batsman of the 1930s, Jack Fingleton, wrote to Greg questioning the wisdom of his going to Pakistan. Fingleton, a cricket writer in Canberra, wrote:

> *...you have to decide what is more important to you, your family and your health or a short tour to a place of dubious health standards...*

Greg had his own suspicions as well. It was the time of the Russian invasion of Afghanistan. Greg rang the private secretary of the Minister for Foreign Affairs, Mr Peacock. Greg was aware that Australian teams were public relations ambassadors to some cricket countries. 'You only need talk to Trade Commissioners and High Commissioners for five minutes to realize how important it is to them, for Australia's products and image,' said Greg. 'If a tour is cancelled it's an international comment on the security of that country.' But Greg had no desire to get caught in Afghan-Pakistan-Russian hostilities. 'We'd have just been blokes in white,' said Greg. 'They wouldn't wait to ask why.' The Foreign Affairs Department assured Greg the tour was safe. 'Would you go?' Greg asked the secretary. 'Not if I didn't have to,' came the reply.

Greg also toured because Kim Hughes had led the ACB Australians to India during the WSC years. This was Greg's last chance to tour one of the cricket nations of the vast sub-continent. This was his tenth year in international cricket. He was not sure which would be his last. Thus on 22 February 1980, he found himself staring into the dark, mean eyes of President Zia-ul-Haq, at a reception in his residence in Rawalpindi. They stayed at international hotels and drank only boiled water or mineral water. Geoff Lawson ate an icecream and Dennis Lillee downed a local drink and both were ill. It was somewhat of a culture shock for most of the team — cripples on skate-boards and beggars at every traffic light. 'Don't, whatever you do, throw coins,' Greg ordered. 'They'll adopt us and we'll never get rid of them.'

In Karachi on the coast, Majid Khan, who played a season in Queensland with Greg, scored a patient 89 which won Pakistan the first Test.

Apart from that minor setback the Australians enjoyed themselves. On the Test rest day they sailed dinghies in Karachi Harbour, fishing for crabs which their hosts then beautifully curried for them on a sandy cay. Pakistan's Muslim law prohibited drinking alcohol except in their hotel rooms. But fast bowler, Sarfraz Nawaz, invited them to a private party of a friend who was Health Minister under Prime Minister Bhutto before his overthrow by ul-Haq. 'The friend, a doctor, lived in a compound, with a security guard at either gate,' said Greg. 'He'd just spent three years in gaol and if police had raided his house he'd be back for another spell.'

No drinking, but Greg and Lillee were offered tickets by the Police Commissioner to a public hanging in the town square. It was due at 4 p.m. but Test play did not finish until 4.30. 'I was quite happy when we couldn't go,' said Greg. 'It would have been a macabre experience. But that was their code. Cutting off hands for stealing, stoning to death for adultery, so violent.'

Having won the first Test the Pakistan authorities made that the series. 'They prepared two of the flattest wickets of all time to ensure there was no result in the final Tests,' said Greg. For the second Test in Faisalabad, Imran Khan warned Lillee, 'If you have any brains do not play in Faisalabad. A fast bowler wouldn't bother turning up.' Sure enough Imran withdrew with an 'injury'.

On that death watch wicket neither team was dismissed once. Greg scored 235 before going lbw to Sarfraz. Despite his disgust at the pitch Greg could still admire Sarfraz. 'We got 617 and we would have got 1,000 but for Saf,' he said. Sarfraz was painted as the heavy ox beside Imran Khan's thoroughbred presence but Greg liked Sarfraz' ferocious mien. 'He had a lot of aggro in him for a bloke that wasn't that quick,' said Greg. In 1975 in England, playing for Northamptonshire, Jeff Thomson bounced Sarfraz and hit him on the gloves. 'Saf's gone absolutely bozo,' said Greg. 'Next day when Jeff batted, Saf's come in and instead of bowling off 22 yards he ran through to 18 and let fly straight at Thommo's head. No attempt to bounce. And as he followed through he said, "Thomson, there's a spare plot in the cemetery. It's got your name on it." A fine competitor, Saf. Just getting the message across.'

In Faisalabad, according to *Wisden*, for the first time since 1884, every player in a Test team bowled. That was Greg's protest against the doleful pitch. 'Bacchus [Marsh] was never going to get a chance to bowl in a Test so that was as good a time as any,' said Greg, who took the gloves for Marsh's 10 overs. 'I made a valiant attempt to get a stumping off Rod's bowling. A lesser 'keeper would have missed it altogether. I just knocked it down.'

The third Test in Lahore near the Indian border, an hour's flight from the Himalayas, was preceded by comical relief. Pakistan officials prepared two strips, one green and fast, the other flat and slow. Lillee at this stage had not taken a wicket in two Tests. 'He knew he'd been shafted,' said Greg. 'They made sure he didn't play any part in the series. But he never refused to bowl. Not once. He handled it pretty well.' He was not the only angry fast bowler. Imran Khan and Sarfraz Nawaz constituted a pace attack the equal of Lillee and Geoff Dymock. 'They reckon we rig wickets in Australia, fast wickets for fast bowlers, but they crucified their own fast bowlers,' said Greg.

The green wicket was if Pakistan won in Faisalabad and therefore took an unbeatable 2–0 lead. The flat pitch was in case of a draw or a win by Australia. Greg and Dennis devised an elaborate hoax to fool their hosts. Practising at Lahore stadium Lillee put on a charade of injuring his back. Greg enlisted aid to carry the anguished fast bowler off the ground and back to the team hotel. 'How does it feel?' asked Greg anxiously. 'Like in '72,' said Lillee loudly, referring to his injury just prior to the ill-fated tour of the West Indies. The rumour was spread that Ashley Mallett was being rushed over to replace Dennis. 'We tried to bluff them into using the green pitch,' said Greg. 'It was a top performance, wasted on the audience really.' Greg even went so far as to call a doctor to Lillee, which was just as well because Lillee then fell, genuinely, very ill. After their practice Lillee, with a huge thirst, threw down a local curd drink. Greg sipped the sour fluid and turned his nose up at it. Lillee drank his too.

By the middle of the night Lillee was wracked by both vomitous and bowel convulsions. 'I've never seen anyone go green and yellow so quickly,' said Greg. 'I was convinced he wasn't going to make it to the morning.' A Pakistani doctor arrived at 1 a.m. and sat with the fast bowler until 7 a.m., administering medicines and injections. Greg ushered the doctor out, thanking him profusely for a performance 'above and beyond the call of duty'. Greg resolved to protect Lillee from all interruption. That afternoon the phone rang and a Pakistani voice asked for Lillee. Not here, said Greg and hung up. The phone rang again. All Greg could make out was the word Lillee. There was no way they were getting past Greg. He hung up again. The third time Greg was angry and slammed the phone down just as he caught the

Above: In May 1984, on holiday on Dunk Island, north Queensland with the three mates who shared much of his career, plus a little holidaymaker *Left:* Judy gives Greg some piano instruction for his debut at a charity concert at which he had to play a nursery rhyme

Far left: A fan pays homage to Greg on his way to 150 not out in the second Test against Pakistan in Brisbane in his last season, 1983–84. When he first moved to Queensland Greg was nicknamed by cricket fans 'God'

Top left: Acknowledging the crowd at the SCG after breaking Sir Donald Bradman's record for the most Test runs scored by an Australian

Top right: The relief and the strain show on his face as Kim Hughes walks back after congratulating Greg on breaking Bradman's record

Left: Time for a joke at last with the Pakistanis after breaking Bradman's record

Right: Taking the catch off Mohsin
Khan which broke Colin Cowdrey's
world record for catches by a fieldsman.
He took one more later in the match to
finish his career with 122 catches
Below: Surrounded by the media in the
SCG dressing room after he announced
his retirement on 3 January 1984

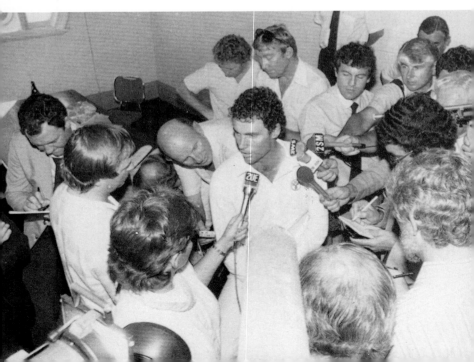

second word of English... 'doctor'. The phone did not ring again. 'Poor bloody doctor,' said Greg. 'If he ever reads this book I'd like to apologize to him.'

Despite Lillee's performance the third Test was played on the flat strip and ground to a predictable draw. Lillee recovered to take three wickets, the first of which brought an ironic cheer from Greg and Marsh. Greg scored two 50s to ring up his 5,000th Test run, but Allan Border hit two 150s, an exceptional performance by one of the ACB's new caps. Greg felt the Australian Cricket Board had let the team down by not ensuring better conditions for the tour. But he now understood the politics of cricket better. If Pakistan had not won their team would have been vilified by the local press. If they were so barbaric about stealing and adultery, what fate awaited a losing XI.

In Lahore Greg and several others went shopping into the Old Town, a walled city within the city, down narrow, twisting laneways into rabbit warren shops, looking for bargain jewellery. By the time they emerged the laneway was crammed with 2,000 curious Pakistanis. Amid confusion, shouting and some anger their guides beat with sticks to clear a path back to the car. It was an experience in sheer mass humanity that Australians could never know. Majid Khan then took them to a carpet factory where Greg bought two double-weave woollen rugs for $700 each, half the Australian price. But he was not happy at the factory, staffed by children who sat daylight to dark sewing in dingy outhouses. 'By the time they are 9 or 10 years old their eyes are gone, the close work and poor light,' said Greg, 'and they turf them out.' Pakistan was an experience he was glad to have had, but was not anxious to repeat.

Greg returned to Australia at the end of March and on 10 April his second son, Jonathan, was born. For the last six weeks of her pregnancy Judy was confined to bed with oedema, fluid retention, and her mother had flown from Sydney to live in. It was no great problem, just one more line in the accumulating debt Greg's cricket owed to Judy and his family. In some ways the end of that season would have been an ideal moment to step down from the captaincy, if not the team. New names were starting to fill Test vacancies, Dyson, Border, Hogg and Lawson, names that would take Australia through the 1980s. Only the Ashes still defied him, but he had beaten Brearley. He was in excellent form, averaging 71 against England and the West Indies and 76 against Pakistan. Ahead lay another harrowing season with both India and New Zealand touring. Yet that was one reason he played on, to try and bring some sanity back into the scheduling of the dual touring nation syndrome. Only a player of his standing would be able to influence the administrators. He still enjoyed cricket but there was an element of duty in continuing, as though he was doing penance for the years of WSC. But it did not save him from purgatory.

19. Changes

A helicopter descended deafeningly into the visitors' dressing-room at Trent Bridge, Nottinghamshire — Greg had flicked high the volume of a transistor blasting out the opening sequence of Pink Floyd's rock tour de force, 'The Wall' (another brick in ...). An Aussie player joked, 'Here's the Boss arriving,' by chopper, as Kerry Packer did occasionally at VFL Park. The heady days of WSC were over but they had acted like drugs on the Australian team. For being swept high, they aged quickly. Only Greg, Marsh and Lillee were left from that great era of the mid-1970s. Name the greatest fast bowler ever, a Nottinghamshire official tempted me. Starts with 'L'. Lillee? He shook his head and pointed to a dedication on his office wall: 'There was no one as fast or as straight as this man.' Harold Larwood. 'Lillee's still good,' the official offered. The signs of decay are imperceptible to the untrained eye — the shallowing arc of a fast bowler's arm, a hundredth of a second delay in the closing of a bat face. Glancing at Greg in that Notts dressing room I no longer saw the fearless, blazing young gun of 1975–76. Instead there was the face of an experienced campaigner, confident in himself, but brow furrowed by the constant demands to perform at his very best because anything less and his team might fail. He had reached that age where for the first time he fully comprehended how difficult were the challenges he had sur-mounted so easily in the past.

Greg was 30, at an enduring peak of physical skills and maturity. A beard, full to the sidelevers, gave him the benevolent presence of a Quaker. This truncated tour of England, his fourth — second as captain — was for the 1980 Centenary Test at Lord's. Though comparisons with Ian still burdened him — that he was a better marksman than a commander — those looking for the superficial showman missed the substance of his real success. He had downed Tony Greig in the Melbourne Centenary Test and had come back after the WSC years to defeat the inestimable Mike Brearley 3–0 in Australia. Why would Ian Botham, now England captain, succeed where the other two failed?

Handicapped from the start by hours lost through rain the Lord's Test drifted into a draw. England, having lost the Australian Centenary, were determined not to lose their own. 'They obviously weren't keen at all,' said Greg. 'They never tried from day one to get a result.' He agreed with Botham that conditions early on the Saturday were not fit for fielders. But he felt the match could have started an hour earlier than it did. So did a spectator in the members' enclosure. As the two captains returned through the members' gate after an inspection of the wicket a young spectator grabbed umpire David Constant and shook him, abusing him for not starting play. It was a modified English version of the riot for similar reasons in the West Indies during the Australian's 1979 WSC tour. Greg grabbed the agitated assailant and said, 'You come with me to the secretary.' Botham assisted him but the man broke away — they weren't policemen after all.

It was an unprecedented incident at Lord's, a spectator attacking the umpires. But just as from Australia's 1977 centenary the WSC revolution was born, so in England's centenary year of 1980 trauma would bruise the game as it felt its way from one century to the next. While Greg was only winged by the backlash to WSC, he was about to take the full blast from an approaching cataclysm.

Before the Lord's Test Australia, twice in three days, had scandalously succumbed to England in one-day matches. Manager Phil Ridings told me, 'One day a statistician will calculate precisely what no-balls have cost Australia in limited over cricket, what runs were struck from the no-ball, plus those off the extra ball in the over.' Australia played unlimited over cricket. At that stage Australia had lost six consecutive one-day matches against England since 1979. Greg had captained those six defeats and that bears examination if nothing else. English cricket writer, broadcaster and raconteur, John Arlott, wrote in 1980 of limited over cricket:

> *Its essence is that the fielding side does better to limit its opponents to 150 for no wickets than to bowl them out for 151 ...*

Wisden records of the 1979-80 Benson and Hedges World Series Cup (where England beat Australia 4-0):

> *Chappell made it clear he disliked such a defensive form of cricket. He attempted to win his matches without resorting to negative bowling or spreading his fielders around the boundary ...*

1979–80 was the first year out of World Series Cricket, when Greg was given that impossible schedule against England and the West Indies. He took a philosophical decision early in that season: the Tests were important, the one-days secondary. He told the selectors that to maintain team spirit he wanted a team picked for the Tests and retained for the one-days, not chopped and changed. 'We probably could have chosen slightly better balanced teams for the one-day games, but the selectors agreed the Tests were the thing,' said Greg. Greg also felt his bowlers were not sufficiently skilled at bowling to defensive fields. He decided to attack, the antithesis of Arlott's one-day axiom. It worked against the West Indies, but England was too experienced.

The whole innovation of one-day cricket, its emphasis on negativism, irritated Greg. The more like normal cricket it could be the better he liked it. Cricket was not meant just for niggardly little medium pace bowlers and batsmen who pushed and ran. 'You have to reward the player who has the ability to hit the ball through the field,' said Greg. 'The most negative, uninteresting cricket I've ever played and watched is one-day cricket. The only exciting thing is that you generally finish up with a fairly close game and get a result. But if you analyse the whole day's play, it's boring and very defensive.' Greg fought hard for the introduction of the two circle field restriction which, after the 1979–80 season in Australia, Mike Brearley refined into the single oval shaped restriction now commonly used. But it was Brearley who also incensed Greg with his application of negativism in the extreme.

In Sydney on 28 November 1979, England beat the West Indies by two runs. On the last ball the last batsman, Colin Croft, needed to hit three to win. Brearley pushed every fieldsman, including the wicket-keeper David Bairstow, back to the boundary fence to prevent a four. Greg watched the match on television in his hotel room and was angered. 'That's the sort of thing I don't like about one-day cricket,' he thought. 'That you're allowed to do that. It's just so unlike cricket.' But Greg respected Brearley's cricket brain and, again in his hotel room, thought the incident through in his analytical stream-of-consciousness fashion — limited over cricket was not orthodox cricket — you could not have a bastardized version of cricket and apply the same tradition to it as Test cricket — what spirit was there in one-day cricket? — Brearley's action was within the rules — if it was permissible Greg would probably have done the same. But it also occurred to Greg that if he had pulled Brearley's tactic he would have been criticized far more than was Brearley.

Ian Chappell also saw Brearley's manoeuvre. Walking behind an SCG stand after the match he happened near England batsman, Mike Gatting. Ian said to his companion, loudly enough for Gatting to hear, 'The way the Poms play this game they ought to be roped and burnt.' When the Australians next played England in that series Ian and Dennis Lillee were the batsmen during the last over. Ian was on strike as Brearley placed his field to restrict slogging. When Brearley looked in Ian's direction Ian pointed at 'keeper Bairstow and said, 'Put him on the fence.' Brearley advised Ian to concentrate on his batting.

Brother Trevor joined Greg and Ian in their dislike of the negativism of one-day cricket. Though a talented all-rounder, an ideal limited-over cricketer, Trevor knew its deficiencies. 'Unless you bat in the first three, you haven't much hope of a decent opportunity to bat properly,' he said. 'After that you make yourself look like a fool half the time.' Few players enjoyed it as much as Shield or Test cricket. To them it was rather like asking a portrait painter to whip up a couple of caricatures. That did not help Greg. 'He used to get really furious when we lost,' said Trevor.

He did indeed. He was continually thwarted by his bowlers giving away no-balls. 'We took them to nets and they'd be fine while you were standing alongside them, but next match ...' He lost track of the number of emergency meetings he called. They had lost two in a row and would miss the finals. 'Then they'd start playing to the best of their ability,' said Greg. It was exasperating. He never had to motivate Australian teams for Tests, it was all in the players' psyche. But walk into the dressing-room before a limited over match and he could detect the difference. Two or three senior players would knuckle down, but the others emanated the feeling: 'Oh, it's just another one-day game.'

Greg knew perfectly well the problem. It was entertainment, for prize money. They were not judged by their one-day performances. It was such a product of the modern age that there were no records with which to compare themselves. No records, no history, no tradition. Greg could not blame his team because he himself had told the selectors before that hectic season the Tests had priority. That put Greg as much at fault as anybody, but, in contrast to all but a few players, Greg never stopped trying in the one-days. He played his heart out, but as often as not the team let him down. 'I got to the stage where I didn't want to captain Australia in one-day cricket,' said Greg.

It was an extraordinary admission by a man whose love for cricket had been proven by his lifetime devotion. Cricket was his mistress sport. Judy could almost be jealous of an obsession like that. The first 100 years of Test cricket in Australia had produced Bradman, an aberration called bodyline and a saying that made the game synonymous with fair play. What had happened in the first blush of the second century — since 1977 — to so alienate Greg?

Eminent historian George Trevelyan, wrote in his *Social History of England*:

If the French noblesse had been capable of playing cricket with their peasants, their chateaux would never have been burnt.

He was alluding to cricket's place as a form of class communication between the English aristocracy and the rest. In eighteenth century England, usually on Sunday, social differences were forgotten as butchers, gardeners and farm labourers became equal under the rules of cricket with noblemen, gentlemen and clergy, in a match on the village green. What this match also ensured, of course, was the preservation of the economic and social status quo. While working class cricketers were sublimating their grievances with bouncers and hooks, they were not routing the privileged from their castles as had occurred in the French Revolution. Cricket in England's Victorian era was a product of, and vehicle for, reinforcing class structures.

The Victorian sporting ethos encouraged amateurism because a professional working class team would easily defeat an amateur team of gentlemen. It emphasized participation over victory because the drive to defeat a team of gentlemen was not to be encouraged in the working class. And it discouraged mass participation because from that would spring working class élites to challenge the status of the gentry. The modern English film *Chariots of Fire* depicted the conflict between classes perfectly in its dialogue between the university dons and Harold Abrahams, when they accused him of employing a professional coach to train for the 1924 Olympic 100 metres in Paris. The exchange proceeded:

Dons: *This university believes the way of the amateur is the only one which provides satisfying results ... Your aim is to win at all costs.*

Abrahams: *You would rather I played the gentleman and lost?*

Dons:	*To playing the tradesman, yes. Your approach has been too plebian. You are the élite and therefore expected to behave as such.*
Abrahams:	*Gentlemen, you yearn for victory just as much as I do ... Yours are the archaic values of the prep school playground. I believe in the pursuit of excellence and I'll carry the future with me.*

Two other Victorian England legacies adhered to cricket. The Christian church praised cricket for allying the virtues of sportsmanship with a pure morality. To this day sermons ring with the metaphors of 'playing it straight' and 'it's not cricket'. John Arlott once found a droll reference on a church door: 'Them as hasn't been at church, shan't play at cricket.' But other similarities are more revealing. The church and cricket combined the ideals of unquestioning acceptance of rules and laws, a social and sporting pacifism which had the effect of perpetuating class discrepancies. And this led to the insidious Victorian myth that the lives of the thinker and the athlete were incompatible. This persists to the modern era where coaches are the brains and the players dumb jocks. Philosopher-cricket captain Mike Brearley was regarded as an oddity among his contemporaries.

The traditions of cricket therefore were those founded upon élitist ideas designed to protect English aristocracy from severe challenge from the working classes. Some American sports analysts such as Mike Novak in *The Joy of Sports* sublimated the class aspects of this Victorian legacy by promoting the 'selfism' of sport. 'A great rival is a great gift,' he wrote, because it enabled the contestants to push themselves to their limit. The ultimate competition was not with others, but with oneself. Cricket arrived in Australia with its class discrimination intact, but under the egalitarian Antipodean sun it metamorphosed, retaining only the mythic phrases of the past and developing into a sporting meritocracy, underlined by Novak's joy of self discovery. This was the hybrid game taught to Greg as an Adelaide schoolboy.

When Greg began his career no cricketer trained seriously. England fielding sides were dubbed Dad's Army because of their lack of mobility. Shield cricketers travelled by train between cities. 'You never had to be fit because if you pulled up sore after a four-day game, you had five days to get over it before the next,' said Greg. Shield matches enjoyed a rest day. Greg's leisurely cricket life disappeared with WSC's emphasis on limited over, televised cricket, which in turn led to night cricket, white balls and coloured clothing. The erstwhile excitement of waiting for a liner to berth bearing a Hutton or a Cowdrey had been replaced by the thrill of a guaranteed match result in one day.

But limited over cricket was not the only change. Test cricket after WSC lost its rest day and gained protective helmets. Increased prize money brought specialization, the crucial factor of which, as much as the money, is time devoted to cricket. As Greg's life demonstrated, he was a 75 per cent fully professional cricketer. Professional cricketers were beginning to defend their earnings with more than their bat and pads.

Under the stress of competition between World Series Cricket and the Australian Cricket Board, cricket became soured by acts of arch competitiveness. Several occurred when the WSC-dominated Pakistan team played the ACB Australian team in 1978–79. Rodney Hogg was dismissed when he wandered out of his crease after completing his shot. The Australians then 'Mankadded' a Pakistani batsman, in return for which Australian opener Andrew Hilditch, handing the ball in a friendly way back to Sarfraz Nawaz, was given out for handling the ball.

Greg the following season had his own problems with Lillee's aluminium bat incident and he foresaw the fate of the West Indians when they stopped in New Zealand for a three Test series in 1979–80. The West Indies' disappointment and anger at New Zealand umpiring was expressed by Colin Croft colliding heavily with an umpire as he ran in to bowl. 'They gave every sign of being an exhausted team when they left us,' said Greg. But the New Zealand series simply took the West Indies season tally to six Tests, the same as played by Australia. The West Indies' reaction in New Zealand was testimony to Greg's great captaincy control as he weathered that season without undue incident, aluminium bats notwithstanding.

Richard Cashman in *Sport, Money, Morality and the Media*, published by the University of New South Wales Press, wrote perceptively: 'Cricket is now plagued by ... conflicting ideas about its conventions.' Conventions are just that — normal procedures backed by nothing more than a past consensus about acceptable standards of behaviour. Without wishing to extend the analogy too far, Federal Opposition Leader, Malcolm Fraser, and Queensland Premier, Joh Bjelke-Petersen, showed how ineffectual were conventions when they swept them aside to bring down Prime Minister Gough Whitlam in

1975. In lay terms that was when two strong mainstreams of Australian culture clashed — the belief that everyone deserves a fair go and the opportunist urge never to give a sucker an even break. Whitlam rode the former to victory in 1974 and was tossed by the latter the following year. In that instance political conventions were simply traditions and no more inviolable to manipulation and flouting than was cricket when WSC awoke the ACB from its Rip van Winkle slumber.

Cricket's conventions were slowly sinking beneath a welter of professionalism, commercialism and rationalization. From the first the players derived new impetus to win, the second placed the game under trial by television and the third had actually introduced a new game. Rationalization involved the logical pursuit of short term goals more easily obtained — limited over cricket. Just as game hunting and shooting bulls became firing a bull's-eye on a target range, so the risk of no result over a five-day Test was replaced by the certainty of a victor in a match viewed from the lounge-room.

Cricket was known by its consecrated places, the SCG and Lord's, until John Maley desecrated the altars by making pitches in concrete tubs and laying them on any unholy ground. Cricket was above all a sport of time, where profane time, the length of the match, was secondary to the moments of heroic time of which Greg had provided so many. Limited over cricket destroyed that by giving priority to profane television time, and let the heroic moments squeeze in where they may. In consequence, Greg can hardly remember an innings he played in one-day games. Cricket was one of the few sports where the metaphor of life and death for victor and vanquished did not hold sway. A draw could be a marvellous result. The one-day match would brook no such prevarication. One side must live, one side die, the vast voyeuristic coliseum that is television demanded blood.

One-day cricket as Greg approached the 1980–81 season at home represented what French sports critic, Jean-Marie Brohm, termed the worst fate of the sportsman victim: his alienation from his sport. One-day matches for Greg had turned cricket from challenge to stress. Instead of leisured time, cricketers had become time's carcass. One-day matches rolled off the assembly line for television and the players became the production line workers. Brohm's theories in *Sport: A Prison of Measured Time*, are straight Marxist interpretations, but no less applicable to one-day cricket for being so. The Australian cricketers, having embraced the rewards of capital investment in their sport, now found themselves subjected to the inevitable corollary of any unalloyed pursuit of profit — the principle of maximum production. In the final result capitalism cannot be sated. The assembly workers on the cricket oval were expected to perform with mechanical perfection, as tirelessly and flawlessly as the cameras which surveyed them.

Greg was no trade union renegade against this oppression. But he remained the supreme individual. He possessed no blind obedience to the moguls of the ACB, PBL or Channel Nine, nor any unthinking devotion to those institutions. The edifice of values that surrounded cricket he saw as a diaphanous veil masking the monolithic commercial enterprise that televised cricket had become. When he began the domestic cricket season of 1980–81 he had diagnosed the schizoid dementia that had seriously unbalanced Australian cricket. He proposed to treat with the reality, not the delusion.

THE FALL (1980–1982)

20. Underarm

Sunday, 1 February 1981, the MCG, 5.15 p.m., Australia versus New Zealand, World Series Cup final. Ian Chappell at the microphone for Channel Nine:

> *Trevor Chappell takes a well-judged catch running back... he's got the ball in his hand and he's going to have to bowl the last over... the man coming in is the well-loved Richard Hadlee... and I doubt we can ask for a better finish... New Zealand 6–221, six balls to go, 15 runs required for victory... 52,000 people and I doubt that any have left the ground.*

Bill Lawry:

> *It's going to be T. Chappell to the demon Hadlee... he's hit that, he's hit it well, out to Max Walker and that's four... My, what a start. Wow, ho ho... 11 required for victory, five balls to be bowled.*

Greg, standing at deep mid-on, was becoming a very angry man. Australia's score of 235 was good under the conditions, with the MCG wicket low and slow. New Zealand opener Bruce Edgar's century had thrown out a challenge, but Greg was incensed by his team's slipshod fielding, fumbles and misses, singles becoming two's, two's into three's. 'Annoying!' said Greg. 'Our blokes knew the situation, but having put our score on the board they played like, "Oh well, just a matter of turning up, they shouldn't get them."' Greg had spelt it out to the team before the match. They were 1–1 in a five match final series. If they won that day, Sunday, and in Sydney on Tuesday, they won the series. They would then have three days off before the final Test against India in Melbourne starting 7 February. 'I needed a rest, so did Dennis and Rod,' said Greg. 'Any blokes who'd had a heavy season. Dennis had done a lot of hard bowling and I'd made a lot of runs as well as captained the one-day side, which was tiring.'

Greg had led Australia to a 2–0 Test series win over New Zealand, and led India 1–0 with the third to play. He had scored 204 against India in the first Test in Sydney after being ill the night before with a stomach virus. Pale and listless he was, but the concentration was unimpaired and the body staggered along for the ride. Both Test series had their upsets. Greg was sledged by several young Kiwis and called them 'cheeky brats' and 'prima donnas' in his newspaper column. The Indians complained about the umpiring. Greg received fan mail and hate mail. One fan was a 76-year-old, terminally ill ex-cricketer whose sister wrote on his behalf of Greg's 204: 'Yesterday was one of his wonderful days as he watched your slashing bat and thrilled to your glorious shots all around the wicket on his television set.' The hate mail accused Australia of blatantly cheating the Indians. One writer was slightly premature: '...I must bestow the highest praise on the Indian captain for not walking off the field with his team...' All of which required comment from Greg at every post-match media conference and later to cricket writers from his hotel. Greg was sanguine about the complaints. It was for Indian consumption. 'If they don't complain about the umpiring, how come they didn't win?' he said.

The match schedule had improved from the previous season. Each Test series was now separated, but the one-day matches still peppered the lot. Greg had criticized the format during the season. There were 35 actual playing days in the 68-day international schedule. But the team had to travel and practise in between playing. As any air traveller knows, even the one hour flight from Melbourne to Sydney expands to a wearying three hours packing to unpacking. 'I think Richie Benaud was involved in the programming,' said Greg, 'and he took my criticism personally. That was when he made his comments about what a wonderful life we led, in the cocktail bar in the sky.' That was all very well for Benaud, stretching his legs in first class, said Greg. But he was sitting up the back with his knees jammed up against his chest. Planes were a nightmare of hostesses or passengers seeking autographs or conversations. 'Sorry to bother you, but would you sign these sheets and get the others to sign as well?' requested the stewardess. It was pressure, not peace. But Greg and Benaud enjoyed a friendship of mutual respect which those minor differences did not really touch.

On 1 February at the MCG Greg shouldered his portion of the bargain he had struck with his team. He scored 90, a long hot innings complete with the controversy about whether Martin Snedden caught him on 52 with a marvellous diving, grass-burning plunge on his elbows at deep mid-wicket. Inexplicably neither umpire was watching. To Greg it was irrelevant whether Snedden caught it or not. All his career his policy could not have been clearer had he advertised it in newspapers. He did not walk. He played the umpire's ruling. They gave him the benefit of their ignorance.

Having moulded a good target, Greg then returned to bowl 10 overs and take three wickets. He had decided to bowl the last over himself but after taking early wickets he bowled out his allotted overs. With one over left Greg had done everything to make the match a winner for Australia bar sell drinks in the stand. Hence his irritation at the laziness and lack of application by the Australians which had let New Zealand creep near. Before that last over New Zealand Prime Minister Robert Muldoon settled in his Air New Zealand seat en route to Wellington from Christchurch where he had just attended the closing ceremony of the summer games. A keen cricketer, he had followed the match and was delighted when the pilot called over the intercom, 'Six balls to go, 15 runs to win.'

If Greg was not happy with Hadlee's four off the first ball of the over, neither was Trevor. He was trying to bowl short so that the batsman went backwards to it, but not so short he gave Hadlee a 360 degree arc to hit it in. 'Bloody good shot for a guy who hadn't faced a ball all day,' said Trevor. In fact Trevor was aiming for a dark patch on the wicket about two feet shorter than the optimal length because he noticed that balls landing on that patch kept very low. As did his second ball of the over, angling in, rapping Hadlee on the pads. Out lbw. Ian Chappell:

> *Well, Hadlee wouldn't be overthrilled about that. He's been struggling all season to get an lbw himself . . . I would say that might have pitched outside leg stump, certainly it would have hit the stumps.*

'Eleven to win, four balls left,' announced the Air New Zealand pilot. Mr Muldoon, like everyone else, put down his reading material and waited. The next batsman was wicketkeeper Ian Smith. Bill Lawry:

Ian Smith... he's counting the fieldsmen, hee, hee, hee... probably thinks they've got the twelfth man out there... lot of pressure out there... he's hit it, hit it well, go for two, and they get it... two balls remaining, Irving? [Rosenwater, Channel 9 scorer] Two? Three balls remaining! I put the pressure on Irving Rosenwater then.

Smith slammed the next for two as well. Two balls left, 7 runs to win. Greg's heart sank. 'Two bad pieces of fielding,' he said. 'Both should have only been singles. Slow to the ball, fumbled one, fieldsman just wasn't thinking.' Next ball Trevor clean-bowled Smith. On the slowed television replay the middle stump leaned drunkenly back at 60 degrees, the bails spun eternally into the air like the thigh bone hurled by the ape in Kubrick's *2001*. Dennis Lillee trotted up and shook Trevor's hand. Ian Chappell:

Eight down for 229. New Zealand's only hope now is six off the last ball for a tie.

On the Air New Zealand flight Prime Minister Muldoon relaxed a little, victory impossible, a tie an honourable improbability. That was the atmosphere in the New Zealand dressing-room too. Geoff Howarth and the players joked to their last batsman, Brian McKechnie, 'Don't worry about getting your eye in.' Howarth knew that on a slow wicket, at the huge MCG, a six would be a mighty effort. But at the back of his mind there was the thought, 'You might just get a lucky blow in.' McKechnie himself was quite relaxed. No one expected a miracle, he was on a winner to nothing.

McKechnie was a man for occasions. An All Black five-eighth, about 178 centimetres, 79 kilograms, he was powerfully built through the chest, with strong upper arms and forearms. At Cardiff Arms Park in 1978 New Zealand trailed Wales 12–10 with minutes to go when they were awarded a penalty. From 30 metres out McKechnie calmly booted the penalty for a 13–12 victory. There was nothing wrong with his physique or nerve. He walked to the wicket wearing a black peaked cap and the Kiwi uniform of fawn with black trimmings. As he walked he looked about and thought, 'Now I'm a bowler. Where would I bowl it so I couldn't be hit for six? Pitch the ball well up to the batsman's feet.' He would work on that theory. The shortest boundary was back over Trevor's head. Just as Trevor bowled he would step outside leg stump and come down, anticipating that line.

Greg was sitting on the ground, thinking how well Trevor had bowled that over, pitched to a nicety and straight. When he saw McKechnie walk through the gate his nerves clamoured and rang. 'If anyone can hit one over the fence, this bloke can,' he thought. His accumulated anger lifted him to his feet. The beast he saw slouching towards the crease at McKechnie's shoulder was not defeat but the wastefulness of so much effort, the futility of a tie, the dread of yet one more fatiguing game of this Philistine cricket. The principles of playing that had loomed in his listening since before he could remember computed an answer. Who would have thought that if you hemmed this man in he would ride down the hosts opposing him? He was apprehensive as he headed for Trevor, but he was not afraid.

Martin Kent at deep mid-wicket grew nervous. He was sure McKechnie had him lined up. That was where a wild swing would go. A ridiculous scenario fled through Kent's imagination: 'If he skies one to me, they'll run two before it comes down. If I fumble it they'll run another one and a half, a stumble and a wild return and they're nearly home.' All so improbable, but the tension was immense. 'As much pressure as I've ever been under in the field, for sure,' said Kent.

Greg reached Trevor, who was spinning the ball from hand to hand, grimacing. Trevor had just spoken with Rod Marsh who advised him, 'Try to bowl exactly what you've been bowling.' The previous ball that dismissed Smith hit the stumps only 30 centimetres from the ground. It seemed excellent advice. But Greg could go one better.

'How are you at bowling your underarms?' Greg asked Trevor.

'Oh, I don't know — why?'

'Well, you're about to find out.'

Trevor looked surprised, then impressed. He thought, 'That sounds like a pretty good idea. That'll make it pretty hard to hit a six.' Greg turned to umpire Don Weser and told him to instruct the batsman the delivery would be underarm. Weser rolled his eyes in amazement. McKechnie looked up to take block and saw Weser heading for square leg umpire Peter Cronin. He thought they were checking it was definitely the last ball. Greg and Trevor, both in Australia's colours of wattle with bottle green panels, stood together for about 10 seconds, Greg in white washing hat, Trevor bareheaded, if his wild, curly mop could ever be called that. Greg set his field and demonstrated to Trevor the delivery, swinging his right arm slightly back as though to bowl underarm. Then he headed back to deep mid-on. Umpire Weser told McKechnie, leaning on his bat, of the proposed underarm. McKechnie replied, 'You've got to be joking!' and dropped his bat in astonishment.

Watching television in Adelaide Martin Chappell turned to Jeanne and predicted the underarm. Sam Trimble in Brisbane actually said aloud to himself minutes before, 'Bowl an underarm'. Old captains think ahead, forever. The Channel Nine commentary hiatus was finally broken. Bill Lawry:

> *It looks to me like they're going to bowl an underarm off the last ball...this is possibly a little disappointing...let's make sure-...would you ever have believed it.*

Greg watched Trevor wave Rodney Marsh back from the stumps. Marsh shook his head and mouthed back, 'No, mate, don't do it.' Trevor shrugged his shoulders and nodded towards Greg. Greg thought perhaps Marsh was declining merely to retreat from the stumps. He had never asked Rod about it. When I queried Marsh he loyally replied he could not remember. But it needs no explanation. Nor does Greg's motivation. 'I thought, "This is not going to be well received",' he said. 'I expected a lot of people would say, "Tch, tch, not cricket," but quite honestly I couldn't give a rat's tail. I was quite prepared for a wrap over the knuckles if it saved us from the extra game.'

The tableau that had gradually collected on field suddenly accelerated into action. Trevor licked his lips, took four paces forward, propped well inside the crease to avoid a no-ball, and bowled the ball as if in a bowling alley. It did not go 'dadum, dadum, dadum,' as Greg and Ian had discussed. It hit the ground centimetres in front of Trevor and sped all along the ground on a slight swerve to McKechnie's leg stump. The batsman had considered his options. No point in a four, which he could have hit. 'Nor did I want to be embarrassed by having a swing and being bowled,' he said. He turned his bat slightly inside out to block the ball, took three paces and flung his bat high into the air, thinking, 'Oh God, this is not cricket, you know.' Trevor watched the results of his handiwork, then collected his cap from umpire Weser. Bruce Edgar, 102 not out, who had not faced a ball in the last over, gave Trevor the two fingers up sign with his gloved right hand.

The New Zealand dressing-room erupted. 'What the hell is going on?' asked Howarth loudly. 'What's the ruling? I thought the ICC ruling barred underarms.' Manager Ian Taylor dived for his briefcase but in the excitement could not find the tour rules. Howarth stalked onto the field in his socks, his trouser waist button undone, to berate the umpires. As he passed Bruce Edgar he said, 'Just hang on, to my mind what's happened is illegal.' Edgar stopped McKechnie. Kim Hughes came over and apologized. Marsh took off his right glove and shook Edgar's hand. The umpires told Howarth it was a perfectly legal delivery. In the New Zealand dressing-room one player dashed his tea cup against the wall in frustration. On Prime Minister Muldoon's flight the tension of several minutes silence since the second last ball was broken when the pilot crackled over the intercom in a shaken voice, 'He bowled it underarm ... and they're all arguing!'

Greg saw Howarth run on out of the corner of his eye as he raced off. The crowd was bellowing a mixture of three-fifths booing, one of applause and the rest were dumbstruck. A small girl, about nine, leaped the fence and grabbed Greg by the arm. He was about to decline an autograph when she shouted, 'You cheated, you cheated!', the defamatory indictment around which cricket commentators were about to carelessly skirt. In the old MCG scoreboard attendant Noel Carter sat for a moment and then rang the scorer to check whether he had missed a signal from the umpires. 'They allowed to do that?' he enquired.

By the time Martin Kent made it up the long aisle to the cream concrete dressing-rooms some spectators were hurling vicious comments at the Aussie pack of bastards. But in the dressing-room it was deathly quiet. 'Like a morgue,' said Greg. 'No one was going to look at me or say anything. They hoped someone else would say the first word to break the ice.' Greg went and showered to give them a chance to talk. Still no one spoke. The brown locker doors gaped ajar, clothes drying machine stood silent and the masseur's bench lay quiet. The players sat as inanimate as the collection of bats leaning against the concrete wall. A white wall telephone jingled. Trevor was nearest. Perth calling for Greg Chappell. Not here, said Trevor. Then it rang again. New Zealand calling for Greg Chappell. Trevor had no illusions. 'No, he's not here, you're on the wrong place.' He did not tell the caller who he was. Greg returned from his shower but still silence reigned. Martin Kent estimated it was half an hour before anyone spoke. Or it seemed like that.

The New Zealand dressing-room was pandemonium. ACB executives Bob Parish and Ray Steele were there apologizing, as was executive director Dave Richards whose job it would be to quell the blow-out. The New Zealanders were irate. They would bowl their 50 overs underarm at the next match. But really they were disappointed and confused. 'We didn't fully understand what happened,' said Howarth. 'It was so momentous. It was the controversy of the century.'

If it was not already Richie Benaud was ensuring it would be. In the Channel Nine commentary quarters, in his post-match summary, Benaud was delivering one of the most astonishing pieces of invective ever levelled at an international cricket captain. He said:

Well, there are 50,000 people here at the MCG today. I would hazard a guess that you might find three or at the very most four who wouldn't have a sinking feeling in their stomach at the moment over that last delivery...

Now you can have your own opinions about that. Let me tell you what mine is. I think it was a gutless performance from the Australian captain. It came about because he got his sums wrong.

Benaud then explained his theory about how Greg really intended Dennis Lillee to bowl the last over but through error ended up with Trevor:

He [Greg] and Kim Hughes and Rod Marsh were doing the sums on their fingers out there. I don't think we'll go too far into what they should be doing with their fingers at the moment.

Benaud was at his most plausible, silver grey hair brushed from left to right, fawn suit, striped tie, unwavering gaze, Nine sports logo over his left shoulder. A man of justifiably great credibility through his experience, but of inordinate influence through his television position, he led the charge of the Lilliputians to pinion Greg with their gossamer arguments.

And just a final thought... it's one of those things about cricket, that there's always a lot of pressure on umpires and players and commentators as well. As regards that last ball what I say is, if you can't stand the pressure, you're too tired, and that makes you make decisions of that kind, then it might be time to have a little rest.

The question is, was Benaud referring to Greg or himself? Benaud was not immune to the hysteria building around the underarm. To summarize it in the heat of the moment was an invidious task, like writing history from the battle-front. Ian Chappell said of his commentary leader, 'Richie's correct 99.9 per cent of the time,' which proves only that he was fallible. His 'captain-getting-his-sums-wrong theory,' which occupied a third of his summary, was sheer speculation. Greg at no stage considered bowling Lillee last over. 'Particularly in Melbourne where the wicket was low and slow,' said Greg. 'The faster you bowl the easier it is to score. Dennis would get reasonable bounce and pace which would allow the batsman just to deflect and get easy runs. With fellows like Trevor and myself they had to really make the effort, take risks to score. Trevor was the perfect bowler for it. Never above medium pace. That's why he got Hadlee and Smith out in quick time, trying to force the pace." Trevor confirmed the plan. 'With Dennis' pace a nick would be four,' he said. 'To hit me for four they had to hit the ball in front of the wicket. If they nicked me somebody would cut it off.'

That demolishes that theory. Yet Benaud had not only told millions of viewing Australians that Greg's performance was gutless, but had held Greg up to ridicule as a captain who could not even get his sums correct. It was a regrettable piece of television editorialising. Bob Merriman, ACB cricket committee co-ordinator, saw Benaud's summary and warned Greg of its inflammatory nature. Greg did not need to hear any more once he faced the press conference. 'They were like buzzards around a dying body, waiting for death,' said Greg. He asked team manager, John Edwards, if he could get out of Melbourne to Sydney that night. If he gave the media time to marshal their troops he would be well under siege at the Melbourne Hilton by morning. Dennis Lillee wrote that Greg joked to him, 'Could be a good idea to get out of the hotel...could be a few bombings tonight.'

In the foyer of the Hilton he saw Billy Snedden, speaker of the House of Representatives, with whom he was acquainted. Snedden waved and came over. 'Just wanted to let you know there's going to be a fair bit of flak over the next few days,' he said. 'I've been through a bit in my time. It's amazing how quickly it blows over. Just keep calm.'

Upstairs in his room Greg paused for a moment, familiar with the peace of the air-conditioner's hum and the fridge's murmur. He rang home. Judy had watched the match and was initially shocked. And then she began her analysis. It was in the rules. Judy trusted Greg's cricket judgement from the day she met him. She saw no reason to change now. The morality concerned her until she remembered Greg's ashen face. 'Dennis and Rod commented afterwards how exhausted Greg was by that dreadful schedule,' said Judy. 'They were on the run, backwards and forwards. And then Richie Benaud made those comments about if you can't stand the pressure and I thought, "Well hang on boy, you've never played one-day matches under those sort of conditions."' Judy knew Greg had done it in the best interests of the team. Beyond that she had shed a tear for Greg whom she had not seen for months and would not see for weeks. She knew her husband to be a very good person, a very fair person, and that he would not have been motivated by ill will. Her loyalty was never in doubt.

Greg in his hotel sanctum stared at the herringbone carpet and asked to speak to his son Stephen. Nearly six now, Stephen had watched the match with Judy. Greg took a breath.

'What do you think about it?' he asked.

'Um, I don't think you should have done it,' said Stephen.

'Well, it's a bit late now, isn't it? How do you feel?'

'I feel sorry for you.'

There, echoing over the line from 1,600 kilometres north, Greg heard the verdict he had been shutting from his consciousness. He had defended his action at the press conference. 'If it is written in the rules of the game it is fair play,' he had said. But he sensed the wave building out of sight, in the cricket community, in the newspapers, in hotels and homes, a racing current of uninformed indignation which no man, no matter how upright his stance, could withstand. He warned Judy to be ready for the onslaught to come, to say nothing. Stephen too. First his brother, Trevor, a victim of his captain's orders. Now his family too. He was spreading a mist of unhappiness wherever he touched. In fact the Chappell phone at Kenmore ran hot, with calls from friends supporting Greg. And Stephen next day at school dealt with his own crisis. An older boy sneered, 'What your Dad did was slack.' Stephen stood up and replied fiercely, 'No it wasn't, not at all. He did what he thought he had to do.' Stephen was proud of his father and no bully boy would say differently.

But in Melbourne Greg was beginning a long, slow slide into weariness and depression. He joined half a dozen other players in a bus to the airport. They had regained their good humour along with their voices. In the dressing-room they had agreed none would comment for or against the underarm. That restored their unity, paralysed momentarily by the unprecedented pressure on their moral nerve induced by Greg's action. All the same Trevor had not been keen to be first to leave the dressing-room in case spectators, unhappy with his underarm, were waiting. But he walked the 500 metres up through a park of maples, gums and Moreton Bay figs to the Hilton unhindered, unnoticed.

In the bus and at the airport the jokes began. 'You know what Greg said at the press conference,' announced Len Pascoe. 'He said, "I don't know why Trev did it!"' Doug Walters remarked that Greg had messed up his childhood lesson that the game was not over until the last ball was bowled. A Melbourne newspaper had recently run a large aerial photograph of the controversial MCG pitch with the word 'DISGRACE'. The paper would probably just repeat the photo on the front page the next morning, they mused. But Walters, as usual, put it precisely. Those 50,000 would have left the MCG feeling as he had after he saw the movie *The Sting*, thinking, 'What the bloody hell did happen?' Greg let the jokes wash over him, relaxing in their cameraderie and unspoken, if not unquestioning, loyalty. No passenger approached to insult him. Perhaps, as Bill Snedden said, it would blow over quickly. But even then a new dimension was being added to an already exaggerated incident.

Prime Minister Muldoon had landed in Wellington and at home had seen the underarm replayed on television. He was angry, as were most New Zealanders, but when his nation's press rang him he replied, 'No comment, no comment,' until the calls trailed off. He went to bed and at midnight — but only 10 p.m. in Sydney — a journalist from the *Sydney Morning Herald* dialled Muldoon's number, which is publicly listed, and it rang in his bedroom. Awakened at midnight Muldoon's suppressed anger broke its traces. 'Look if the bloody Australians want it they'll get it fair between the eyes,' he said. And he proceeded to damn Greg's underarm order as 'an act of cowardice' and that it was appropriate that the Australians were dressed all in yellow.

Late at night, in his Sydney hotel room Greg rang the hotel switchboard and asked for no calls before 10 a.m. On that particular subject he would have liked to have requested no calls ever again. But it was only just beginning.

21. Epiphany

History works in strange ways. So often it turns upon a man who is made of the very best mettle, the champion of his era, and demolishes him to demonstrate that the times have changed. It took nothing less than the collision of two ages of cricket to bring down Greg Chappell. Like two worlds which brush, they momentarily crushed him between their ponderous weights, before the past receded and the future cleared. The underarm worked like a Joycean epiphany for cricket, a moment of near spiritual clarity which enabled its minions to gaze wondrously at the new soul. The tragedy was that Greg had already examined its heart as had few others. He knew that though the name remained the same, the game had not. Had he not given half his life to cricket? From childhood Greg was directed down the paths of cricket righteousness by home, school and church. MBE and ABC awards for his sportsmanship were recognition that he was a dedicated disciple. Was it likely that he, of all people, would sully the name of cricket? There is a hint of the martyr in Greg and the underarm. Unknowing and unwilling, yes, but in that moment he bartered his reputation to play the reality of the one-day game as he saw it.

My own view, published then in the *National Times*, was that Greg's professionalism had proved equal to the demands of modern cricket, whereas the ACB's administrators had not. If they had been thorough in their preparation for the one-day series they would have outlawed the underarm delivery as had been done in England. A good measure of the fury engendered in so many official breasts was due to Greg's exposing the ACB's inefficiency. It is hard to escape the conclusion that the heartburn in the Channel Nine pillbox and among the crowd was their disappointment at being denied a spectacular, grandstand finish. But 1 February at the MCG was not a circus with a programmed finale. Neither the crowd nor the commentary team had to play the extra match if McKechnie pulled off the improbable. Surely Greg would be derelict in his captaincy if he had a resource to prevent a tie and did not use it?

Benaud called it gutless. Howarth didn't know whether he would have the guts to use it. Well, which was it? Perhaps it lacked discretion, which maybe is what courage is. Whatever, Greg snatched the purdah from the face of limited over cricket. The appalled mullahs, Benaud and the ACB, who both nurture and exploit cricket, were not about to let him forget his sacrilege.

On Monday, 2 February — The Day After — Greg was woken in his Sheraton Hotel room at 6 a.m. by an ABC reporter who had circumvented the switchboard by booking in and dialling internally. 'Very ingenious,' said Greg. 'I'm going to be equally ingenious. When I'm finished talking the next sound you'll hear is the phone going down.' Messages were sliding under his locked door, 'AM,' 'Willesee,' a stream of messengers passed his door. The foyer was packed with media. All the ancient rules of the hunt attained. Greg was at bay.

The chairman of the ACB, Phil Ridings, saw the match on television in his Adelaide home and from 7 p.m. that Sunday evening his phone did not stop ringing with calls from the public, the cricket electorate and board members. Early on Monday the ACB executive director, David Richards, rang Ridings and they arranged for a telephone hookup of the board executive for 2.30 p.m. that day. Richards rang around and picked up the vibrations as he went. There was no sympathy for Greg. As a general rule those who were close to international cricket were more balanced than those who were not. Those who were at the game were swifter to cool their emotions than those who saw it on television. Richards then rang Greg.

To listen to the bio-rhythms of our captain that morning would be to hear a long, thin, dispirited sigh as he surveyed his own impotence. He threw the morning's newspapers on the floor and discerned that this was a moment to step back from confrontation with the ACB, rather than to continue arguing with Martin on the porch. 'In the cold light of day I could see that I just couldn't ignore it,' said Greg. 'I could not say no comment. Nor could I say I would do it again tomorrow if I had the chance.'

Richards was more than an acquaintance, less than a close friend. He appreciated that after WSC Greg had made an effort to establish a good rapport with the ACB. Richards' own opinion of the underarm was not generous. He thought Greg snapped under the enormous pressure. But he did not condemn Greg for that. It was essential for Richards to see Greg as guilty, but a first offender, to play the part of the ACB counsellor. 'The single best thing that Greg did after he stopped defending his position, was to recognize that it was a bit bigger than a legitimate tactic to prevent a very unlikely New Zealand tie,' said Richards. His advice was that Greg should don a cloak of humility. The consequences of being pig-headed could mean his departure as captain. To which Greg said, 'Quite honestly, if they want to do it, good luck to them.' He knew several ACB members had not forgiven him for his Packer defection. 'I couldn't have given them a better excuse,' he said.

But Richards was there to conciliate, not aggravate. He wanted to go to the board telephone hookup armed with an expression of regret. Was there any danger of Greg losing the captaincy? I asked. 'Yes,' said Richards. Between them Greg and Richards compiled a statement. 'He coughed and swallowed a few times, chose a few different words,' said Richards. 'Whether deep down he believed it or not didn't matter a damn. It was politics at that stage and he plays his politics quite well.' Mere politics or an abrogation of Greg's own soundly held principles? Greg spoke to Richards, Ridings and Bob Merriman by phone that morning. If the handpiece had been a rubber cosh they could not have more effectively subdued him. Of the Australian team in the hotel only Marsh, who popped his head in, and Lillee, who stayed, actively and demonstrably supported Greg. PBL liaison officer and WSC original Austin Robertson also offered assistance.

Richards took Greg's statement to the phone hookup, but he was armed also, it is said, with advice from the ACB's solicitor. Greg believed it was to discover whether they could sack him. Richards: 'It wouldn't surprise me if we did seek legal advice. That season was my first as executive director.' But he could not recall such advice. He might have double checked the ACB constitution, ensured no decisions trespassed the Trades Practices Act, he said. 'I like to know where I'm going before I debate these things.' Richards did not believe it would be fair to sack Greg. 'I could not see there was sufficient evidence to say, "Let's discard Gregory Stephen Chappell, great player."' Instead they humbled him. At 5 p.m. Monday a press conference, without Greg, issued two statements. Phil Ridings, on behalf of the board, deplored Greg's action which, though legal, 'is totally contrary to the spirit in which cricket has, and should be played'. Then Greg's:

> *I have always played cricket within the rules of the game.*
>
> *I took a decision yesterday which, whilst within the laws of cricket, in the cool light of day I recognize as not being within the spirit of the game.*
>
> *The decision was made whilst I was under pressure and in the heat of the moment.*
>
> *I regret the decision. It is something I would not do again.*

Before that Greg and Lillee were shepherded down a service lift by a security officer, out a back entrance and slipped off down the street to catch a taxi to a friend's for the afternoon, their anonymity miraculously intact. Greg was grateful for Lillee's company. He had felt completely abandoned and, though calm, and resigned, a shrill, primal defiance sang in him: Was it so wrong? Did he deserve this? Newspaper posters trumpeted the furore. Richie Benaud had repeated his obloquy in his afternoon newspaper column. This time he added a defence of the 'integrity' of one-day cricket. Precisely what that was, in a cricket format which, in three years since 1978, had been impaired by three major changes of fielding rules and others to bouncers or wayward balls, only Benaud knew.

Brother Ian had also weighed in with his newspaper column, but left his criticism at the cash level: 'Fair dinkum, Greg, how much pride do you sacrifice to win $35,000?' More than anyone those two ex-Australian captains, Benaud and Ian, dismayed Greg. They knew the pressures on captains. A more balanced reaction by them might have dampened rather than fed the hysteria. Greg's only criticism of Benaud was that if Benaud considered Greg got 0 out of 10 for his actions, Benaud deserved no more for his performance. Benaud has never expressed any contrition to Greg. Greg has never raised the incident with Benaud. Since then they have played golf together and they and their wives have dined together. Greg retains a respect for Benaud's career as a cricketer and as a commentator and journalist. In the years following the underarm Benaud never stinted in his praise of Greg as a cricketer. But if you could lay open the flesh of their relationship there you would find, dormant but unhealed, the canker of the underarm. Benaud did not mention it in his admirable book, *On Reflection* published in 1984, but I did come across the words which, in context and out, say it all. He wrote:

> *There is, other than the names of the participants, no connection between Test cricket and one-day cricket.*

Just so.

Jeanne and Martin Chappell were distressed by Ian's criticism. Jeanne rang Ian, 'I would never say anything against you if you did something wrong. I'd always support you, even if you were on a murder charge.' Ian understood that. Loyalty was his strong suit. But he thought Greg was wrong. 'If that's all he ever does wrong in many years of first class cricket then that's not bad,' he replied to Jeanne. 'But I don't think I can just sit back and make no comment or make a wishy-washy comment.' That was Ian's first year in television. It taught him the power of the medium. Because of that, although he had been writing newspaper columns for years, he would be less harsh on Greg if he had to write it again today. 'It's a very hard, touchy situation,' he said, 'but I think I'd still take the same stance.'

As for Benaud, Martin and Jeanne reeled back through their memory tapes and stopped, inevitably, at Benaud's appeal that dismissed West Indian Joe Solomon when his cap fell on his stumps in Melbourne in 1960. But Jeanne, who never once mistook a spade for a shovel, did not really see anything wrong with that. Or with Mankadding. 'I mean it's out. It's in the rules. Exactly the same as the underarm,' she said. 'I can't for the life of me see why they put on such a bloody turn.' Later when Martin asked Trevor if the underarm was his idea Trevor replied, 'Gosh, I'm not quick enough to think of that.' Then added puckishly, 'Anyway, what would I want to bowl underarm for? I could have got him out.'

By Monday night the stream of denunciation of Greg was in full flood. Tony Greig called for his sacking, Keith Miller said one-day cricket had died and Greg should be buried with it. The Prime Minister, Malcolm Fraser, could see no excuses for Greg's action under any circumstances. Harold Larwood deplored it, Bill O'Reilly felt humiliated. Sir Donald Bradman very cautiously stated, 'I totally disapprove of what happened yesterday. Action should be taken immediately to ensure it can never happen on a cricket field again.' Of the first 40 callers to the *Courier-Mail* in Greg's home town of Brisbane, only one defended Greg. At the ACB in Melbourne, which eventually received over 1,000 letters, the tide was running 90 per cent against Greg. Abusive mail began streaming in for Greg. One classic, from Madras, India, Greg had framed. It began:

> *Hello! Read the letter completely without fail. Greg Chappell: You are not fit to be a captain. Don't lead the team right from this moment... You and your companions are fit to play only North Ireland, Malaysia, Fiji and Israel.*

The author signed himself off in red ink, 'Big Bullshit to All.'

In New Zealand over the next few days it was not wise to declare your Matilda nationality. A coachload of Australian tourists were involved in a brawl while sightseeing. A magistrate strode into court and declared, 'I hope there are no Australians coming before me today.' It must be remembered that in New Zealand we are dealing with a country which equals Queensland on the Richter scale of inferiority and xenophobia and which depended upon its sportsmen, John Walker and the All Blacks to make an impact internationally. Their priority was sport before butter and it was quite in keeping that the chairman of the New Zealand Cricket Council, Robert Vance, suggested the ACB 'might care to cancel' Sunday's result. To Greg's satisfaction this was not possible. 'It wasn't against the rules,' said Greg. 'It was legal under the tour conditions. They couldn't fine us, they couldn't do a bloody thing.'

Not all cricket lovers had deserted Greg. When one man told retired masseur Dave McErlane after the underarm, 'That's the end of Australian cricket for me,' the Doc replied, 'I wouldn't call you an old fool, I'd just call you sentimental.' By Tuesday morning, 3 February, the backlash against the previous 24 hours of vilification had begun. Cables and letters started arriving in batches at the Sheraton and the SCG where the fourth final was to start that day. One telex came from Barry Maranta, his business colleague in Brisbane. It read: 'Permission to write you a script for Benaud. First word is Get ...' Greg rang him. Maranta devilishly suggested, 'In today's match when you get your first 50, turn to the TV commentary box and give them the old you-know-what.' In all the brouhaha it was overlooked that cricket was about batting and bowling and that Greg could provide 50 almost at the asking.

Sydney police escorted the team from their hotel to the SCG. A few crackpots had made threats. The team assembled at the SCG No. 2 to practise and nearby a bus halted and disgorged a band for pre-match entertainment. Ian, who had not spoken to Greg since writing his column, arrived at the same time. As Ian approached Greg gestured towards the musicians and said to him, 'You should have come on the bloody bus with all those other bastards who are on the bandwagon.' Ian stopped. 'I'm a journalist, pal, I give my opinion. If you don't agree, that's your problem.' Ian was not bothered that it would harm their long-term relationship. They had argued all their lives and would again.

In the dressing-room the team began papering one wall with telegrams supporting Greg, and another with those against. The wall supporting Greg quickly filled, the other was nearly bare. They came signed by little old ladies, from teenagers, from whole families, from fan clubs, cricket clubs and shop employees. From Mackay to Dubbo, Burnie to Texas, Orange and Canberra. A flood came from Perth, a State that understands isolation and loves winning. Simple cables like, 'Hang in there Greg' and 'Hit a ton and ignore them' and longer versions such as, 'The boys from the west are behind you Greg win at all costs nobody salutes a loser and you're the winner to us, good luck today.' Another read, 'Get out there and win don't let your critics including Piggy [Muldoon] dismay you answer with a century.' There were 91 for and 10 against. To read through those telegrams is to have faith restored in the humanity of Australians after the early acrimony heaped upon Greg. As one writer said: 'Now you can see how easy it was for Christ to get crucified.'

Greg tested the temper of the SCG crowd when he inspected the wicket and again when he and Geoff Howarth tossed. He had Graeme Wood's white handkerchief in his pocket to wave if the reception was hostile. He need not have worried. The cheers overlaid the boos. When he came out to bat, the senior director of television for Channel Nine's cricket, Brian C. Morelli, in his outside broadcast van, instructed his cameraman, 'OK give me a shot of Killer.' It was just a name that sprung to mind but it stuck with the camera team until Greg retired. They almost addressed him as such when they spoke to him off-field. Geoff Howarth knew Sydney was full of Kiwis who would look for blood at the slightest encouragement from the New Zealand team. He instructed no player to ignite the fuse of a potentially explosive situation. When Greg came out to bat Howarth was fielding near Greg's path to the crease. To Howarth Greg was simply 'a great bloke'. As Greg passed they exchanged a few pleasantries and Howarth patted Greg on the bottom and wished him good luck. Greg was nervous and not unappreciative. 'Geoff was good; the whole New Zealand team was good actually,' he said.

It did not save them. Greg played an implacable innings, turning to the keystone of his public life, his batsmanship, to restore his shaken ego. The nearer to 50 his score, the wider became Barry Maranta's grin. 'You wait, you watch,' Maranta told his puzzled family, called to scan the television screen. At Greg's half century the SCG cheered and Greg turned straight around and upped his bat to the Nine commentary box. Thanks for your understanding, fellas, he thought coldly and proceeded to 87, sufficient for an Australian victory. And the series.

In the next two weeks the tide fully turned. The Anglican Dean of Brisbane, Reverend Ian George, wrote in his *Courier-Mail* column:

> *Greg Chappell... has always displayed a graceful demeanour with a modest smile and rarely has any word of acrimony crossed his lips even when considerably provoked...*
>
> *Let it clearly be said that he was perfectly within his rights, he was within the rules of the game, he was involved in a business activity for the purpose of winning considerable sums of money for his little company or team.*

A Melbourne priest, Father Michael Long, wrote in his Moreland parish newspaper:

> *I, for one, am jealous of Greg Chappell (and his family) as sportsmen... I am prepared to stand beside him and stand for him anytime. In my view the people who condemned Greg Chappell have made very little contribution to sport and to say the least- ... their motives for condemning him are suspect.*

Four days after the underarm the *Courier-Mail* had received 199 unsolicited letters on the underarm, the most ever received on a single subject. Of these 81 criticized Greg, 78 defended him and 40 seemed neutral.

One supportive letter, from Sister Ann O'Conor, of the Xavier Hospital for Children, Brisbane, published in the *Courier-Mail*, intrigued me. It emerged Greg 'played' cricket for several years with their physically handicapped children. 'The first few visits to Xavier I dreaded it,' said Greg. 'I wished something would prevent me from going but nothing ever did.' One boy, who walked on his knees, tossed a plastic ball high up to a bed-ridden mate who belted it with a toy bat, to be fielded by another boy entirely encased in a material to stop his skin peeling away. It tore at Greg's heart. Then he began to enjoy the visits because it took so little to make the kids so hugely happy. Sister O'Conor's letter returned Greg's kindness.

I asked Greg whether a little bit of his love for cricket died during that horrendous week. No, he said. It just confirmed his belief that many people closely associated with the game did not understand how quickly it had changed. 'I tried to tell the administrators it was a symptom,' he said. 'More such incidents would occur if they didn't relieve the captain of pressure. I'd said for years, "I shouldn't be expected to do as much as I have to." ' From that trauma emerged media managers and other support staff for the Australian captain. The ACB discovered precisely Greg's calibre when his successor, Kim Hughes, lasted less than two seasons as full-time captain.

No part of this biography was as hard to obtain as that just retold. It was painful for Greg, like undergoing psychotherapy to unearth wounding memories — memories he would prefer to forget than relive for yet one more catharsis. He heaved his shoulders, was uncomfortable, stared at the table for so many seconds sometimes I wondered whether he would reply. If I offered an opinion he gazed hard at me in case he could divine new light from my words. There existed some people in cricket who would like to have seen him like that, vulnerable, stripped of that Clint Eastwood, flint-hard face, and straight bearing — seen him wilting, the innate dignity faltering. But they never caught him out because it did not change him on the surface, where his opponents dealt with him. It changed him deep down, in his understanding of human nature. To see him like that was disturbing because I glimpsed the passing of an original innocence that most of us have long forgotten or foregone.

For some hours we ploughed back and forth across those barren days, raking over the stumps of unkindnesses, the potholes of ill-will, turning up a rare gem, like Lillee's loyalty, and then, increasingly, the semi-precious telegrams of support, and the vivifying columns by the servants of God. 'This will be the last time you will have to relive this,' I offered sympathetically. He looked up and grinned. 'No, mate, they will never let me forget.' When he retired he had played 48 Tests as captain of Australia, five days per Test: 240 days, at six hours a day — '1,400 hours as captain of Australia and I cocked it up for 30 seconds and I'll probably be remembered more for that than the other 1,400 hours.'

Not really. With time it may be seen that Greg represented an exalted ideal of conduct thrust upon him by a nation that sought celluloid romanticism from their television screen idol. He fitted the image so easily, proud bearing, stern of face, that damned illusionary batting stance. He became the focus for a national identity, carrying on the myths proposed in the bush and seconded at Gallipoli. He was lionized as the Australian who became a world beater without ever transgressing some superb, intangible code which Australians asked him to keep because they could never themselves. Greg was not averse to accepting that role because he is something of a perfectionist. But grafted onto that quality stock was the new breed of Australian whose morality is success legitimately achieved and that was how the myth and the man were cleft by the underarm. When Greg fell he turned the mirror upon his makers and if they were aghast it was because he had failed them in their own impossible vision. But that was inevitable — life imitating art is forever dangerous for being unreal.

For months, years afterwards, at the slightest opportunity cricket crowds brayed their reminders to Greg. But slowly the incident became depersonalized from Greg himself, to enter the folklore of New Zealand and Australia as a symbol of the perfidy of the great and glorious continent towards that island ingenue. Three and a half years later, New Zealand's newly elected Prime Minister, David Lange, in an interview with Huw Evans on the ABC's 'Pressure Point', said New Zealanders had no desire to join an Australasian commonwealth, but not because of 'that macho stuff, us and them, underarm and all that', and viewers understood exactly what he meant.

Trevor was briefly razzed every time he played in a match which developed a tight finish: 'Bring on the underarm bowler.' It annoyed him at first until he became reconciled. The media soon dropped off him, not even a phone call after a few days. He could have refused to bowl the ball. 'But it was in the rules and there to be taken advantage of if the situation called for it,' he said. 'When I look back, I think they over-reacted. It just wasn't that bad.' Strangely he had never spoken to Greg about it from that day on. Neither of them ever brought it up. But then again, what was there to say? Much later when Ian and Greg were yarning Greg said with a smile, 'I guess it's just as well you didn't agree with the underarm, because I ordered it, and Trevor bowled it, and if you'd agreed with it they would have thought we were all bloody mad.' It was a magnanimous family peace gesture from Greg. He hated disputes or feuds no matter how low current they were. And he knew that once Ian had taken his stance a caterpillar tractor would not move him.

In New Zealand a favourite question in sports quizzes became: Who was the batsman at the non-striker's end when the underarm ball was bowled? Nine out of 10 fans can't remember, even though Rod Marsh rated Bruce Edgar's century as one of the finest he had witnessed in one-day cricket.

And that was the season that was. All except for the third and last Test against India in which captain Sunil Gavaskar, enraged at being

215

given out lbw, ordered his batting partner Chetan Chauhan to leave the field with him. In an ordinary season such a bizarre occurrence — the second time in Greg's career a captain risked forfeiting a Test by walking off (the first was Illingworth) — might command massive media attention. But in that summer of sensation it paled in importance. Greg was sympathetic to Gavaskar, who had a lean batting trot in Australia. 'When things are going bad you tend to notice your bad luck,' said Greg. 'Things seem a lot worse than they really are.' Impossible as it may seem, the awful irony of that insight Greg was about to discover for himself.

22. Ms Judy

In the weeks following the underarm Judy went about her usual life in the expansive L-shaped bungalow she and Greg had bought from Ashley and Helen Cooper in Kenmore. The tennis court waited empty, swept by summer leaves, the swimming pool lay still and blue, reflecting the limitless sky. Greg had been on the Test trail for months. She had seen little of him. Nothing new. But the underarm had hurt. It marked the beginning of the end. She had put off as long as possible confronting cricket knowing all the time that sooner or later she might have to.

In just over 10 years of marriage Judy rarely complained to Greg of how alienated cricket could make her feel. She was nearly 22 when they married. She could never have anticipated cricket's totalitarianism, but she had submitted as the loyal little housewife women were expected to be at the start of the 1970s. Her own interests, music, church and teaching career fell away, wholly, amazingly, like the backdrop of a changed stage scene. She learned new etiquettes — never walk in front of a sight screen, don't move to your seat until the end of an over. On the 1976 Wanderers' tour of South Africa she became aware of how unremittingly a man's man Greg's fraternal upbringing had made him. In between matches when other players joined their wives sightseeing Greg would as likely join Ian and Richie Benaud for a game of golf. She occasionally interrupted his preoccupations. She looked back amusedly at the time the refrigerator door fell off. Greg was playing golf. Judy thought, 'Someone's got to help me and it's got to be Greg.' She rang the clubhouse and paged him. 'What's broken?' he asked. 'Your leg?' No, the door, the door of the fridge. 'Oh,' said Greg. 'Everything else OK?'

When he left for tours the first week for Judy was always the worst. One night, at 1.30 a.m., pregnant with Belinda, Stephen only two years old, she heard footsteps on the roof. She lay petrified, fear prickling her skin as the steps searched the gutters for a way in. It was what she had feared, her living nightmare, that encumbered with unborn Belinda, she would not be able to pick up Stephen and flee. She gathered her courage, crept to the telephone and breathlessly dialled her neighbour. He rushed over to shine his torch at a possum on the roof. In the end Judy developed a policy: 'Blow them, I'd rather not know about it. They can rob me while I'm asleep.' She needed that rationale for her sanity. More mundane challenges she overcame. Fuse wires were a snap, tap washers were less easy.

Even when Greg was at home during the cricket season their privacy was violated by the telephone. 'He saw what happened to Bill Lawry who was abrupt with the press and then with Ian who tried to help the press,' said Judy. 'He resolved to take a middle road, but they took advantage of him.' She sat in their family room listening as Greg repeated his views to callers who exhibited the apparent sensitivities of a fence post. 'You've explained that to them a thousand times,' she would call, shaking her head as Greg's verbosity stole the hours. Judy grew to resent cricket officials and went through a brief period of rejecting them, eschewing their company at matches, pulling the telephone plug out if a controversy was brewing. But she knew that to reject any portion of cricket was a contradiction in terms, married to Greg. Then there were the written requests, three or four a day, to appear, to talk, to be a guest, to judge, to raise funds for inevitably worthy causes and, a hundred times, requests for his favourite recipe — but we all know what that is, Doc McErlane told us: banana and mustard on toast.

When Greg and Judy moved from Adelaide to Brisbane she joined Chapel Hill Uniting Church, which reminded her of Bexley Methodist of her childhood. She began bible study: 'An incredible book.' But as her children arrived, her time diminished, though her faith remained, a personal combination of fundamentalism and pantheism. She would stand at her kitchen sink, looking out at a glorious blue Queensland summer's sky, set against grey-green trees and silver trunks and think, 'I know You're outside there,' or inside her looking out. She could not share it with Greg. Salvation and the eternal spirit were not his concept of a greater omnipotence. Prayer was a source of strength to Judy, especially at those moments when her own tolerance was stretched to misery point. She had said a prayer for Greg during the underarm crisis. She used to remonstrate with herself, 'Righto, don't give up hope because you know that just through asking for help, some good will come, even if not in the form you want it.' Judy marvelled at the number of times, having uttered that prayer, a friend would arrive on the doorstep or the telephone would ring: 'Bring Stephen over for the day.' Or the Marantas: 'Come over and sleep the night,' whereupon the Marantas' three daughters would take over the children.

The satisfaction of learning to survive by herself — almost as a deserted mother during the five month England tours and three month West Indies tours — was offset by the adjustment necessary when Greg returned. Instead of being an independent person, thinking, 'I'm going there, I'm invited to that,' it became the plural and sent Judy's sense of identity skew-whiff again. Absence did not make their hearts grow fonder. Said Judy, 'I used to believe that. But I don't now.' Sometimes when Greg returned they were almost shy with each other, unused to the intimacy of daily life together — marriage. Said Judy, 'It was so unnatural. We didn't share in the nitty-gritty of life. We couldn't laugh over little things.' Then Greg would start to recount memories of the tour and gradually a picture of his life for the missing months would emerge. And the processes of renewal and rediscovery would unite them again.

Judy was not immune to harbouring resentment towards Greg's free-wheeling summer life — he's having a great time while I'm slogging away with the kids — and to top it, he might innocently remark when he returned, 'Gee, it's hard to adjust back to home life after travelling.'

The children had different modes of coping. Stephen was in conflict about Dad's departures. He was proud of him as Australian captain but he missed him too. He would grab Greg's arm and say, 'Don't go,' and maybe shed a tear. Belinda had her own defence: a pretence that she did not care. She would not wave goodbye and proffered a kiss only if asked. Jonathan was too young to know. Greg brought back little gifts for them, usually a doll for Belinda, but it was never compensation nor meant to be. As the children grew older they too began to resent the unwelcome attentions of autograph hunters and oglers when the family went out. For privacy and safety Greg and Judy banned publicity for them. One day, at the 'Gabba, a club attendant advised Judy he had seen Stephen go by with Peter Meares, the ABC cricket commentator. The good-natured Meares was an acquaintance, Judy relaxed, and then jumped up: an interview! She intervened just as the hapless Meares was about to start a live television interview — friends watching television recognized Judy's skirt as she swished in and out of focus. Meares was all apologies. He had seen photographs of the children in a magazine, presumed them recent and that she and Greg had changed their minds.

Judy's first stirrings of discontent with her cricket wife's life surfaced through her love of music. She did not have the equivalent of Greg's love of cricket — if she had she would have succeeded Joan Sutherland. But Judy had perfect pitch and learned to read music at school. Consequently she was always landed with the alto harmony parts in choirs while the mob galloped on with the melody. In 1979 she took private tutor lessons to ensure her vocal cords were still in key and joined the Queensland Light Opera Company. Greg proudly saw her sing in the chorus of *The White Horse Inn* at Her Majesty's Theatre that year. For two mad months her rehearsals turned the house haywire. Greg returned from cricket practice early to find dinner on the table, the children bathed and fed and Judy a choralling vision splendid, disappearing out the door. A small step towards redressing the balance of careers in the house.

Jonathan's birth in early 1980 was the turning point. As mother-in-law Jeanne put it, 'You can cope with two, take them most places, but you haven't got three hands. That's when she put the weights on.' Well, not quite like that. Judy tended to repress her feelings rather than broach them, not a useful habit for problem solving. But the approach of the 1980–81 summer provided a stark contrast in husband and wife perceptions.

Judy: *About a month before the club season I started to get uptight. It was a feeling of tension, 'Oh, here we go again. He's off again.'*

Greg: *I always found the cricket season relaxing. The leadup was hectic tying up loose ends at work, bit of trauma at home, family getting edgy because you're always going on tour.*

Judy was not untouched by the feminist revolution which by 1980 revealed to women of the western world their chains, even if it did not unshackle them. At the very moment Judy was awakening from her 10 year marital sleep she read two books which helped focus her feelings. *Passages* by Gail Sheehy neatly compartmentalized the stages of life which bind women. It also presented a typical male syndrome, the wunderkind, with which the sports world was peopled. Wunderkinds played to win, and blurred dividing lines between work and private life. Wunderkinds invariably married caregivers, wives who formed a sanctuary which freed the men to work, or play, at the cost of the caregiver's own freedom.

The second book was *The Cinderella Complex* by Colette Dowling, which in essence showed how Judy, only 21, sacrificed her own substantial achievements when she opted for Prince Charming Greg as he strode by in his baggy green cap. One chapter, Flight from Independence, even described a contralto singer, Carolyn, who ignored an opera career for the security of marriage and two children. She was desperately unhappy by 30 and divorced at 40. Carolyn seemed too close for comfort.

Both those books identified the fear growing in Judy's mind that her years of motherhood had left her a bland, uninteresting person. She had the children, yes, and good friends. But she paid for their comfort with her isolation. She had scarcely read, seen films, attended theatre or concerts. She had grown inwards, explored and expanded nowhere. Now she longed for life's true promise, to be inspired. What hit Judy at 30 she shunted straight at Greg because she felt almost in a panic that they should talk about it. She had long repressed her objections, easily done with Greg whose family background did not encourage enquiry into feelings. 'For me to suddenly speak out was probably a bit of a shock to him,' said Judy. 'He used to go away and walk around and think it out.'

If Greg required any convincing of the pressure cricket was putting on his family the Year of the Underarm provided it. 'I was being paid for the stress of it,' he said. 'It wasn't part of their job. They just had to cop it.' As an ancillary, though not necessarily related matter, Ian and Kay Chappell's divorce sent shock waves through the Chappell clan. Greg calculated that if it had not been for World Series Cricket he would probably have been out of Test cricket by 1980. Ian had begun in 1965, retired in 1975. Greg began in 1969. 'The normal expectation in modern times was 10 years,' he said. 'I'd been playing that long, been away for almost half of it.'

Judy's anxiety gave Greg pause. 'I think I made the assumption that she was happy in her role as a mother with the children,' he said, 'and that she fully understood how much cricket meant to me. But I came to realize over the years — if I made a mistake — it was that it went on too long. It got beyond the realms of the reasonable.' Judy made it clear to him that she and the children had suffered, that trying to be mother and father was wearing her down. She said, 'It's up to you. I'm just letting you know how I feel. You're the one that has to make the decision.' Greg caught the nuances. She was not saying anything that she knew could rebound on her, or them, for the rest of their lives. But the time had come. Greg withdrew from the 1981 tour of England. No more long tours. That was the compromise.

It sounds almost comical in its gravity. It would have been less like drawing a tooth but for the underarm. Though disenchanted with cricket in some respects, Greg was also anxious to redeem himself in the eyes of the world, not just New Zealand or Australia. An England tour, coming so soon, would have been ideal, rather than having to wait for the domestic 1981–82 season. Judy discerned that Greg would love to have toured. It made his withdrawal all the more significant. If Kim Hughes succeeded in England Greg might never regain the captaincy, would never regain the Ashes, the loss of which he felt so personally — might never restore his reputation.

23. *Ducks*

Greg's philosophy of life embraced a rather stoical Christianity-cum-fatalism, revolving around a theory of balance — that there is an evening up process. No one is given things or has them taken away all the time, perhaps a personalized version of Job 1.21, 'The Lord gave and the Lord taketh away.' Greg believed in an omniscient spirit but saw no reason to attend church. 'He could just as easily come to my place as me to His,' smiled Greg. Nor did he use his faith as a crutch, more as a thanksgiving for his family, for Judy and three healthy kids. He believed life was part of an overall plan in which each person had a blueprint wherein they came to crossroads and got to make a choice. A test. Make the wrong decision, live with it. 'Perhaps it is sent to punish you, to test your mettle,' theorized Greg. 'To take you to the limit of your suffering to make you a better person.' But if you lived a reasonable life, close to the Christian ethic, there would be more good days than bad. That was the bargain He struck.

When I defended Greg's underarm command in the *National Times* that week in 1981, I noted that in his expressions of regret he did not once use the word 'apologize'. For what? To whom? It was not difficult therefore to see how his holier-than-thou critics might interpret the season about to descend on him. They would turn to the opening lines of Ecclesiastes and brandish them to his face: 'Vanity of vanity ... All is vanity.'

During Australia's calamitous 1981 tour of England Greg stayed up the crucial nights to watch. 'In a situation where you couldn't lose it, they lost it,' said Greg with a disbelieving shake of his head. He resolved in the small hours after Headingley to at least play on the side that won the Ashes back before he retired. If he could captain the side, so much the better. Greg was unambivalent about the captaincy. Decorum demanded he declare himself happy to play under Kim Hughes. But he fooled few, least of all David Richards, executive director of the ACB. Richards read the headlines: 'I'm A Good Captain — Chappell' and 'Hughes Must Fight for Place — Chappell'. Greg may not have written the headlines but he spoke his mind when interviewed. Said Richards, 'It was almost like he was running a campaign. I've always felt he was a little indiscreet.' The ACB had adopted a policy of not penalizing players for missing tours. Thus when Hughes was held responsible for Ian Botham's superhuman feats Greg was offered the captaincy for 1981–82 in a far from unanimous vote. Greg sounded out Rod, Dennis and other England tourists. The response was universal. 'For God's sake take it. If you'd seen what happened in England. Don't bail out on us.'

In a way Hughes' failure in England assuaged some of the pique Greg had felt about his own reputation as captain. 'Ian was a better captain than I was,' he said. 'I did a workmanlike job, he did a very skilful job.' Even so Ian always had the same nucleus of players, whereas Greg's captaincy straddled the decline of one era and the formation of another. Compared with Ian, Greg's ability was devalued; compared with Hughes, Greg looked brilliant. He would like to edge a little closer to Ian.

The season began inauspiciously. In the first Test against Pakistan in Perth, Lillee aimed a kick at Javed Miandad, who sought to reply by crowning Lillee with his bat. Greg did not endear himself to press or public by defending Lillee. He argued that Miandad, while pretending to look to fine leg, knew precisely where Lillee was standing. Furthermore, when they collided Miandad gave Lillee a quick little jab in the stomach with his bat handle. They had been niggling each other, as they always did, and both were to blame. More reports, more explanations. But Greg had a gutful of media inquisition. He marched into the post-match press conference and demanded militantly, 'Well, would anybody like to talk about cricket?' By the time the extended press conference was finished and explanations tendered he was late for a theatre booking he had made for himself and Judy, who was on holidays in Perth. Dangerously late when the artist in question was Barry Humphries, but Edna, obviously a cricketophile, let the late-comers off the hook.

In Brisbane for the second Test, Stephen, now nearly seven, took umbrage at television criticism of his father's form. Greg had scored only 48 runs in his previous five innings. He told ABC commentator, Peter Meares, 'I feel fine. There's a big score just around the corner. I'm just not quite sure how long the street is.' To Stephen he confided, 'I'll get 100 for you.' When 76 not out at stumps he expanded it, 'I'll make it 200.' Stephen was at the 'Gabba when Greg reached his double century and waved his bat to his son in the stand.

Greg led Australia to a 2–1 Test series win over Pakistan and averaged 50.20 runs, close to his career target. But in Melbourne in the third Test, second innings, he was caught Miandad, bowled Sarfraz for a duck. That was 15 December 1981. Two days later, in a one-day match against Pakistan in Sydney, he was out for a duck again. Three days later, 20 December in Perth, another duck in a one-day against the West Indies. And then six days on, 26 December, on the first ball of the first innings of the first Test against the West Indies in Melbourne, his fourth consecutive duck. For a batsman of Greg's world standing it was an unprecedented sequence of failures — four ducks in 11 days went beyond the laws of coincidence. West Indian doctor, Rudi Webster, who had first diagnosed Lillee's spinal fracture eight years before in the West Indies, dropped into the Australian dressing-room. 'I don't want to get on the bandwagon with this advice, but I just wondered if you had thought about whether you were watching the ball?' he said. Greg smiled and thanked him and returned to his dolour. Of course he was watching the bloody ball, what else would he watch?

The magnitude of those ducks bewildered Greg. If he was to maintain his career average of 50 odd (even his one-day match average was over 40) he would have to score 250 in his next innings. He made just 12. That was in the first innings of the second Test against the West Indies. In the second innings, another blot. He told himself this street was just a little longer than the one he had talked about in Brisbane with Peter Meares. If he just kept applying himself. The cartoons started, funny at first, but dripping water tortures in time. Arriving for matches schoolchildren stood silent as their teetering idol passed and then the bravest would squawk, 'Quack, quack'. Greg would mutter, 'You rotten little so-and-sos' and return them a strained, good natured smile. Once at the MCG a duck was shoved over the fence as Greg walked out to bat. 'They'd gone to a bit of trouble to get the duck so they deserved a laugh,' he said.

But in the dressing-room he was not laughing. Fewer people were talking to him and he, an inveterate talker, was saying less. He was tense, worried about his footwork, anxious at the crease and thinking, 'Come on, bowl so I can score.' It was a desperate rush for runs, destined to fail, all exacerbated by his desire to prove his captaincy, prove himself after the underarm. His Year of Recovery was collapsing from within. He resigned himself to his fate. 'You almost see it happening to someone else so you can live with it,' he said. 'I didn't feel as though I was going insane. I wasn't going to slash my wrists. It was just a matter of time.' For what? The pressure had to find a release and it did.

The MCG, 10 January, a one-day against the West Indies, 25 days after the start of the duck sequence. *Wisden* records: 'Batting was never easy on another poor Melbourne pitch...' Behind that mild criticism lay explosive action. For three years Greg, Clive Lloyd, Desmond Haynes and many others had criticized the MCG pitch as disgraceful. But Greg criticized it most because Australia played on it most. Greg lost the toss and Lloyd sent Australia in. Joel Garner knocked Bruce Laird's helmet off in his first over and Graeme Wood narrowly missed being struck. Greg was livid. 'They had watered the pitch to hold it together and the first couple of balls went straight through the top,' said Greg. He was next in. He turned to Allan Border darkly. 'Get the bloody pads on. I've got something to sort out here and if we lose a wicket you'll have to go in.'

Greg strode from the players' room to the executive room next door and confronted Bob Parish, immediate past ACB chairman, referee for that day. 'That bloody wicket's dangerous,' said Greg. 'If you don't call the game off, I will. Somebody's going to get hurt out there today.' Greg's voice was tight and clear. A roomful of Victorian Cricket Association guests turned from the cricket to this rival attraction. Someone pulled a concertina room divider to separate the VCA view room and guests from Greg and Parish. It was not soundproof. Parish was incredulous. 'We can't call the game off,' he said. 'We've got

70,000 people here. They'll howl the place down.' Greg said he would howl the place down if one of his players was hit. 'If that happens I'll call them off. The responsibility is laid fairly at your feet, not mine.' And strode out.

Greg was right. The pitch was a minefield. The previous month, December 1981, the ACB resolved that the VCA require the MCG fix the pitch or else. 'That was made known because we were finally making sure GC and his team got the support they deserved,' said ACB chief executive David Richards. 'Greg has never been known for his patience and he jumped in the deep end again. He put himself in a position that was not winnable.' A man like Parish, virtually managing director of Australian cricket administration for the previous five years, would not take kindly to being addressed like that in the public gaze. Said Richards, 'It made it hard for Greg's supporters to argue why they should continue to support him.' On that evidence Greg's confrontation was unjustified. But leafing through Greg's dog-eared correspondence I came across the carbon of a letter he wrote to Richards in December 1980, more than a year earlier. It formally registered his dissatisfaction with the state of the MCG, which he had complained about for the past two seasons. He wrote urgently recommending:

No further first class fixtures should be played at the MCG until a trial proves that first class playing conditions can be provided at the ground.

For three seasons Greg had warned about the MCG pitch — three seasons to provoke the ACB into action. While the niceties of protocol were certainly ignored by Greg, cricket captaincy constantly requires an individual to make decisions on behalf of his team. It encourages a superior confidence and when under pressure Greg trusted himself. He is adamant he would have made his full frontal assault on Parish whether his form was good or poor. My own view is that it also showed he was on a short fuse.

In his next two one-day matches Greg scored 36 and 61, but then in Sydney on 19 January, he was lbw to Roberts for another duck. The bad streak had become national news. Letters and phone calls began to mount up again, remedies, tonics, suggestions and cures, some sensible, some crank, nearly all kind-hearted. Judy insisted Greg follow up one suggestion from former Olympic sprinter, Mike Agostini, who told her about a sports psychologist, Dr Arthur Jackson, in Sydney. Jackson decided Greg was caught in the classic bind of all top sportsmen, the fear of failure which causes them to fail further. He diagnosed Greg's problem as trait anxiety, that which occurs only in specific situations. He hypnotized Greg and implanted confidence building suggestions and cues for concentration and relaxation. 'Greg had always used a lot of mental rehearsal, so it wasn't difficult,' said Dr Jackson. 'He was highly hypnotizable, probably because of his powers of concentration and relaxation.' Did it help? Did it work? Well, something did eventually. But not yet.

Trevor Chappell knew what was wrong: 'He kept nicking 'em,' he said drolly. Once Trevor and Steve Rixon were driving to Newcastle, listening to the cricket on radio. Greg came in to bat, Trevor left the car for a minute to ask some fishermen on a bridge if they were biting and when he climbed back in, Greg was out. Ian commented to Greg that he did not seem as well organized mentally as in the past. 'If that continues for any length of time, you've got to think that it might be the right time to get out,' said Ian. 'Once you start those signs it's either getting close or the time has come.'

That moment appeared to have arrived on 24 January at the MCG, where so much of Greg's destiny seemed to have been decided in the past 12 months. The previous day, the first one-day final against the West Indies, Greg went lbw to Garner for four. This day he did worse. Garner bowled him for one. According to Rod Marsh in *The Gloves of Irony*, Greg returned to the dressing-room, shook Rod's hand and said, 'Well, that's it pal, thanks for all the good times we've had during our careers, I'm officially retired.' Greg did not recall retiring at that moment. What he did say, 30 seconds after he slumped in the dressing-room, was to the twelfth man, 'Get me Phil Ridings.' Ridings, ACB chairman, arrived within minutes and he and Greg sat down in a huddle for half an hour. Greg declared his despondency. 'I'm sick of it. I don't feel I'm doing the team or myself any good. No one has talked about leaving me out of the side. I'd like to bring it up.' Greg had thought for some days that his illustrious career was working against him. A younger player would have been dropped to find form. Greg's record was so consistent that everyone thought it was just a matter of time. They gave him more and more chances to fail over and over.

Ridings replied exactly that. 'Your form is not always going to remain like it is,' he said. 'There has been no suggestion inside the selection room that you be left out of the side.' He was chairman of selectors, he would know. Greg then suggested he step down from the captaincy, let Kim Hughes take over and Greg concentrate on batting. Riding replied, 'I think you're unwise doing that, but it's up to you. I'm prepared to accept your resignation, but not before you sleep on it overnight.' Ridings was returning to Adelaide. He would call Greg in the morning. Ridings told me, 'He had tons of support, from the board and the selectors. There was no one in the side to compare with him.'

There was something forlorn about that conversation. It was almost a plea. Greg's confidence was so shot that he was testing the shadows for threats that did not exist. Aged 33, financially secure, loved husband and adored father, it seems unimaginable that sport could bring him so undone. But cricket was a hard mistress. However much he had enjoyed its charms, cricket could call in that debt.

That night, early morning to be exact, Rod Marsh, imbued with the team spirit engendered by a late meeting of most of the players, woke Greg. The team was behind Greg, said Marsh. 'You stay as captain, I'll do all the work,' said Rod. 'You just stand there and relax and enjoy your cricket.' Marsh was genuine, no doubt. But he also knew who would succeed Greg as captain — they had experienced Kim Hughes in England. The next morning Greg told Ridings, 'If there is genuinely no pressure to stand down, I'll stay. If the selectors want to make a change for the tour of New Zealand, that's fine.' Ridings told him anything they could do to help, they would. Two days later, in Sydney, in the third one-day final, Joel Garner bowled Greg for a duck.

Where did Greg go from there? He sat down and thought about it. 'I felt in control of myself, as much as you can in a situation totally out of control,' said Greg. He had played 10 years but suffered comparatively few bad trots. For not having a dispersed record of small failures, he was suffering a large lump of them all together. He ruffled through the pack of causes to blame. The backlash from the underarm. Whenever he went to Melbourne he could be sure of a smart alec underarm quip. Not Sydney, just conservative Melbourne. Then there was the MCG pitch, that hallowed turf, which he had blasted. Some Melbourne newspapers were offended. And there was home. He knew that Judy was upset about his being away, even for the domestic season. 'If she could have argued me out of it, she would have, but she wasn't game to,' he said. 'But she couldn't hide her disappointment and frustration.' Whenever Greg returned home, even if he had only been away for the day, he was aware, if the children had been cranky, there was stress in the air. 'I had real qualms about what I was doing,' he said. 'I felt guilty and yet I knew deep down I had to do it. It was not going to solve Judy's problems or mine if I stopped.'

In this quandary he flew to Adelaide for the last Test against the West Indies and here the Gothic horror story that had become Greg's season reached its denouement. It began with him having his eyes tested. It seems ludicrous in retrospect, the man who would take a world record number of catches, most of them in slips where nicks flew like shadows, who saw fast bowling so early he played the quickest with grace, doubting his eyes. The optometrist prescribed weak reading glasses which he now uses for the fine print.

The day before Greg arrived in Adelaide, John Coomber, an experienced Australian Associated Press journalist in Wellington, New Zealand, idly leafed through a souvenir programme for the forthcoming tour by Australia. It contained an article by Sir Donald Bradman. Towards the end of the article Coomber read a paragraph referring to New Zealand's 1980–81 tour of Australia. It said:

> *The sportsmanship of the captain, Geoff Howarth, was quite outstanding, especially in a moment of extreme provocation, a blot on the spirit of the game which no apology from the Australian captain could erase.*

Coomber extracted that paragraph and wrote a brief story which was published in Australian newspapers on 28 January under a variety of headings typified by 'Sir Donald Blasts Underarm Incident'. In Adelaide the *News* published a placard reading: 'Bradman Lashes Chappell'. Bradman's article was over 1,000 words long, and the paragraph which ignited such headlines contained just 34 words. Bradman's defence was that the paragraph did not mention Greg by name, nor the underarm. It is a specious argument. Who else was the Australian captain, if not Greg? What was the 'blot' if not the underarm?

Sir Donald's article was an otherwise historic, moderate and constructive piece in praise of the progress of New Zealand cricket. But his own experience with the media should have warned him to stay his hand with any gratuitous, scarcely camouflaged, references to the underarm. With Greg almost certain to lead the Australian team on tour in a matter of weeks the New Zealanders needed no reminding.

Bradman may not have known the exact timing of the publication of his article in the souvenir programme, but when would have been a good time for such a remark? Bradman and the rest had their say in February 1981. Any further reference inevitably raised suspicions, however incorrect, of malice aforethought. Greg read the news reports of Sir Donald's article. He did not call for his pen and ink, he did not rend his shirt, he did not seek to address the Houses of Parliament. He made no comment.

In Brisbane Judy joined the fray over Greg's poor form. 'Until now people have treated him like a superhero,' she told one newspaper. 'They didn't realize he was human.' Seven ducks in 16 innings from 15 December to January 27 had proved that. But what really depressed Judy were the rumours that his bad run was caused by an imminent marriage break-up. Sheepish reporters knocked at her door and mumbled the question: Were she and Greg living together? Judy tried to make light of it all. 'As a matter of fact, we're not,' she would smile. 'Greg hasn't been living here for the past six weeks and he won't be for another six yet. But we're not separated in the sense you mean. He's playing cricket.' In the end she rang Greg and put her position. The rumours were not going to die a natural death. She was sick of them. The longer they were allowed to fester the worse they would get. 'It's about time I said something to kill them,' said Judy. 'Are you happy with that?' Greg supported whatever she decided. From that agreement came a front page story across six columns in the *Australian* newspaper. Over a large photograph of Judy ran a headline: 'It's a short-term job and life-long love' — Judy's description of the role of cricket in Greg's life. The story was written by a journalist who Judy knew, Jacky Archer, daughter of Ron Archer, former Australian all-rounder in the 1950s era. Judy was frank in the interview. The continual separation was hard, sportsmen's wives played second fiddle and, 'I guess I'm living proof that it's hard to get used to loneliness.' The rumours were rubbish, she told Archer. She and Greg had a giggle about them.

Judy was not laughing. She was lonely. The *Australian* story appeared on 28 January, the same day the Bradman story hit the newspapers. Husband in Adelaide and wife in Brisbane could hardly be at a lower ebb. The underarm had seemed the nadir of their fortunes, but this concatenation of events was plunging them further. 'Oh, I'd love to be with Greg right now,' Judy sighed. Not to declare their fealty but to share their marriage and the burden of defending it. As so often happened when Judy uttered her mini-prayers, they were answered. Friends who read the *Australian* story phoned to offer their support. She thanked them. That too took its toll. Then one couple, Pat and Ian McCarthy, said, 'We know everything's all right. We've seen you and Greg together. We want to do something constructive.' The upshot was they took Stephen and Belinda, the Marantas collected Jonathan, and Judy booked her flight to Adelaide. She rang Greg who was about to leave by helicopter for the Yalumba vineyards on a team day out. 'Save me a piece of bienenstick,' said Judy, attaching a sweet memory of the vineyard's yeasty German cake to the sweet thoughts of flying to Greg.

In Adelaide Greg had been contemplating a tiny light at the end of his abyss — Rudi Webster's remark about watching the ball leaving the bowler's hand. He remembered getting out first ball to Colin Croft in the Sydney Test and turning to look at the background as he walked off. He had not 'seen' the ball. Webster's remark acquired new wisdom. In the nets in Adelaide Greg began deliberately focusing on the bowler's hand. That extra split second suddenly found his feet in position, his stroke instincts poised. Confidence flooded back. Judy flew in and laid to rest one more doubt; if he was going to keep playing, then for goodness' sake make a success of it. Give it 100 per cent. That's what she wanted.

Greg walked onto Adelaide Oval to bat more relaxed than he had been for months. 'It was as though someone had lifted a curtain from in front of my eyes,' he said. Released from so much doubt he played his best innings since the 201 aeons ago in Brisbane. If we may divert from Greg's crisis to the cricket for one moment, Australia were 4-17 when Greg went out to bat. The West Indies immediately peppered him with bouncers, presuming they had his number. After three overs of five bouncers an over from Colin Croft, Greg called from his crease down to umpire Robin Bailhache, 'I thought there was something in the rules about intimidatory bowling?' Bailhache more or less ignored the remark. Croft did not. 'Oh man, you expect us to bowl half volleys?' Greg replied, 'No, but I do expect you to bowl some in our half of the wicket.'

At the end of the over Greg told Bailhache, 'For Christ's sake, Robin, they can't just keep running in and whistling them around our ears all the time. Somebody's going to get hurt.' Two overs later Croft sent two range finders fizzing head high, one down the leg side and the next past the off. Greg stared at Bailhache. The next ball jumped at Greg's eyes, smashing into his hand as he warded it off. 'I knew as soon as it hit, my knuckle was broken,' said Greg. He put his hand down, feigned no injury, pushed a single and reaching Bailhache, said, 'I hope you're happy. The big bastard's just broken my hand.' Greg was 20 and refused to go off. His rediscovered form killed the pain as surely as morphine and he made 61 runs on the strength of it, becoming in the process, the third Australian, after Bradman and Neil Harvey, to score 6,000 Test runs.

His Test batting average that season against the West Indies reflected the anguish of his form, 14.33 runs. His overall first class average for the season was 35.46, the lowest of his career in Australia. As if to compensate for his batting, Greg felt he never captained Australia better than during that season. In their subsequent books his two mates, Dennis and Rod, made similar perceptive remarks about that 1981–82 season. Marsh in *The Gloves of Irony* said Greg's failures taught him to understand batsmen less blessed in talent than himself. 'I think he will be a better captain for it,' wrote Marsh. Lillee wrote in *Over and Out* that Greg's failures made him a wiser, more mellow man. 'Almost overnight he became a more understanding captain.'

Greg listened to those quotes and conceded some substance. He had asked no more of anyone than he had of himself. 'It's a harsh judgement,' he said. 'I didn't expect any miracles, but I expected players to play to their potential. There were three or four players who could have tried harder not to fail.' They thought him schoolmaster-ish, but neither Marsh nor Lillee would have seen Greg quietly counselling team members while all eyes were on the action in the centre. Unlike Ian, Greg did not wear his sympathy on his sleeve at the bar.

A comic note concluded the Australian season. Greg played that Adelaide Test under death threats. The police allocated extra men at the ground and told Greg they were confident they could screen spectators for high powered rifles. They could not guarantee hand guns but if Greg stayed away from the boundaries he was safe. Greg assured them he would stay in slips. He felt obliged to tell the team. On the first morning two detectives arrived to collect him. 'Anyone for a lift?' asked Greg. Rod Marsh absentmindedly accepted. Once in the car he exclaimed, 'Jeez, what am I doing here?' The police entertained them with stories of Sprinkler, the cop who had 13 bullet holes in him. On the field whenever Greg sauntered near Marsh, that fair-weather friend shouted, 'Get away from me, I don't want to get hit by the ricochet or the blood.' At drinks Greg sidled into the centre of the group until someone said, 'Hey, what are you doing here?' and they scattered.

Listing Greg's misfortunes from February 1981 to February 1982 is rather like listening to the conclusion of a rampant Beethoven symphony, each momentous surge topped by yet further crescendos, until one is never sure where the crashing drama-filled movement will end. The end of season tour of New Zealand became a gratifying coda to Greg's concert of woes. He and New Zealand had a mutually therapeutic assignation to keep.

Greg was welcomed to those gallant isles with a quiet warning that radio stations had received threats to assassinate him. The underarm of course. New Zealand Cricket Council chairman, Bob Vance, offered Greg a bodyguard. He graciously declined. We have seen how he treated death threats. In Auckland Lillee, Border, Alderman and Greg stepped out to buy some music cassettes. Greg found New Zealanders as anxious to mend fences as he was. Their hosts had already taken the first conciliatory step by banning a television promotion for the series which featured the underarm. In the street it was, 'Glad you're here' and 'Hope you don't get a hard time.'

Prime Minister Muldoon set the tone. He invited Greg and New Zealand captain Geoff Howarth to meet him privately at Parliament House. The underarm was not raised. Greg felt that Muldoon's 1981 remarks were an over-reaction, like everyone else's. 'I gave him the benefit of doubt, that it wasn't a personal assault, it was a political one, for publicity,' said Greg. He was right on the over-reaction, wrong on the publicity. Mr Muldoon told me, 'Greg's a good bloke, an ornament to Australian cricket. I've got a theory that you can forgive a bloke one error. That was a mistake.' If that is true then so were Mr Muldoon's 1981 remarks. Second only to Benaud, the Prime Minister's remarks served to pervert rational debate on the merits or demerits of Greg's tactics. But memories could not destroy Greg's bonhomie. He found he did not dislike the squat, tough Kiwi Prime Minister, who displayed more than a passing knowledge of cricket. When Muldoon later welcomed the whole team to Parliament House Greg apologized ... for the team not wearing the yellow shirts that Muldoon had found so fitting. Greg then demonstrated his Prince Alfred College history lessons were not wasted. He said he had heard that the only person who had ever entered Parliament with honourable intentions was Guy Fawkes.

In the first one-day international the ground was tense, a few hecklers started up and when Greg came out to bat a lawn bowl wobbled onto the field. Greg saw and ignored. He was as determined as ever to reply as he knew best. He hit 108 and every run chipped and chiselled at whatever grudge New Zealand held against him. When he was finally out a busty young woman burst from a crowd of wellwishers and bowled him over in her enthusiasm. Knocked flat, he knew he was back.

In that first match left hand opener Bruce Edgar lost his bail but was given not out. Greg had decided beforehand that if the team started to query umpires they would not endear themselves to anyone. When several players wanted to take issue over the bail Greg warned them, 'Piss off, I'll talk to the umpire.' The umpires were not sure the ball had hit the stumps. End of argument.

On a similar note, in their match against the President's XI in Christchurch John Bracewell was given out caught by Greg for 14. Bracewell was one of the 'brats' who sledged Greg in Brisbane during New Zealand's 1980–81 tour. Greg did not hesitate to ask the umpire to call Bracewell back because the ball had not carried. The crowd warmly applauded, but as Greg said, it was not something he would not do in normal circumstances. He had in the Centenary Test against England in Melbourne. 'People were looking for us to be good blokes,' said Greg. 'Anything we did was terrific.'

Judy arrived before the second Test in Auckland and spent three days sightseeing with Greg. It was the first time in 10 years she gained access to Greg mid-tour, instead of just at the end. During the Test she sat next to the Governor-General's wife, Lady Norma Beattie, who promptly organized a luncheon for Judy the next day at Government House with New Zealand Cricket Council wives. One of them was the mother of Martin Snedden of the catch-that-was-not fame the day of the underarm. 'They managed some small references to the under-arm,' said Judy. 'But they were all light-hearted and designed to put me at ease. I suspect it was partly a square-off for how the New Zealanders criticized Greg the previous year.'

Trailing 0–1 in the series at the third Test in Christchurch Greg laid it on the line to the team. 'Anyone can lose one Test, but if you get beaten twice in a three Test series, you've had a bad tour,' he said. Some reputations would suffer. But not his. He scored a masterly 176, an innings he classed among his best, qualified only by the standard of the attack, Richard Hadlee excluded. As always Hadlee lacked support at the other end. Greg respected the wiry, fast-medium all-rounder. 'He was a fighter with the bat, some of it bravado, but he made a lot of runs,' said Greg. 'He wasn't as quick as Dennis Lillee, but faster than Geoff Dymock. About Geoff Lawson's pace. But Richard was a better bowler than his speed suggested. He had a lot of variations and bowled a good bouncer, well disguised. He was quick enough to worry everybody.' Except Greg this innings. On 76 not out overnight he passed Neil Harvey's 6,149 Test runs to move into second place behind Bradman. Returning to the Avon Motor Lodge he found the manager had in a stock of Queensland Fourex beer. From stumps to midnight Greg drank 17 cans of beer, about three times his normal quota. 'I don't know, just got the taste for it,' joked Greg. 'I still got eight hours sleep. Can't go to bed too early.' The clues were there that at last Greg had really relaxed from 12 months of acute stress. Certainly the beer was not detrimental to his batting. The next morning he hit the first ball from Hadlee for four and was away. He was 176 at lunch, registering his first and only 100 in a Test session, the feat for which he admired Doug Walters so much. But it made Greg the only captain in history to score a century before lunch in a Test. Fast scoring does not become the captains of posterity.

Dennis Lillee in his book, *My Life in Cricket*, rated that 176 one of the best innings he had ever seen. He wrote:

> *I watched him on the television monitor in the dressing room and he was picking up the ball just short of a length and flicking it high in the air to whatever part of the field he wanted. Sometimes it went for 6, sometimes in between the fieldsmen for 4 ... I just cried out, "Eat your heart out, Viv Richards."*

That won the Test for Australia to square the series, but not before another coup of which Greg is justly proud. Greg made New Zealand follow on. Rod Marsh was not keen. Lillee had broken down and Thomson was weary from a superb first innings spell. Greg told Rod, 'I've always been taught if you've forced the follow-on, you bloody well enforce it. I've seen a few blokes come adrift for not.' Greg opened the attack with himself and Len Pascoe and then threw the ball to Bruce Yardley and Allan Border. Marsh was all for bringing Thommo back on. 'No, we can always go back to the quicks, but if we burn them out now we'll have nothing to fall back on,' said Greg. 'We'll give the spinners a chance and see.' Yardley took four wickets and Border three to wrap the Test up. Greg did not need the quicks at all. Some time later Rod said to Greg, 'That's one of the best pieces of captaincy I've ever seen.' Greg told me, 'Rod doesn't remember saying it now, but I do. From him it was a tremendous compliment.' It has to be seen in the family context. Marsh and Lillee always declared, if asked, that Ian was the best captain they had played under. That never bothered Greg. He agreed. But after downing 17 cans, fulsome praise from Lillee and a contested compliment from Marsh, Greg reckoned he must be close to Ian. To cap it all Greg was awarded the Sportsman of the Series — the underarm formally forgiven or New Zealand donning sackcloth and ashes for their national calumny? Whatever, it was one of Greg's best ever tours with an average of 79.25, the third best of his career, enough to make you want to keep playing.

REDEMPTION (1982-1985)

24. Ashes

Kim Hughes lost the 1981 series in England 3–1, and the 1982 series in Pakistan 3–0. He fought the former without Greg, and the latter without Greg and Dennis Lillee. I put it to Greg that he was partly responsible for Hughes becoming a caretaker captain, the scapegoat for away losses who never had the chance to redeem himself at home.

Greg's reply was that tours were an ideal opportunity for Hughes to obtain experience away from the home spotlight. When the ACB decided he was the man for the job full-time, he would be the better for it.

In keeping with his new policy of no long tours, Greg did not go to Pakistan in the early Australian summer of 1982. He was aware that every time he gave the captaincy away the likelihood of his regaining it grew less and less. 'Kim had only to do half a decent job and he would have kept it,' said Greg. 'It was not that he lost, but the way he lost. It was a capitulation. He started off boom, boom, boom, with all the hype in the world and then it just disintegrated.'

In Greg's growing disenchantment with the humbug of cricket politics, he no longer could be bothered nicely parrying endless, moronic media questions. 15 October 1982: Did he consider himself the best man to lead Australia against England that summer? 'Yes.' In Pakistan a week later Hughes replied that he would like to keep the captaincy against England. He had a point. However much Greg sought revenge for having lost the Ashes in 1977, Hughes equally wanted to redeem himself for his humiliation in England, in 1981.

As with that England tour, reports of the Pakistan tour filtered through to Greg. 'The same sort of answers came back, a fair-weather leader,' said Greg. 'It was disappointing to hear because I would have been happy to have handed it to Kim or anyone else. It was obvious he wasn't equipped to do it.' What if several of the players had told Greg: 'Kim wasn't great, but we think he's probably turned the corner'? Greg replied, 'I would have made myself unavailable for the captaincy.' 'I would have said, "Go to it."'

It must be remembered that Greg was one of the four senior WSC players who advised against Packer offering Hughes a contract in 1977. At that stage the four, Greg, Ian, Marsh and Lillee, considered Hughes immature and unready. Marsh's relegation behind Hughes for the Western Australian captaincy would have made him a biased observer of Hughes' performance in Pakistan, but Greg knew how to read beneath that antagonism. Over the years he grew to understand the Hughes character. He had a sunny disposition, could be excellent company, dancing, singing and performing tricks at team parties. But the other side of him bore a naked and overwhelming ambition which, while appearing to defer, sought to further its ends whenever possible. That end was the Australian captaincy. His ambition, when it surfaced, unsettled Australian teams. Having been ACB captain during one WSC year, he was frustrated by Greg's occupancy. Yet he was never able to exhibit the leadership qualities necessary to win the selectors' confidence over a part-time Greg. Strangely enough, though Greg never sought Hughes' company off the field, they could bat well together and put together two fine partnerships in the England series. 'He could take an attack apart at times,' said Greg. 'He was unwise to harbour such desires to captain Australia. He was better value to himself and the team when he played his natural game, which he never seemed to do when captain.'

Greg celebrated his reinstatement with a century in the first Test in Perth against Bob Willis' Englishmen. It was Greg's twenty-first Test century, equalling Neil Harvey's tally, second only to Bradman's. It was the start of a statistical count-down that would last for the next two seasons. But the match was marred by the injury to Terry Alderman when he tackled a young spectator who had run on and chiacked him. It was another depressing season's start. 'I just didn't need it,' said Greg. 'Three years in a row, the bloody aluminium bat, Javed Miandad and then that.' To cap it all Lillee, the culprit in the first two on that list, broke down with a knee injury and was out for the season.

Australia drew in Perth and won in Brisbane, so Greg led the team to Adelaide in great spirits. He rang his father, Martin, and apologized for forgetting his birthday the previous week. 'I'll make it up to you,' said Greg. 'I'll make 100 against the Poms here.' Greg had never made a Test 100 in Adelaide. Martin duly received his gift of runs, 115 of them. The previous year Greg had promised son Stephen a century and made 200. He gave himself a century gift on his twenty-first birthday playing for Somerset and in 1972 predicted, to Ashley Mallett, the century he made at The Oval. Now his father's birthday and the next year, 1983, he gave Judy a century birthday present in Brisbane against Pakistan. Greg's explanation was that by making the promises he made himself concentrate. But he never made the promise without delivering. To predict one's own glory is surely the stamp of an amazing greatness.

Pursuing the Brearley theory of 1977 Bob Willis had bounced away at Greg in Perth. Ian Botham hit Greg in the shoulder but Greg hooked him for six. All square. In Adelaide Greg took up the gauntlet and hooked free and easily, striking 19 fours. 'England bowled unintelligently,' said Greg. 'At the end of his over Bob Willis was marching to mid-off to field and the next over he'd come running in and bowl another one short. I kept taking him on. David Gower tried to offer advice from time to time, but Bob was on another planet. He was definitely somewhere else.' Greg's former Prince Alfred College coach, Chester Bennett, saw that Adelaide century from the members' stand with his son Christopher, a school contemporary of Greg's. Bennett watched with pleasure the profit of hundreds of hours of coaching Greg. He did not attempt to speak to him. 'I have a little bit of an antipathy to being looked upon as a barfly,' said Bennett, who is the antithesis of the genre.

Came Melbourne and at last England's bounce theory worked. Greg, caught Lamb, bowled Cowans, 0. 'When I hit it I thought, "Gee, that's out of the ground",' said Greg. 'But wrong shot, wrong ground. If it had been Adelaide Oval it would have been 30 yards over the boundary, it was still 15 yards inside the Melbourne fence.'

Describing Greg in *Decision Against England*, published in 1983, English cricket writer Robin Marlar wrote:

> *His batting was often brilliant but it now has that brittleness popularly associated with elegance. England invariably went at him as if they thought he would break up like slab toffee under the hammer... Even against such a barrage he was the only player to hit two centuries in the series.*

Melbourne was memorable not for Greg's duck but Allan Border and Jeff Thomson's fighting stand of 70 runs that took them to within four runs of what would have been an historic victory. Border was batting at number five having failed at number three in the first two Tests. Greg was trying to groom a batsman to succeed himself. Ever since brother Ian, Redpath and finally Walters, retired, Greg had withstood the pace assaults of teams who knew that once they got Greg they would have little trouble with the rest. 'Allan was not 100 per cent in favour and I think that's what made it psychologically counterproductive,' said Greg. Border's form suffered but he rein-stated himself in Melbourne. With 40 runs required overnight Greg and the team joked at Thommo's expense. 'Surely we don't have to go down there and warm up just for one ball,' they said, and then at the MCG carpark in the morning, 'Look at all these people, won't even see a full over of cricket.' And, 'These are the ones with season tickets who want full value.' Thomson, possibly inspired by his team-mates of little faith, held on until, as Greg put it, 'He got out to the only shot he played. The rest he'd been blocking or leaving.' The team then had the job to console the two diehards who felt they had let the team down. As a match incidental, Greg broke Bobby Simpson's Australian record of 110 fielding catches, which left only Colin Cowdrey ahead of him on 120.

Australia duly drew the last Test in Sydney to regain the Ashes. If that sounds anti-climactic it may be because the subject himself was starting to exhibit an uncharacteristic lassitude. Greg was keyed up for the start of that series and ran headlong into the Alderman incident. Centuries in Perth and Adelaide sapped him mentally. After Adelaide his form fell away until his end-of-season average toted just 39, only four runs better than the previous year, his worst. But call it selective performances because the two seasons do not compare. He had regained the Ashes, a great coup since most of the team had been involved in one or both of the 1977 and 1981 defeats. It was a thrill to be met by Bob Willis inside the boundary fence for a congratulatory handshake and it nicely rounded the record. But Greg also spared a thought for those who had been on the receiving end in England in 1981, particularly Kim Hughes. 'He must have gone through hell in England,' said Greg. 'It was tremendous to see his face, and Rod Marsh's, when the final ball was bowled.'

Significantly that was the second full Test series against Greg in which England's champion, Ian Botham, was unable to assert his matchwinning talents. In 1977 in England Botham played only two Tests against Australia and he captained England to the 1980 Centenary Test draw at Lords. But, in the post-WSC years, he toured Australia twice, in 1979–80 under Mike Brearley and now with Bob Willis. In eight Tests in Australia, England won one, Australia five. Greg had no doubts about Botham's ability. 'The most aggressive English player I have seen, no one was more competitive,' he said. Australians tended at first to class Botham as a lucky player, but they learned better. Said Greg, 'Ian is the kind of player who is happier trying to get a batsman out rather than trying to contain him with tight bowling. In this he's not unlike an Australian. And he spends all his time trying to make quick runs. When it comes off, it wins Test matches. When it doesn't, the critics can easily find room to hammer him.' Greg's success was in never underestimating Botham's skill and he insisted his team play him accordingly. 'Though his bowling might appear occasionally wayward he could give you an absolute jaffa,' said Greg. 'Similarly I told my bowlers to give him nothing but line and length. No trying to bounce him out. We reduced him from the man we knew in other Tests, who could walk on water, to a normal human being.' To contain Botham so consistently at the height of his career, to handcuff the man's huge hitting, was testimony to Greg's matured captaincy.

Greg was just beginning to glance at the wall plaques of *Wisden* to wonder how he would polish up a few years hence. But having plotted the chart of Greg's career I sensed at this point a shallowing and flattening of the oscillations, as though the recording needle was being sent less urgent vibrations. The Ashes in 1982–83 could not mean the same as from 1969 to 1975. The young, thin, fearless batsman of the early 1970s saw those Ashes victories engraved in men's hearts, not just in history. The faces of Illingworth and Denness remained as memories of cricket when the challenges were simple and uncluttered. So much had altered cricket and Greg. Even this England team lacked Boycott, Gooch and Emburey, banned for touring South Africa. Political and commercial wrangles had rent the game so often in the past five years cricket was reduced by its controversies. Bob Willis therefore came and lost and left almost as an afterword in the curling scrolls of Greg's cricket life.

It did not, however, dampen the celebrations one whit. Dennis Lillee joined Greg, Marsh and the team in Sydney. Marsh wrote in *The Inside Edge*, published in 1983, 'I only wish I could remember the night more clearly.' Greg smiled. 'No, Rod doesn't remember,' he said enigmatically. First they hit the Woollahra Hotel in Paddington, where they ate al fresco in the Bees Garden Restaurant and then adjourned to the Cauldron night club in Darlinghurst.

The Cauldron was once a morgue, a paradoxical place for a victory night. But it possessed all the essentials for cricketers at leisure, sandstone walls, low, low ceilings that troubled Joel Garner when he visited, adzed timber beams, alcoves and crypts and discreet lighting. It had the feeling of catacombs, perfect for the subterranean nightlife of sun-scarred cricketers. As with the Different Drummer, where Ian led the 1974–75 Ashes celebrations, the Cauldron is nothing if not like the MCG dressing rooms. The bar had heavily polished, sculpted wooden stools on stands as thick as an elephant's leg and from one of these an equally heavily thighed member of the Australian team, in the middle of a sensible, dignified conversation, slowly, quietly slipped sideways to conclude a marvellous night out.

Rod Marsh missed captaining Australia by possibly one or two votes. When Greg withdrew from the 1982 Pakistan tour the Australian Cricket Board vote is said to have stood at 7–6 for Hughes over Marsh when chairman Phil Ridings cast his vote to make it 8–6. At 7–7 who knows what might have transpired? From then on Marsh knew his chances of the leadership, the culmination of his occupation-pastime, were slim. When he returned from that Hughes-led débâcle in Pakistan, he was an angry man and muttered to Greg once, 'If they offered it to me now I probably wouldn't accept it.' But he would have, said Greg. And made an ideal captain at that. Said Greg, 'He stood next to Ian and myself for 14 years and you know from the advice someone offers you whether he knows what he is talking about.' But Marsh also stood too close to Ian politically and as much trouble as Greg gave the ACB, it was no secret who that august body of men considered the mongrel of the Chappell litter.

Marsh's tally of 28 victims for that Ashes series was a record for a series between any countries. Greg admired Marsh's fitness, the more so because he carried cartilage injuries in both knees. 'Every day he came off the ground, every session virtually, he packed one or other of his knees in ice,' said Greg. 'But when he got out there again he just said, "Bugger the knee" and forgot about it. Occasionally I'd see him buckle in pain, but he never said anything.' Marsh played many times with chipped bones in his fingers which he nursed through the pain of taking the fast bowlers. Greg would tell him to have it X-rayed.

'What for?' replied Marsh. 'They'll tell me it's broken. It's not going to stop me playing.' Test after Test Greg watched his stout friend's agility and mobility and concluded, 'His fitness was sheer willpower.'

Greg handed over the captaincy to Kim Hughes for the one-day matches and then, at their conclusion, resigned forever from the job. He would continue simply as a player. It was no cataclysmic decision. As Greg wearied of each portion of the game he gave himself time to be sure and then stepped down; first long tours, then one-day captaincy and finally Test captaincy. With 48 Tests as captain he had far outstripped Bob Simpson's previous record of 39. But if the World Series Supertests are included he was not so far ahead of brother Ian, 49 matches to 44. Greg's record of 22 wins from 48 Tests and one Supertest is actually superior to Ian's record of 18 wins from 30 Tests and 14 Supertests. No one is suggesting that some of those Supertests in 1978, when Ian led WSC Australia against phenomenal Best World XIs, could be compared with an ordinary Test. Nor that Greg was the motivator of players that Ian was. But Greg regained the Ashes, as did Ian, and fought the West Indies tooth and nail to square the home series in 1981–82 when the Caribbean countries were on their world ascent. Greg won 44.9 per cent of Tests and Supertests he captained, to Ian's 40.9. Richie Benaud won 42.8 and Bob Simpson 30.7. Statistics don't lie.

Having resigned Greg then contradicted himself and accepted the ACB's invitation to lead Australia on a short end-of-season tour of Sri Lanka. Kim Hughes had argued from Pakistan that the captaincy was a full-time job, but he was left stranded mid-wicket in the debate when family pressures compelled him to withdraw from Sri Lanka. Greg declined to make capital from it. He never saw himself as opposed to Hughes. 'A lot of players will find that if they want to keep playing cricket, they will have to make the same decision,' said Greg. Such as Marsh, Lawson and Thomson who did not tour. Dennis Lillee did, returning from injury, raring to go, joining his mate on a tour very likely their last.

Greg and Judy tossed up whether she should go too but decided against it because of the unknown health factors. In the capital, Colombo, Greg's room in the Intercontinental opened onto a balcony which overlooked an internal courtyard where a string quartet sawed and plucked in the evenings. Greg rang Judy one evening and she heard the music through his open door. 'She'd have loved it,' said Greg, now with regret.

In Kandy, city of festivals, the casino was taken over for the shooting of the film, *Indiana Jones and the Temple of Doom*. Dennis Lillee led a commando raid one night and met Harrison Ford. The rest of the team amused themselves firing garden-stake-sized skyrockets from their hotel roof. 'It was like Cape Canaveral,' said Greg. 'One got loose, and whoosh, through the restaurant, but luckily missed the glass doors.'

Another day Greg, Allan Border and three others drove high into the mountains to play golf at a cloud-top course. They were told it was an hour but it was three times that, a giddying, twisting trip of switchback S-bends that wound higher and higher through vertical tea plantations — and then back down again. In true Aussie humour the trippers cleared their addled brains sufficiently to convince the rest of the players to take a bus trip there. 'They were sick when they got back,' said Greg. 'Didn't they give us buggery.'

Australia beat Sri Lanka in the one Test but lost both one-day matches ... no explanation needed. Greg re-injured his neck in Sri Lanka. He ricked it first in Adelaide in 1981–82 when so much else was going wrong I spared the reader that extra agony. The injury saved Greg from the 1983 Prudential World Cup in England, when Australia lost a first round match to Zimbabwe. The strange thing is that despite his injury, and the fact that he had already toured England four times and it would have extended the season unmercifully for Judy, Greg was inexorably drawn by the prospect. They have not made the mass spectrometer to detect the addiction in Greg's blood for cricket, but the fix was certainly there.

25. AB and Kim

Before the start of the 1983–84 season Greg took Allan Border for a round of golf at the Royal Queensland Golf Club. He wanted to convince Border to take over the Queensland captaincy. Greg had not yet decided this would be his last season, but he was beginning to tie up loose ends. Getting Border to agree was no simple task. He had taken Allan for a similar game and put the same proposition the year before. Border's reaction then had been direct. 'I don't want the responsibility. I've seen what has happened to you and Kim and I don't want to know about it.' Greg was disappointed then but had understood Border's view. 'I even thought perhaps he was smarter than the rest of us,' mused Greg. Now he tried again. Border had recently returned from the World Cup in the UK where Australia, under Kim Hughes, had performed disastrously. Greg cast Border into the future to a hypothetical moment when Hughes might not be captain of Australia. The ACB would not have Rod Marsh as captain. Kepler Wessels had been vice-captain to Greg for Queensland but Greg believed the ACB would never make the South African-born Wessels Australian captain. That left Border. If Allan was to captain Australia he would first have to captain Queensland for experience. 'Twelve months ago we had this conversation,' said Greg. 'I think it's more important now. What about it?' Border studied the lie of the course before him, remembering the traps the Australian side had dug itself into and finally replied, 'Well, having seen the cock-up Kim's making of it, I might as well do it myself.' Border became Queensland captain that season and Australian captain midway through the next.

Greg first saw Border bat on television during the WSC years. Border played his second Test in Sydney in January 1979, and Greg watched him take on the England spinners, John Emburey and Geoff Miller so confidently he remained not out in each innings. *Wisden* recorded Border was in a 'lonely class of his own'. Greg noted he had observed a bloody good player. Before moving to Queensland in September 1980, Border flew north and sounded Greg out on the likely problems. Border's admiration for Greg was unbounded. 'He's such a fantastic player,' Border told me the season he became Queensland captain. 'It's an inspiration just being involved with the guy. He's not a captain who psyches the team up openly, but if you make elementary mistakes he'll go and stand at the door and say, "That was shithouse today" and give you a bit of a dressing down. He's an aloof character that everyone looks up to. He just stares at you and you think, "Well, I'm expected to do my job" and that's that.'

Border's admiration was reciprocated. Greg thought Border the best left-hander he had seen since Graeme Pollock and Gary Sobers. He found Border to be the ultimate professional. 'If he had been born in England he would have been the ideal county cricketer,' said Greg. 'All he wanted to do was play cricket.' Border also possessed a remarkable cool under pressure. Beaten repeatedly outside off stump he would remain unfazed. 'He was a gutsy player,' said Greg. 'His idea was that the next ball was the important one.' Whenever critics commented that Border, with his short back lift, was more a tradesman than a talent, Greg would reply, 'He may not be elegant, but he's the most efficient batsman I've seen in a long time.'

Greg also got to know the Border personality. In slips Border, like Marsh, always had an idea, a suggestion if his captain sought some inspiration. But Greg also stumbled across Border's dark, implacable alter ego and clashed with him in occasional fiery exchanges. Such a skirmish occurred during Border's run of outs when Greg had him batting number three for Australia against England in 1982–83. One morning at the 'Gabba, before play, Greg asked Border to spend five minutes talking to a group of kids in a coaching class. It was a mildly onerous, rostered task all the players had to endure. Said Greg, 'What do you want Allan, the good news or the bad?' Border declared blackly he had too many problems to talk to the kids. 'Well I guess you know the bad news,' said Greg cheerfully. But he had underestimated precisely the depth of Border's mood. There ensued a running battle of request and refusal, Border opening with small arm insults and escalating into heavy anti-personnel obscenities. The engagement lasted 30 minutes, sweeping from the dressing-room out onto the 'Gabba dog track and back into the changing room with Border not giving an inch.

'He was in a shocking temper,' said Greg. 'Angry Anderson, Grumpy, Puggsley, you name it, he lived up to all his nicknames.' Though he was not too thrilled at the time, Greg examined the incident afterwards and suddenly knew that the good side of that fanatically determined, even selfish, character, contained the makings of an Australian captain. 'He'll make more runs and knock my record over and go so far past it won't matter. He'll play 120 Tests and make 8,000–9,000 runs. He's a very rare breed.'

That same season, before the Pakistanis arrived, Greg decided to act on all the feedback he had received from Australian players about Kim Hughes' captaincy. The occasion was a meeting of the players' sub-committee of the ACB with Bob Merriman at the Hilton hotel in Melbourne, August 1983. Greg made a point of rooming with Hughes and in the morning had breakfast delivered so conversation would not be disturbed. At 7.30 a.m., their breakfast trays before them, Greg embarked upon some unsolicited shock therapy.

If Kim was under the impression that all the players supported him, he was wrong. He had not brought unanimity to the team. It was not just the senior players. There was a strong feeling from the majority of players who went on the 1981 England tour, the 1982 Pakistan tour and the 1983 World cup, that all went well with Kim until the tour hit a hurdle and then the team went downhill very quickly. It was not so much that they lost, but how they lost. The feeling was that the guys would like a change. Rod Marsh was the ideal choice but if the Board would not have him then perhaps Allan Border.

Greg told Kim, 'Why put yourself, your family and your form under pressure? Do yourself a favour, draw back now, make yourself unavailable voluntarily and give yourself time to regroup. You might be able to come back as Australian captain a couple of years down the line. The danger you face if you keep hanging in there is that you'll lose the captaincy, because the Board won't keep supporting you for ever. And the pressure of the captaincy is going to make your own form suffer so badly you'll finish up out of the side.' Greg kept at it for a straight half hour. Kim had always said he only had the interests of Australian cricket at heart, Greg said. If he meant that he had to step down.

Hughes sat dazed, his breakfast untouched. He did not speak, did not interrupt. Greg concluded and sat back in his chair. He knew Kim to have a quick tongue if he disagreed with anyone. 'If he disbelieved what I said he had either to argue or hit me,' said Greg. For 30 seconds Hughes sat silent. Then he stood up and said, 'I'll go and see if Bob and the others are ready.' And walked out. Greg's rationale for his broadside was that he felt Hughes was the wrong man to captain Australia. He said, 'I didn't blame Kim for that. I didn't think he should have had the responsibility thrust upon him. I was one of the senior players in the team and I knew he respected my opinion. I thought somebody, who he was likely to believe, had to set him straight, give him the opportunity to weigh his position up. It was not something I looked forward to.'

Greg's advice may have been well meaning but it hardly seemed appropriate. He was not exactly a consort of Hughes'. Indeed Hughes could regard Greg as a member of the old mafia who for so long had appeared to frustrate his captaining ambitions. And here he was telling him to resign. Yet Greg's words had their effect. Within a week or so of that Melbourne meeting Hughes decided to resign during a conversation at his Perth home with Bob Merriman, co-ordinator of the cricket sub-committee and a good friend of Kim's. Merriman flew out of Perth with a signed statement but when he arrived at his Geelong home that evening there was a message from Kim rescinding the resignation. Subsequently, Greg received a rapid-fire phone call from Kim. He had thought over Greg's comments, talked it over with his wife, Jenny, and his advisers, and was rejecting Greg's advice. He rattled off, 'I've decided I'm the man for the job, I can do it, I'm going to make a success of it. And I'd like you to be my vice-captain.'

Now it was Greg's turn to be nonplussed. Greg could not possibly accept. The media would slaughter them both. 'If I'm seen to be giving you a lot of advice I'll be accused of pulling the strings, if I'm seen not to be giving you advice, then I've abandoned you. Either way neither of us can win,' he said. It would be far better for Kim to have Allan Border as vice-captain. It could be seen that they were close friends and Kim was running the job. Greg then gave Kim the assurance that went part way to repairing the damage that his Hilton assault may have inflicted. 'I'll be as happy as anything to give you any assistance I can in the background,' he said.

Those events preceded Hughes' eventual resignation by just 15 months. In that intervening period Greg did not raise the captaincy issue with Kim or anyone else again. He served Kim loyally on the field and was pleased to be part of the Hughes-led victory over the touring 1983–84 Pakistanis. But fate decreed that Greg should be present to bear witness to Hughes' final abdication. In November 1984, Greg, now a selector, arrived in Perth a few days before the start of the first Test against the West Indies. Kim approached him at the nets. Kim had been working on his footwork in the off season, would Greg mind having a look at it? Greg watched and thought, 'Gee, there's something different.' He walked around for a side view and spotted the change immediately. Kim had widened his feet to an Ian Redpath-like stance, his bat between his toes.

At the end of the session he asked Kim, 'When did you change your stance?' Hughes explained he was worried about his footwork. He wanted to be able to move into position more quickly against pace bowlers. Greg was uneasy. He had always admired Hughes' footwork. 'You always looked perfectly balanced Kim, feet closer together,' Greg said. He recounted his own bad experience in 1978–79 with WSC. He had tried to design a set of footwork to counteract the West Indian bowlers but only succeeded in designing a set of footwork to suit them. He said to Hughes, 'It put me on the back foot in front of the stumps and that's what you're doing now. You'll get out lbw more times than you can count. The worst thing is you're such a good driver, if you're on your toes, when they do pitch it up you've got a chance of hitting it. Now if they pitch it up you won't be able to hit it anyway. And if you do your weight will be on your back foot and you'll hit it in the air.' But Kim felt good and was keen to try.

The Australian team collapsed in the first innings in Perth for 76 runs. Hughes scored 4. It had all the earmarks of the débâcles overseas under Kim. Greg was not alone in detecting a crisis surfacing in the Australian team. He spoke to Bob Merriman for any feedback on Hughes' state of mind and to fellow selectors, Rick McCosker and Laurie Sawle. Apart from expressing their private dismay there was nothing the three selectors could do.

On 21 November, two days before the second Test in Brisbane, Kim invited Greg to address the team at the Sheraton Hotel. Greg gave them the well rehearsed Chappell charge about how the team had lain down and let the West Indies run over them. Greg had heard it from Ian on tours of the West Indies in 1973 and 1979. 'If you're going to do that for the rest of the series it's going to be an absolute disaster,' he told them. 'You've got to get up and fight, show some spirit, believe in yourselves. If you blokes feel as if you've done your best, all I can say as a selector is we'll have to start looking somewhere else.' Greg did not single out Kim, rather he supported him. It was not the captain's sole responsibility. It was the teams, the vice-captain, the senior players, everybody. If they did not support their captain he was hamstrung. Nevertheless it was significant that it was Greg who was lecturing the players. The ship seemed so rudderless that Greg was speaking like a de facto captain. It could not but reflect poorly on Hughes' leadership.

The second Test lasted only four days, Australia managing just 175 in the first innings on a good batting strip. Peter Blucher wrote in the *Courier-Mail* on 24 November:

> *The extravagant promises from captain Hughes of guts and determination and national pride amounted to nothing...*

On 25 November Keith Stackpole commented in his syndicated column:

> *I doubt whether our cricket has ever been in such a pitiful state. And unless something is done quickly our Test team and the funeral standards of cricket right throughout Australia are going to keep deteriorating.*

The next day, 26 November, the last day of the Test, Bob Merriman rang Greg at home at 8.30 a.m. Merriman had just had breakfast with

Hughes. 'Kim wants to have a talk with you. Can you get to the ground virtually straight away?' Nothing more was said but after Greg put the phone down he turned to Judy and said quietly, 'I think Kim is going to resign.' He cancelled his office appointments and drove thoughtfully to the 'Gabba, arriving at 9 a.m.

He, Merriman and Hughes went into the empty office of the QCA secretary, Grantley Evans. Merriman left Greg and Kim alone. They both sat down. Hughes told Greg how low he felt, how he had given matters a lot of thought and that he intended to resign. It was a painful moment. The curtains were drawn on the large picture window looking out to the oval. Rows of *Wisden* in Evans' bookcase looked down on the scene, witnesses to what they would eventually record. Greg listened with a sense of inevitability. It was plain Hughes was at the end of his tether and Greg felt sorry for him. Despite their different paths Hughes was a cricket colleague of some seven years' standing. But Greg did not let his sympathy sway his judgment. When Hughes finished Greg said, 'Kim, the decision has got to be yours. But if you're talking to me in the hope that I'm going to tell you not to do it, and try and talk you out of it, I'm afraid I can't. You know how I feel. I really believe that what you're doing now is in the best interests of Australian cricket. I know it must be difficult for you, but I think it's the right decision.'

Merriman returned and a plan of how Hughes should release the news was formed. Their decision was that as few people should know until Kim was ready for them to know. Consequently Hughes did not immediately inform the chairman of the ACB, Fred Bennett or the executive director, David Richards. The effect was that neither had much chance to talk Hughes out of his decision had they been of a mind to do so. English writer Henry Blofeld wrote in the *Australian* on 27 November:

> *I have felt for some time that as a tactician Hughes was a captain who lacked awareness...*
> *It is no discredit to a man that he does not have it in him to be a good captain...*
> *There is no doubt that he badly wanted the captaincy but I am not sure that he really understood or faced up to the responsibilities of the job.*

The saga of Hughes' descent from Australian captain to be omitted from the 1985 tour of England is one of the saddest in contemporary cricket and again Greg was inescapably involved. In the third and fourth Tests against the West Indies Hughes scored 0, 2, 0, 0. By the fifth the selectors were in a quandary. The West Indies were hammering Hughes into the ground. 'We felt he had undergone such a traumatic experience, resigning, we had to get him away from the West Indies,' said Greg. 'Give him a couple of Shield matches to get a few runs and bring him back for the one-day matches.' Was that a unanimous decision? Greg replied that the teams were not selected by majority rule. 'We discuss the problem and then it's a consensus decision,' he said. 'It never gets to a position where one person is being outvoted. We talked it around and, for his sake, and for the team's sake, that's what we agreed.'

Hughes' form was so poor that his being dropped scarcely raised a ripple. Since then Greg has been reminded that when he was undergoing his horror stretch of ducks the selectors had stuck by him. Greg replied that though he was glad of the selectors' confidence in him, what he had really needed at the time was to return to Shield and make a few runs. 'That would have been the best thing that could have happened to me,' he said. 'I could understand what Kim was going through but really, whilst you don't want to be dropped, the best thing is to be given a rest.' And that Hughes was given on 27 December 1984. He had lasted one month since his resignation.

Hughes rested, returned but never quite recaptured form. Though the selectors sent him to Sharjah for the one-day series they were worried about sending him to England. During the Sheffield Shield final in Sydney in March 1985, the three men spent much of their time debating the Hughes question. All were reluctant to leave him out. To send him was the easiest answer because the newspapers would probably be less critical. But that would ignore the potential disruption to new captain Allan Border, and a young touring team, if Hughes' form continued to desert him and English newspapers began needling him over his captaincy resignation. It reached the stage where none of the selectors was game to make a decision either way. In the end they decided they had more to gain than lose by leaving Hughes at home. Border would return with his captaincy consolidated. With Hughes' proven ability he would make so many runs at Shield level in the 1985–86 season he would return on merit to the Test team no matter how well the Australian team performed in England. 'There was no doubt in my mind about that,' said Greg. 'If he came back we had ourselves a very good player who had played 70 Tests and made over 4,000 runs who would be the better for having been down and made it back to the top.' But that plan reckoned without South African rands.

In retrospect it may be seen that what Greg essayed back in that 1983 pre-season was nothing less than the deliberate manipulation of the future of Australian cricket. Greg's advice to Hughes at their Hilton breakfast displayed a considerable arrogance. There was an authority empowered to judge Hughes' fitness to captain Australia. It was the ACB, not Greg. Perhaps it was no secret to Hughes that Greg did not consider him the right man to lead Australia. But Hughes then had to live with the humiliating certainty that the most senior player in his team, already the second greatest Australian batsman of all time, did not believe in his leadership and also that, on his word, nor did the rest of the team. If Greg had set out to undermine Hughes' confidence he could not have done better.

That is one view. It condemns Greg on circumstantial evidence of a campaign, deliberate or incidental, to unseat Kim Hughes. But that misses the target. Greg's campaign was not against Hughes, it was for Australian cricket. All Greg's actions must be examined in the light of his intense involvement in, and concern for, the future of the game he loved and was soon to leave. Nobody could accuse him of disinterest. He would never pretend to be unbiased. He had watched Kim since 1977, acknowledged him as his deputy after WSC and respected him as a batsman. But he could not ignore, as the seasons passed, the persistent alarms that were sounded by players under Hughes on successive tours. Greg began feeding hints to influential ACB officials, to no avail.

He made his first approach to Border in 1982 to assume the captaincy of Queensland so that Border could succeed Hughes, not depose him. After the World Cup failure of 1983 Greg sensed that the ACB intended to stick with Hughes as captain, partly hoping he would come good but equally through a sense of loyalty to Hughes who had been their flag-bearer during the WSC years. As Henry Blofeld wrote in the *Australian* after Hughes finally resigned:

> It was no fault of Hughes that he was chosen as the champion of the Establishment when the Australian Cricket Board and World Series Cricket were at each other's throats.

Thus when the ACB, for all the wrong reasons, continued to support Kim they renounced their responsibility to Australian cricket and

Hughes became their victim. Greg feared that the ACB might continue to ignore the problem to the point where Hughes would still be at the helm for the 1985 tour of England. It would be calamitous. He saw a new generation of young players emerging — Craig McDermott, Greg Ritchie, Simon O'Donnell — whose education under Hughes would be learning how to lose. If the ACB was not prepared to act, Greg was. He knew that in declaring his beliefs to Hughes he stood a good risk of being accused of undermining him for some ulterior motive. He was not deterred. 'I felt I did what I had to,' he said. 'I'd be less able to sleep soundly if I'd stood by and, because no one was prepared to do anything, let the worst happen.'

Greg believed that Hughes, in his heart, accepted what Greg had told him at the Hilton. 'He knew the truth that day in Melbourne,' he said. 'That's why he later resigned to Bob Merriman. But somewhere along the line he changed his mind.' There never had been, and subsequently was no, personal animosity between Greg and Kim. That is why Hughes asked Greg to be his vice-captain, why he sought Greg's advice on his new stance in Perth and why he invited Greg to address the team before the second Test. But most significant of all it was why Kim called for Greg when he finally decided to resign. He did not ask for ACB executives, David Richards or Fred Bennett, to consult about his decision. In a way Kim's summoning Greg on such a significant occasion was his admission that Greg was right in his advice 15 months earlier.

Greg's matins with Hughes at the Hilton say much about Greg's self-perceived role. He was a retiring Prime Minister seeking to choose his successor, adopting the mantle of wise, elder statesman shaping the destiny of the Australian cricket entity while he still had his hand upon it. That Greg had assumed that elevated status was undeniable. Allan Border told me in September 1983, 'Greg was playing Tests while a lot of the guys were still at school — he was when I was. When you are suddenly playing with these guys it can be a little overpowering.' Greg acted over the captaincy as he always had when he saw clearly that a path existed which others would not see. He dispensed with subtleties and hoped that his own position would be protected by the righteousness of his cause. His behaviour was that of many great sporting, and political, leaders, acting with a black and white certainty which can sweep opposition aside by its sheer force of momentum. It was also behaviour which could cause pain as it relentlessly sought its end.

Whether Greg comprehended precisely how powerful a figure he was in that 1983–84 pre-season, even though no longer captain, seems in question. Yet once Hughes rejected that Hilton approach, Greg retreated. Having done what he considered his duty he was prepared to accept the inevitable and support Hughes. He turned his concentration to his own setting career. The season did, after all, present its own considerable challenges.

26. Finale

A barefooted well-wisher dashed onto the 'Gabba ground, kissed Greg's gloved right hand, genuflected and then dashed back to his place on the hill. Police ignored the intrusion. Pilgrims paying homage to the man who bore the soubriquet of God were to be tolerated in this his last year — the Year of the Record. The occasion was Greg's century against Pakistan in the second Test of the summer of 1983–84. Though he had declared himself unavailable for the long tour of the West Indies at the end of the season, as far as Australia knew he might keep playing for several more seasons. But from the moment Pakistan arrived an air of melancholy accompanied Greg's every walk to the crease. And every step he took was to the drum of a statistical countdown towards a record held by the man whose image had hovered wraith-like on the periphery of Greg's squinting scan — Sir Donald Bradman.

Sir Donald held the record for the most Test runs scored by an Australian, 6,996 runs. Greg's 150 not out in Brisbane left him just 83 runs behind. Greg made his opinion clear from the start. 'There is no comparison between what Sir Donald did in 50 odd Tests and what some other bloke may have done in 80 odd,' he said. 'It would be almost sacrilegious to pass him.' Sir Donald would be interested to know that 56 per cent of Greg's runs in that 'Gabba 150, including 12 of the 17 fours, were scored on the off-side. Nearly 17 years earlier, when he scored his first Shield century, only 31 per cent of his runs came through the off. Greg's 'Gabba innings showed how delighted he was to have done with the migraine of captaincy. He joked with the Pakistani fieldsmen and when he finally departed leg-spinner Abdul Qadir, who dropped Greg on 47, threw an arm around Greg's shoulders and said, 'Well played.' Greg replied with a grin, 'Thanks for your help.' Greg was never inclined to laugh and joke on the field, he was too busy concentrating for that. But having become a multi-

253

media personality he was now expected to relate John Newcombe-like to the viewing audience complete with jokes, laughs and gestures to show what a wonderful all-round human being he was. It was encouraged in the name of entertainment but its true nature lay way back in its Victorian roots, with the university dons who advocated victory without apparent effort, the absolute antithesis of what Greg, like Harold Abrahams, knew to be victory's secret.

Once the season started Greg developed problems. After the 150 in Brisbane he scored 6 and 4 in the Adelaide Test. The 4 was a run-out, Greg's fault. 'Out by three yards,' he said. 'Just never on. My mind was completely blank.' That irritated him. It was impossible to ignore the talk about records. It had been discovered he was also just one short of Colin Cowdrey's world record of 120 catches by a fieldsman other than the wicketkeeper. He would have liked to have broken Bradman's and Cowdrey's records in Adelaide if anywhere. That motivated him for the fourth Test in Melbourne but, batting down the list at number six, the score was 354 by the time he came in. He scored six runs and took no catches. Batting at number three or four all his Test career Greg had developed a rhythm of mental and physical preparation. To make number six more like three he tried ignoring the match. He did not smoke or play cards, so he lay down in the dressing-room until his turn came. But the adrenalin remained blocked. He decided in Melbourne that the fifth Test in Sydney would be his last.

He wanted to make a fist of it and the best way to motivate himself was to bat where there was batting to be done. He went to Hughes. 'I'm used to three and four. My record suggests I've done a good job of it. I'd like to bat there in the last Test. If you and the selectors don't want me to I'd rather not play.' Greg did not tell Hughes he was retiring after Sydney. Nor did he confide in his team-mates. Lillee was playing his career day by day. Marsh seemed ready to last forever.

And so we come to Sydney to witness the farewell of a champion. Behind him lay the history of cricket, a land as large as the imagination, a province which would endure beyond even this very best of batsmen. The strong thread with which Greg was attached to cricket, and which had grown thinner as it wound around the world more times than Judy cared to count, was about to snap. His renunciation was at hand. Judy was in Sydney with the children, staying with her parents. He told her first. She tested his resolve, but Greg was firm. The message for which he had waited had been delivered on the Adelaide and MCG scoreboards as clearly as though in tablets of stone.

Jeanne and Martin had come east for the Test, so they soon knew, as did Trevor and step-grandmother, Peg Lester, who had taken to watching most of Greg's Tests because she could never be darn well sure which would be his last. The tribe was gathering as if for some celebration, not a wake. Greg somehow gave that promise. You could rely on him.

He was not so sure. This would be his eighty-seventh Test, the bogey number for Australian batsmen, being 13 from the century. 'It looked like out first ball and three dropped catches would be the order of the day,' said Greg. To turn that hard gaze one last time upon fate Greg severed his line of retreat. He would make the announcement of his retirement before the Test rather than afterwards. That way, if he failed to break the records, he would not be tempted by second thoughts. 'Always seemed to have played my best under that sort of pressure,' he explained lightly.

The first day of the Test, Monday, 2 January, was almost washed out but in the few overs bowled Pakistan lost two wickets. The second, Qasim Omar, was a nick off Lillee, which flew towards Greg at first slip. Allan Border, perhaps half a metre in front of Greg at second slip, dived across and caught it. Greg fell with his hopefully cupped hands empty. In the instant before the usual jubilation besotted Border, he realized, looked up at Greg sheepishly and said, 'Oh, sorry.' Greg brushed it aside. 'As long as you caught it, that's all that matters.'

On the morning of the second day Greg returned from practice and quietly informed Phil Ridings of his retirement. 'Thanks and congratulations on a great career,' said Ridings. From there Greg told Rod and Dennis and Kim Hughes. As the word spread, and the media girded its loins for nostalgia, Greg tickled the tear ducts along. Soon after lunch he caught Mudassar Nazar off Geoff Lawson to equal Cowdrey's catching record. Greg had no need for humility. He took his 120 in 87 Tests, Cowdrey required 114 Tests.

At tea exuberant New South Wales all-rounder, Greg Matthews, said to Greg, 'There's a rumour going around you're retired?' Greg kept deadpan. 'No, it's not.' Matthews looked baffled. 'It's not a rumour, I have,' said Greg. Matthews shot back quickly. 'What size shoes do you take?' With respect, as far as cricket was concerned, they were the shoes of the fisherman.

Ian met Greg at stumps with a Channel Nine crew to enact one of those uncomfortable scripts interviewing close relatives. It produced this good line. Why make the announcement with the records still unbroken? 'I needed the incentive,' said Greg. 'Rodney Marsh's great quote, "A drowning man would clutch at a serpent."' His team-mates clapped him from the field and the crowd stood to applaud too. The press conference, in the battered dressing-room of the equally old, but gracious members' stand, produced front pages laden with sorrowful prose and praise the following morning. Statistics ruled. He still needed 69 runs to break Bradman's record and one catch to outstrip Cowdrey.

The next day, 3 January, Greg walked out to bat at 12.24 p.m. to tumultuous applause from a crowd of 17,000. Half an hour before lunch was an awkward period. The way the Test was progressing he would only have one innings. The Pakistan team sensed advantage in the occasion. Had not Bradman gone for a duck in his last innings? They bowled straight and tight. 'I decided to tread all over them, fall on them, kick them away, anything but get out,' said Greg. After lunch he still kept risks to a minimum as his score crept to 65, four runs short. At drinks Greg said to Kim Hughes, his partner, 'I can't see where these four runs are coming from. They'll be the toughest I've ever scored.'

In the M. A. Noble stand Judy sat with the children, her mother and father and Jeanne and Martin. Jonathan, not yet four, muttered, 'When my daddy breaks the record we're going home,' but just why his father would want to smash nice music he could not fathom. Jeanne sat, as always, with all four fingers on each hand crossed, fists full of knots to match those in her stomach, hoping that her star batsman-son could match such great expectations. It was so much more tense than when Ian played his third last Test on the same ground exactly four years before. As Ian walked out the spectator in front of her growled, 'Here comes that bastard Chappell.' Jeanne rapped him on the shoulder and said with a glare, 'I happen to know he's not. I'm his mother.'

Greg, on 65, farmed about, left the crease, grimaced, held the bat blade in his hand, focused, consolidated, concentrated and... missed a leg glance. He threw his face skywards, eyes closed. If for one critical millisecond he did not devote his entire being to this task he knew his innings, like an unguarded flame, would snuff. It was at such moments that cricket struck straight to the heart of matters, compelling him to exclude extraneous data and open himself to the purity of challenge.

Next door on the SCG No. 2, brother Trevor was practising with others in the New South Wales Shield team, Rick McCosker, Steve Rixon. As the roars next door warned of the approach of some

worthwhile miracle they left off and walked through to the members'
stand to watch.

Greg took block with his back foot on the popping crease, bat just
behind the toe of his right foot and lifted his bat as Sarfraz wheeled
in on his stuttering run. Greg's mouth opened drily. Sarfraz pitched
marginally short and Greg put his left foot well down the pitch for
a defensive push into cover. Tony Greig on Channel Nine:

> *A quick single, in comes Mohsin [Khan], he'll shy at the stumps,
> Chappell's home and . . . there's overthrows! This could be it, Chap-
> pell turning for the second, he'll be back for the third, Hughes is
> flying, he'll come back for the fourth and that run makes Greg
> Chappell the most prolific scorer of runs in the history of cricket
> in Australia.*

Greg threw his right hand into the air, and saluted with his bat as well.
Hughes came down to shake hands and tapped Greg's pads with his
bat. Greg looked out of contact, tired, relieved, holding his green
Australian cap in his hand, waving to Judy who was signalling back.
Green and gold flags shook deliriously. Strange ceremonies were
abroad in the stands to mark the felling of Sir Donald's record. Peg
Lester had never been kissed so often in her life. Javed Miandad and
several other Pakistan players shook Greg's hand. Greg had a theory
about those overthrows. Mohsin Khan's attempted run-out was a low
percentage throw. 'I've never asked him . . . the Pakistanis are very
record conscious. It's just a suspicion I have. I don't think it would
bother him that overthrow. I think he'd have been delighted to have
been part of it.' Part of the final hours of Greg painstakingly pressing
together the last pieces in the mosaic of his career. Each innings, like
this, had been created from nothing, each had to escape the tyranny
of the empty scoreboard. The applause was in recognition of this
retrospective of Greg's art. It lasted about a minute, then it was over.
Finished. Trevor and Co. returned to their practice. The next ball was
bowled.

But the rites were not quite concluded. Four runs later Greg became
the first Australian batsman to post 7,000 Test runs. That meant more
delays for applause and on 74 runs Channel Nine crossed to Ian talking
with his father Martin, who ruined any pretence at objectivity by
calling Ian 'Son'. When the pride quivered in Martin's voice it became
clear how much he would miss Greg at the crease. Martin had never

let go of cricket. He had managed the South Australian Shield side and scored for WSC. Every one of Greg's 7,000 runs was an affirmation of the rightness, the worthiness of his devotion to coaching his sons. It was cricket perpetuated in his own image. He would have moved to Brisbane to coach Greg's son, Stephen, but Jeanne had too many friends, too much life in Adelaide to leave. 'You would have to take some credit for Greg equalling Cowdrey's catching record,' said Ian. 'Well, if a million hours throwing balls at you three amount to anything I probably had something to do with it,' said Martin. And if Greg could make a century in his last Test? 'Yes, it would be lovely. I hope he has his head down with that in mind.' A taskmaster to the end.

Greg was 79 not out at stumps but when he came in friend Lillee produced his own surprise retirement which almost superseded Greg's continuing feats. The day was awash with emotion, a mixture of rejoicing and regret. That evening, in Adelaide, Sir Donald Bradman, 75, released a statement congratulating Greg. It said in part:

He has generously pointed out the disparity between the number of innings we played. But don't let us be uncharitable about that. He is a worthy holder of the honour because, for many years, he has been Australia's premier batsman and his runs were made with aesthetic and imperious quality which few others in history can emulate.

Sir Donald also sent a telegram to Greg in which he thanked Greg for lifting a great weight from Sir Donald's shoulders. One of the burdens of being the best was to be forever the yardstick for new performances. The measure was now Greg.

That evening the extended Chappell clan dined out in The Rocks, Greg and Judy, Ian and his wife, Barbara, Trevor and Lorraine, Martin and Jeanne, the Donaldsons, Peggy Lester, Judy's sister Elizabeth and her husband Dennis and so on. Peg collected Greg in a cab outside the Wentworth Hotel en route to The Rocks. 'Congratulations,' she said quietly. 'I've waited a long time for this.' Greg replied, 'I did it for Vic.'

The next day, 4 January, just before midday, Greg hit his twenty-fourth and last Test century, the only batsman ever to score centuries in his first and last Test innings. Cricket is full of such gee-whiz memorabilia. The cameras caught Judy clapping with her hands above her head, blonde hair clipped short above a grey and white pinafore.

It was like an award winning serial for Channel Nine, this Test. Stephen was beside himself. 'This is the greatest day of my life,' he declared proudly. Belinda had promised that if Daddy made 100 today she would be good for the rest of her life. Greg should have got it in writing.

After reaching 100 Greg moved into overdrive, displaying all the élan of one released. The Pakistanis actually bowled a few half volleys. For years the West Indies had fed him a wasting diet of non-stop, short-pitched bowling verging on pure bodyline. It was a pleasure for him to skip forward to on-drive with that characteristic kick of his right foot like a Scottish dancer. He was always the most graceful of players. John Arlott once described him as, 'All ease and elegance, fit to play before the Queen in Her Majesty's parlour.' Slowly Greg drew the edges of his innings together, collecting fours and attaching them securely to his century. He could hear the crowd's murmur, the echoes of victuallers calling in the stands and occasionally the wind carried the far-away voice of transistors, counting and prophesying. All this would go on without him, yet remain with him because, God knows, how he had given himself to it. Difficult to know whether to feel consoled or condemned. Perhaps that was the burden that Sir Donald had passed to him.

Yet even on this most climactic of occasions Greg had an eye for the cameos of cricket. Sarfraz Nawaz, as always, was bowling sturdily, hitting a green patch just outside off stump and making the ball nip and cut both ways. Sarfraz was not initially selected for the tour but had been flown out midway through. Said Greg, 'He was cackling away in Urdu to Imran at mid-on, laughing and chatting every time he walked back. I said, "Enjoying yourself Saf, bowling on this?" Sarfraz grinned at me. "The bloody idiots (selectors), if I'd played in Perth I'd have got 14 wickets!"' Greg smiled back. Sarfraz might have too, the way that first Test wicket had seamed about.

Eventually Greg was out for 182 when 'my arms had stopped moving and the legs weren't much better'. He took a long look at the SCG, as he had all the grounds that season where he would not bat again, and walked off, more serious than sad, acknowledging everyone with his bat. After all the keening of the past three days, his absence left a faint uneasiness, as though the passing of greatness detracted from those who had witnessed it. Perhaps no man is an island.

It was late afternoon when Greg reappeared for the last act, through a guard of honour for him and Dennis as they emerged for Pakistan's second innings. Kim Hughes had said, 'Come on, we'll get out and wait for the two geriatrics to show.' Greg and Dennis had developed the habit of walking on last since Greg shed the captaincy. Dennis was simply a tardy dresser, but it suited them, both drifting out of the game together. In the first innings catches had flown either side of Greg at first slip, some caught, some dropped. Second slip seemed the hot spot. Greg asked Hughes, 'Why don't I field at second slip and see if I can catch a few. It'll be good for a number of reasons.' Hughes nodded. Whatever Greg thought.

Off the fifth ball of Geoff Lawson's first over, Pakistan opener Mohsin Khan, who had proved so obliging with his overthrows, was again the means towards Greg's record. He slashed outside the off-stump and the ball flew at Greg's face. He snatched at it in self defence and flung it high into the air. As he leapt Aussie Rules style to retrieve it he realized he had the record. A gleeful Lawson was first to shake his hand, then Rod Marsh. 'I would have broken it weeks ago if you hadn't poached so many,' Greg grinned at his Groucho Marx moust-ached mate. The next day Greg caught one more to finish with 122 catches, a world record. His Australian record of 7,110 runs left him behind only Hammond, Cowdrey, Sobers, Boycott and Gavaskar on the world Test ladder. But if Greg's WSC Supertest innings were added on he totalled 8,525 runs, ahead of Gavaskar's record of 8,384 at the time Greg retired. That made him the most prolific scorer of all time. Of course the Supertests will never be recognized. That would not be cricket. But it would be the truth.

27. A Great Love

When the bathos finally subsided it was possible to divine the nature of the man cricket had bequeathed. Physically he was a little worse for wear. He did not have a good skin for such a sun-drenched sport. Skin cancers had been removed. A melanoma, benign, was cut from his right upper cheek, the roots of which extended almost to his eye, ear and nose. He grew beards, experimented with sunscreens and finally designed his own sun-hat, one whose brim did not tip on his nose when he looked up for a catch. He sent one to Sir Donald Bradman. In December 1984, during the centenary of Test cricket at the Adelaide Oval, Sir Donald was to ride in an open car on a blazing day. He had his G.C. hat handy. 'How much is it worth to you for me to wear it?' he jovially called. Greg replied, 'Sir Donald, we couldn't pay you what it's worth, so just wear it.' And he did. Old misgivings were dying there.

Greg's ricked neck was diagnosed as degeneration of the fourth and fifth vertebrae in the cervical spine, the legacy of peering up a hundred pitches at hundreds of thousands of balls. It forces him to hold his head somewhat ... regally. More evidence to mistake as aloofness. Another curiosity that gave him and Judy a fright one day was that his right upper body, wrist to chest, was massively enlarged compared to his left. Greg had dye tests which showed simply that years of bowling had exaggerated the muscle development of his whole right side, leg as well.

At the end of the Pakistan one-day series Rod Marsh followed his two geriatric mates into retirement. 'I think he might have had a look around the dressing room and thought ...' said Greg. Much later he and Rod, mulling over the memories they prized most, agreed it was the players. Each had played with about 150 cricketers in their first-class careers — Greg with South Australia, Somerset and Queensland — and shared another 100 or so Australian team-mates in Test cricket. 'I reckon that out of those there were only one or two I couldn't get on with,' said Greg. 'They weren't bad blokes, not nasty, just a bit strange.' The rest had survived the peculiar baptism of fire that is any Australian cricket dressing-room. Weaknesses were exposed, deficiencies addressed, truths enforced. 'If you were a weak bastard you were told, selfish you were told, boastful the same,' said Greg. 'It taught players to be honest with themselves. Rod, Ian and Doug Walters and Thommo, would probably be the most honest men I've ever met. Would never tell you a lie. Just couldn't.' That sort of trust was more rare than a precious ointment.

Rod had been more genuinely Ian's mate, but once Ian retired it became the three musketeers, Greg, Rod and Dennis. Greg and Judy worked out that in his 15 year first-class cricket career, Greg spent over four years actually on the cricket field. Add on another four or so travelling and it approached half his adult life. But whereas at home Greg worked during the day and saw Judy at night, during cricket tours players were jammed in each other's company day and night, on flights, on field, in dressing-rooms and hotels. Greg roomed with Dennis on a couple of tours and saw him at his best and worst. 'I can remember seeing Dennis absolutely distraught about his bowling,' said Greg. 'In the first year of World Series Cricket he could have given the game away. We took turns in baby-sitting him. We knew he was

only a bagful of wickets away from being in high spirits again.'
Similarly Dennis had been loyal to him during the underarm and Rod
the same during the run of ducks. Over the years what began as
sporting mateship transformed into a deeply personal knowledge of
each other's character. 'There were very few secrets we could have
from each other,' said Greg. 'It was an intimate understanding, so close
words weren't even necessary. We probably knew more about each
other than our respective families.' Marsh and Lillee lived in Perth,
Greg in Brisbane, separated by a continent, but Greg thought the
friendship would last a lifetime.

I said Greg's love of cricket was something Judy could be jealous of,
but the mateship element revealed forces latent in the breasts of
Australian cricketers to excite the interest of sociological study. In an
age when that last bastion of male exclusivity, the surf lifesaving
movement, has long fallen to female membership, Australian cricket
wives, until the 1985 UK tour, were not permitted to accompany their
husbands on tour, to book on the same flight or in the same hotels.
Once Judy married into that she was contending with cultural ineq-
uities too large to fight by herself. At first her will subsided beneath
Greg's, weighed down by the history of cricket's discrimination.
Australian cricket rides on the back of its subservient and underpriv-
ileged women. It took the underarm and its repercussions, when
cricket showed itself unequal to Greg's perfect devotion, to split the
paternal bond forged between Greg and his game as a child. For Greg
that was as painful as any divorce, but it restored him to his family.

Throughout those trials Judy's endurance proved equal to Greg's.
Their relationship did not crack under the barren heat of cricket. It
matured and toughened until Greg recognized the debt he owed his
family and withdrew them from cricket's blasted heath. Well, almost.
In June 1984, Greg accepted Phil Ridings' invitation to become a
national selector. Rod Marsh could not believe it. 'You've only been
out of the game five minutes and now you're getting back. It's
diabolical.' He and Dennis had different ideas. They were going to
reee-lax. Judy understood Greg would have to wean himself from
cricket. She also recognized the financial security cricket had given
them. Since Greg had joined forces with Barry Maranta their insurance company had given way to various successful enterprises,
culminating in a large property growth trust. The walls of Maranta's
boardroom were devoted to cricket — Russell Drysdale's famous
painting of a boy bowling against an old building in the outback, and

a large framed poster of Greg superimposed over W. G. Grace, signed from Greg to Maranta, 'In appreciation of his assistance and support'. Within these walls Greg had become an assets millionaire.

During that last season rumours were abroad about Greg entering politics. 'I'm available for Prime Minister,' he joked. He was already the Prime Minister of cricket. Greg once attended a National Party launch in Queensland and a fleeting glance at his views reveals a true conservatism — conservation fine, but who paid for it?; erotica OK, pornography no; was Aboriginal land rights back-door apartheid?; export uranium and retain the US nuclear alliance. But it seemed likely that the only politics that would enmesh Greg would be cricket politics. As a selector he began mending bridges with men like Bob Parish and Norm McMahon, ACB administrators with whom he had become an unwilling adversary during the WSC years. He had embarked upon an administrative path in the footsteps of the one Australian whose legend he did not surpass, Sir Donald Bradman.

Having retired from Test cricket Greg played for Queensland, captained by Jeff Thomson, in a fighting Sheffield Shield loss to Western Australia — directed by Dennis, starring Rod — in the final in Perth in March 1984. That elusive Shield was becoming the America's Cup for Queensland cricket. It was Greg's last first-class match. He did not officially retire from all levels until 27 August 1984, having given himself the winter to ensure that no spark remained which might be rekindled. The ashes were cold. The concentration was still there if the interest was not. Asked to play 'Twinkle, Twinkle, Little Star' on the piano at a packed charity concert at the Brisbane City Hall, Greg sweated over nights of rehearsals at home with Judy. One black note looked like another to him. He did not get it right once in the nets, but on the night was, breathlessly, note perfect. It was an amusing, lighthearted, but symbolic gesture that he should apply that famed concentration to a culture that cricket had excluded from his life.

Though not officially retired until after that winter, the cycle of Greg's career was really completed right at the end of the 1983–84 summer, after his last Test, last Shield, last ... He was in Adelaide and he and his father went for a game of golf. Martin became breathless with chest pains on the course and was admitted to hospital with a mild heart attack. He had seen all his sons recently and now all his friends called in. He recovered quickly and was home on Saturday, 28 April, to watch Ian compere Channel Nine's Wide World of Sports. He and Jeanne then drove to the Glenelg esplanade for a walk but with a chilly wind whipping around, Jeanne brought him home. He was watching a football replay with Jeanne when he suddenly slumped over and was gone.

Ian wrote an obituary, more a eulogy, in his newspaper column which he may never hope to better. It began:

> Give him a couple of weeks and they'll have the best damned cricket team Heaven has seen in a long time.

The sons flew down and found in the garage their childhood cricket and baseball gear which Martin had kept. It spun Greg through a time warp, memories too sharp to be enjoyed without grief. Martin had begun Greg's career and somehow, now, he was ending it too.

The cremation was at Centennial Park, about 16 kilometres from Glenelg. A bronze plaque on a wall there reads, 'Martin Chappell, 28th April, 1984, aged 64, Loved by All'. Just to the left is another plaque: 'Victor York Richardson, 30th October, 1969, aged 75'. The wall is set against a background of the Adelaide Hills, only a bird's call away, where eucalypt tops seem to brush the clouds as they whisk south towards the Glenelg seafront, a shimmering blue haze in the distance. That was where it all began for Greg, the boy in whom they instilled such a great love.

G. S. Chappell — Some Facts and Figures

by *Irving Rosenwater*

If a film was taken of a long innings by Chappell and then, for some reason, the game of cricket was lost to civilisation, the entire art of batting could be deduced by a future generation when the film had been discovered. It has not been possible to say that about many batsmen.

— Henry Blofeld on G. S. Chappell, 1984

G. S. Chappell has captained Australia in more Tests (48) than any other cricketer, exceeding the previous record (39 by R. B. Simpson) v. New Zealand at Wellington, 26 February-2 March 1982. He has also won more Tests (21) as captain than any other Australian, establishing the new record (his 16th victory as captain) v. Pakistan at Brisbane on 1 December 1981, exceeding the previous Australian record held jointly by D. G. Bradman (15 Test wins) and I. M. Chappell (15 Test wins). His total Test captaincies (48) is second only in Test history to the 74 Test captaincies of C. H. Lloyd (West Indies).

Of those who have played in five or more Tests, his Test average (53.86) among Australian batsmen is bettered only by D. G. Bradman (99.94) and S. G. Barnes (63.05).

On 4 January 1984, during his 79* (continued to 182) v. Pakistan at Sydney, he became the first player to reach 7,000 Test runs for Australia. He reached this landmark in 151 innings and in his 87th Test, in the process exceeding the previous record Test aggregate of runs for Australia (6,996 by D. G. Bradman in 80 innings and 52 Tests).

On 30 January 1982, during his 61 v. West Indies at Adelaide, he became the third player to reach 6,000 Test runs for Australia, following D. G. Bradman (6,996) and R. N. Harvey (6,149). He reached this landmark in 129 innings and in his 73rd Test, compared with 68 innings (45 Tests) by Bradman, and 134 innings (78 Tests) by Harvey. On 19 March 1982, when he scored the first 76 of his 176 v. New Zealand at Christchurch, he exceeded Harvey's Test aggregate, in 133 innings and 76 Tests, compared with 137 innings and 79 Tests by Harvey.

His 55 Test innings of 50 or more (24 centuries, 31 fifties) is a Test record for Australia, exceeding the 48 such innings by K. D. Walters (15 centuries, 33 fifties). He exceeded Walters' record on 19 March 1982, when he was 76* at close of play v. New Zealand at Christchurch, an innings increased to 176 on the following day.

During his 235 for Australia v. Pakistan at Faisalabad in March 1980, he became the fourth Australian — after D. G. Bradman, R. N. Harvey and R. B. Simpson — to reach 20,000 runs in first-class cricket. He reached this landmark on 8 March 1980, in his 447th innings.

During the 1980–81 season in Australia, he passed R. N. Harvey's career aggregate of 21,699 runs to put him in second place behind D. G. Bradman (28,067) in the table of leading Australian run-getters in first-class cricket. He exceeded Harvey's total during his 52 for Australia v. India at Adelaide on the afternoon of 26 January 1981, in his 471st innings (64 not out), compared with 461 innings (35 not out) by Harvey.

On 20 March 1982, when he reached his century during his 176 for Australia v. New Zealand at Christchurch, he recorded his 68th century in first-class cricket, exceeding R. N. Harvey's career total of 67 centuries to put him in second place behind D. G. Bradman (117 centuries) among Australians in first-class cricket.

On 1 December 1981, he became the third Australian other than wicketkeepers, after R. B. Simpson and I. M. Chappell, to take 100 catches in Test cricket, when he caught Ejaz Faqih (Pakistan) at Brisbane. He became the sixth fielder in all Test cricket to take 100 catches. He reached this landmark in his 69th Test, his brother I. M.

Chappell having likewise taken his 100th catch in his 69th Test (v. West Indies, Melbourne, 1975–76). G. S. Chappell's 122 Test catches is a world Test record for any country (excluding wicketkeepers).

His total of four double-centuries in Test cricket is second only, among Australians, to the 12 double-centuries of D. G. Bradman. His total of 24 Test centuries is second, among Australians, behind D. G. Bradman (29).

By scoring 108 for Australia v. England at Perth in 1970–71 and 182 for Australia v. Pakistan at Sydney in 1983–84, G. S. Chappell became the first player to score centuries in both his first and last innings in Test cricket.

He is the only Australian cricketer since the Second World War — and one of seven Australians in all — to score a century before lunch in a Test, taking his score from 76* to 176 on the second morning (20 March 1982) for Australia v. New Zealand at Christchurch, 1981–82. He is the only Test captain in history (for any country) to score a century before lunch in a Test.

He is the only Australian to score a century in each innings of a Test match on two occasions: 247* and 133 v. New Zealand, Wellington, 1973–74 (this being one of only four instances in Test history of a double-century and a century in the same Test); and 123 and 109* v. West Indies, Brisbane, 1975–76, when he became the only cricketer in history to score centuries in both innings of his first Test as captain. His aggregate of 380 runs in the Test v. New Zealand at Wellington in 1973–74 is a world Test record, exceeding the 375 runs (325 and 50) by A. Sandham for England v. West Indies at Kingston in 1929–30.

He has scored a century in each innings of a first-class match on four occasions — a record for an Australian cricketer, shared with D. G. Bradman. Apart from his two instances in Test cricket (above), Chappell has also scored 129 and 156* for South Australia v. Queensland, Brisbane, 1969–70, and 180 and 101 for Queensland v. Victoria, Brisbane, 1973–74.

He has twice — like, too, his brother I. M. Chappell — scored three centuries in consecutive innings in first-class cricket: 1975–76 — 123 and 109*, Australia v. West Indies, Brisbane, 124, Queensland v. New South Wales, Sydney; 1980–81 — 113, Queensland v. New South Wales, Brisbane, 102*, Queensland v. Victoria, Brisbane, 194, Queensland v. Western Australia, Brisbane. (These three innings were preceded by 94 in the first innings for Queensland v. New South Wales, Brisbane.) His three successive first-class centuries in 1980–81 were all in the Sheffield Shield for Queensland, a feat otherwise performed for that State only by L. P. D. O'Connor in 1926–27.

On 9 March 1981, during his 35 for Queensland v. Western Australia at Perth, he became the fourth player — after D. G. Bradman, L. E. Favell and S. C. Trimble — to reach 8,000 runs in the Sheffield Shield. He reached this landmark in 148 innings, second to the record of 86 innings by Bradman.

In 1973–74 he became the first player to score 1,000 or more runs for Queensland in a single Sheffield Shield season, with 1,013 runs, av. 92.09. This exceeded the previous Queensland record of 990 runs by W. A. Brown in 1938–39. Chappell's record for the State has since been exceeded by A. D. Ogilvie (1,060 runs in 1977–78) and K. C. Wessels (1,015 runs in 1981–82).

April 1985

*Not out.

CAREER STATISTICS

Gregory Stephen Chappell

CAREER STATISTICS

1. All First Class Matches.
2. Test Matches.
3. Centuries — All First Class Matches.
4. Test Centuries.
5. All First Class Matches for South Australia.
6. All First Class Matches for Queensland.
7. All Sheffield Shield Matches.
8. Analysis of Dismissals in First Class Cricket.
9. Bowlers from whom Test Catches taken.
10. Career Figures — One Day Internationals.
11. Career Records — Australian Players — First Class Cricket — Batting Aggregates.
12. Test Career Records — Australian Players — Highest Batting Aggregates.
13. Most Catches — Test Matches excluding Wicketkeepers.
14. Catches in One Test Match.
15. Australian Captains.
16. World Series Cricket Supertests.

NOTES

1. In bowling for G. S. Chappell, wides and no-balls have been debited as runs.
2. Career figures — One Day Internationals, are from the following:
   (i)   *International Limited Overs Cricket Records* by Victor H. Izaacs.
   (ii) *The Book of One Day Internationals* by David Lemmon.
3. Most Catches, Test Matches excluding Wicketkeepers and Catches in One Test are taken from *Wisden* 1984.
4. Australian Captains are from *Cricket Year 1983* — edited by Ken Piesse.
5. World Series Cricket Supertest figures are from *Wisden* 1979 and 1980.

BOB SPENCE
BRISBANE
14 JANUARY 1985

Gregory Stephen Chappell

CAREER STATISTICS Compiled by Bob Spence

1. ALL FIRST CLASS MATCHES
BATTING AND FIELDING (X indicates not out)

SEASON	M.	INNS	N.O.	H.S.	RUNS	AVER.	100	50	C.
1966–67	8	16	2	104	501	35.78	1	4	5
1967–68	10	17	1	154	659	41.18	1	5	8
1968	27	47	8	148	1163	29.82	1	7	11
1968–69	10	17	3	107	707	50.50	2	4	8
1969	25	45	1	144	1330	30.22	2	5	21
1969–70									
Aust.	8	15	2	156X	856	65.84	4	3	8
New Zealand	7	11	2	94	519	57.66	–	5	9
1970–71	14	23	2	133	854	40.66	3	4	23
1971–72	10	18	2	197X	736	46.00	2	2	12
1972	18	28	10	181	1260	70.00	4	3	26
1972–73									
Aust.	9	15	2	129	772	59.38	2	6	11
West Indies	10	17	1	154	1109	69.31	4	7	13
1973–74									
Aust.	11	18	3	180	1288	85.86	5	5	15
New Zealand	6	10	2	247X	592	74.00	2	1	8
1974–75	14	25	1	159	1484	61.83	5	11	24
1975	12	20	3	144	762	44.82	2	4	17
1975–76									
Aust.	15	26	8	182X	1547	85.94	6	7	17
South Africa	4	8	0	35	172	21.50	–	–	7
1976–77									
Aust.	9	15	0	187	859	57.26	2	6	9
New Zealand	5	9	0	130	333	37.00	1	1	8
1977	16	25	5	161X	1182	59.10	5	2	18
1979–80									
Aust.	10	19	4	185	1066	71.06	4	2	15
Pakistan	3	5	0	235	381	76.20	1	2	3
1980	4	6	0	101	303	50.50	1	2	4
1980–81	14	22	2	204	1502	75.10	5	6	24
1981–82									
Aust.	9	15	0	201	532	35.46	2	1	8
New Zealand	5	6	2	176	317	79.25	1	1	4
1982–83									
Aust.	11	20	2	126	703	39.05	3	1	21
Sri Lanka	2	2	0	66	92	46.00	–	1	–
1983–84	15	22	4	182	954	53.00	3	3	19
Totals	321	542	72	247X	24535	52.20	74	111	376

BOWLING

SEASON	BALLS	MAIDENS	RUNS	WKTS	AVER.	B.B.	5 W.I.
1966–67	313	4	203	4	50.75	3–19	
1967–68	79	0	57	3	19.00	1–3	
1968	1342	56	712	26	27.38	4–20	
1968–69	288	6	138	7	19.71	3–32	
1969	2590	86	1255	45	27.88	7–40	3
1969–70							
Aust.	992	26	327	14	23.35	3–40	
New Zealand	444	23	187	7	26.71	2–20	
1970–71	1992	39	763	17	44.88	3–41	
1971–72	655	12	295	7	42.14	3–19	
1972	1238	51	495	19	26.05	7–58	1
1972–73							
Aust.	1046	30	424	14	30.28	5–61	1
West Indies	1287	66	472	13	36.30	4–57	
1973–74							
Aust.	828	22	309	15	20.60	4–47	
New Zealand	502	10	196	8	24.50	4–31	
1974–75	400	5	189	6	31.50	2–23	
1975	288	16	152	5	30.40	2–22	
1975–76							
Aust.	708	16	251	12	20.92	3–27	
South Africa	192	9	90	6	15.00	2–0	
1976–77							
Aust.	360	14	120	3	40.00	2–14	
New Zealand	280	8	87	2	43.50	1–15	
1977	636	28	305	6	50.83	3–45	
1979–80							
Aust.	684	43	227	11	20.63	4–42	
Pakistan	204	9	75	3	25.00	3–49	
1980	96	4	51	2	25.50	2–32	
1980–81	1367	69	550	23	23.91	4–28	
1981–82							
Aust.	300	14	133	3	44.33	1–6	
New Zealand	210	10	58	1	58.00	1–30	
1982–83							
Aust.	411	15	189	4	47.25	3–31	
Sri Lanka	6	0	2	0	–		
1983–84	1212	51	462	5	92.40	2–45	
Totals	20950	742	8774	291	30.15	7–40	5

2. TEST MATCHES
BATTING AND FIELDING

v.	M.	INNS	N.O.	H.S.	RUNS	AVER.	100	50	C.
England	35	65	8	144	2619	45.94	9	12	61
Pakistan	17	27	2	235	1581	63.24	6	6	22
West Indies	17	31	6	182X	1400	56.00	5	7	16
New Zealand	14	22	3	247X	1076	56.63	3	3	18
India	3	5	0	204	368	73.60	1	2	5
Sri Lanka	1	1	0	66	66	66.00	–	1	–
Totals	87	151	19	247X	7110	53.86	24	31	122

BOWLING

v.	BALLS	MAIDENS	RUNS	WKTS	AVER.	B.B.	5 W.I.
England	1867	70	682	13	52.46	2–36	
Pakistan	1076	37	418	12	34.83	5–61	1
West Indies	932	48	323	8	40.37	2–10	
New Zealand	1314	43	474	13	36.46	3–54	
India	120	10	27	1	27.00	1–4	
Sri Lanka	6	0	2	0	–		
Totals	5315	208	1926	47	40.97	5–61	

3. CENTURIES — ALL FIRST CLASS MATCHES

1.	104	South Australia–Queensland	Brisbane	January 1967
2.	154	South Australia–W. Australia	Adelaide	February 1968
3.	148	Somerset–Middlesex	Weston-super-Mare	July 1968
4.	107	South Australia–NSW	Adelaide	December 1968
5.	102	South Australia–NSW	Sydney	March 1969
6.	101	Somerset–Leicestershire	Leicester	July 1969
7.	144	Somerset–Worcestershire	Weston-super-Mare	August 1969
8.	126	South Australia–Queensland	Adelaide	December 1969
9.	129	South Australia–Queensland	Brisbane	January 1970
10.	156X	South Australia–Queensland	Brisbane	January 1970
11.	106X	South Australia–NSW	Adelaide	February 1970
12.	108	Australia–England	Perth	December 1970
13.	102	South Australia–England XI	Adelaide	December 1970
14.	133	South Australia–Queensland	Adelaide	December 1970
15.	115X	Australia–Rest of World	Melbourne	January 1972
16.	197X	Australia–Rest of World	Sydney	January 1972
17.	181	Australia–Essex	Ilford	June 1972
18.	131	Australia–England	Lord's	June 1972
19.	113	Australia–England	The Oval	August 1972
20.	141X	Australia–Kent	Canterbury	August 1972
21.	129	South Australia–NSW	Adelaide	November 1972
22.	116X	Australia–Pakistan	Melbourne	December 1972
23.	106	Australia–Jamaica	Sabina Park	February 1973

24.	142	Australia–Barbados	Kensington	March 1973
25.	106	Australia–West Indies	Kensington	March 1973
26.	154	Australia–Guyana	Bourda	March 1973
27.	180	Queensland–Victoria	Brisbane	October 1973
28.	101	Queensland–Victoria	Brisbane	October 1973
29.	165	Queensland–New Zealand	Brisbane	December 1973
30.	115	Queensland–Victoria	Melbourne	January 1974
31.	158X	Queensland–South Australia	Adelaide	January 1974
32.	247X	Australia–New Zealand	Wellington	March 1974
33.	133	Australia–New Zealand	Wellington	March 1974
34.	122	Queensland–England XI	Brisbane	November 1974
35.	159	Queensland–W. Australia	Perth	December 1974
36.	144	Australia–England	Sydney	January 1975
37.	102	Australia–England	Melbourne	February 1975
38.	122	Queensland–Victoria	Brisbane	March 1975
39.	144	Australia–Glamorgan	Swansea	July 1975
40.	126	Australia–Sussex	Hove	July 1975
41.	105X	Queensland–NSW	Brisbane	October 1975
42.	123	Australia–West Indies	Brisbane	November 1975
43.	109X	Australia–West Indies	Brisbane	November 1975
44.	124	Queensland–NSW	Sydney	December 1975
45.	182X	Australia–West Indies	Sydney	January 1976
46.	131X	Queensland–Victoria	Brisbane	January 1976
47.	187	Queensland–Victoria	Brisbane	October 1976
48.	121	Australia–Pakistan	Melbourne	January 1977
49.	130	Australia–Wellington	Wellington	February 1977
50.	113	Australia–Somerset	Bath	May 1977
51.	102	Australia–Gloucestershire	Bristol	May 1977
52.	100X	Australia–Worcestershire	Worcester	May 1977
53.	112	Australia–England	Old Trafford	July 1977
54.	161X	Australia–Northamptonshire	Northampton	July 1977
55.	185	Queensland–Victoria	Brisbane	October 1979
56.	124	Australia–West Indies	Brisbane	December 1979
57.	169	Queensland–NSW	Brisbane	January 1980
58.	114	Australia–England	Melbourne	February 1980
59.	235	Australia–Pakistan	Faisalabad	March 1980
60.	101	Australia–Lancashire	Old Trafford	August 1980
61.	113	Queensland–NSW	Brisbane	October 1980
62.	102X	Queensland–Victoria	Brisbane	October 1980
63.	194	Queensland–W. Australia	Brisbane	November 1980
64.	204	Australia–India	Sydney	January 1981
65.	172	Queensland–South Australia	Adelaide	January 1981
66.	162	Queensland–Pakistan	Brisbane	October 1981
67.	201	Australia–Pakistan	Brisbane	November 1981
68.	176	Australia–New Zealand	Christchurch	March 1982
69.	126	Queensland–England XI	Brisbane	October 1982
70.	117	Australia–England	Perth	November 1982
71.	115	Australia–England	Adelaide	December 1982
72.	150X	Australia–Pakistan	Brisbane	November 1983
73.	182	Australia–Pakistan	Sydney	January 1984
74.	129	Queensland–Tasmania	Hobart	February 1984

CAREER STATISTICS

4. TEST CENTURIES

1. 108	v. England	Perth	December 1970
2. 131	v. England	Lord's	June 1972
3. 113	v. England	The Oval	August 1972
4. 116X	v. Pakistan	Melbourne	December 1972
5. 106	v. West Indies	Kensington	March 1973
6. 247X	v. New Zealand	Wellington	March 1974
7. 133	v. New Zealand	Wellington	March 1974
8. 144	v. England	Sydney	January 1975
9. 102	v. England	Melbourne	February 1975
10. 123	v. West Indies	Brisbane	November 1975
11. 109X	v. West Indies	Brisbane	November 1975
12. 182X	v. West Indies	Sydney	January 1976
13. 121	v. Pakistan	Melbourne	January 1977
14. 112	v. England	Old Trafford	July 1977
15. 124	v. West Indies	Brisbane	December 1979
16. 114	v. England	Melbourne	February 1980
17. 235	v. Pakistan	Faisalabad	March 1980
18. 204	v. India	Sydney	January 1981
19. 201	v. Pakistan	Brisbane	November 1981
20. 176	v. New Zealand	Christchurch	March 1982
21. 117	v. England	Perth	November 1982
22. 115	v. England	Adelaide	December 1982
23. 150X	v. Pakistan	Brisbane	November 1983
24. 182	v. Pakistan	Sydney	January 1984

5. ALL FIRST CLASS MATCHES FOR SOUTH AUSTRALIA
PERIOD 1966–67 to 1972–73

BATTING	M.	INNS	N.O.	H.S.	RUNS	AVER.	C.
Sheffield Shield	49	89	9	156X	3725	46.56	52
v. India	1	1	0	55	55	55.00	1
v. New Zealand	2	3	0	59	95	31.67	1
v. West Indies	2	3	1	36	65	32.50	1
v. England	2	3	0	102	179	59.66	6
v. World XI	1	1	0	14	14	14.00	2
Totals	57	100	10	156X	4133	45.92	63

BOWLING	BALLS	MAIDENS	RUNS	WKTS	AVER.
Sheffield Shield	3447	75	1405	46	30.54
v. New Zealand	96	4	45	1	45.00
v. West Indies	96	2	42	3	14.00
v. England	352	8	159	4	39.75
v. World XI	32	0	27	0	–
Totals	4023	89	1678	54	31.07

CENTURIES FOR SOUTH AUSTRALIA
SHEFFIELD SHIELD (10)

104	v. Queensland	Brisbane	January 1967
154	v. Western Australia	Adelaide	February 1968
107	v. New South Wales	Adelaide	December 1968
102	v. New South Wales	Sydney	March 1969
126	v. Queensland	Adelaide	December 1969
129	v. Queensland	Brisbane	January 1970
156X	v. Queensland	Brisbane	January 1970
106X	v. New South Wales	Adelaide	February 1970
133	v. Queensland	Adelaide	December 1970
129	v. New South Wales	Adelaide	November 1972

OTHER MATCHES (1)

102	v. England	Adelaide	December 1970

6. ALL FIRST CLASS MATCHES FOR QUEENSLAND
PERIOD 1973-74 to 1983-84

BATTING	M.	INNS	N.O.	H.S.	RUNS	AVER.	C.
Sheffield Shield	52	84	11	194	5037	69.00	56
v. New Zealand	2	3	0	165	213	71.00	6
v. England	3	6	1	126	400	80.00	11
v. West Indies	1	2	0	33	45	22.50	2
v. Pakistan	3	4	1	162	210	70.00	3
Totals	61	99	13	194	5905	68.66	78

BOWLING	BALLS	MAIDENS	RUNS	WKTS	AVER.
Sheffield Shield	3978	146	1629	56	29.08
v. New Zealand	145	8	48	4	12.00
v. England	72	4	17	0	–
v. West Indies	48	2	19	0	–
v. Pakistan	50	1	33	0	–
Totals	4293	161	1746	60	29.10

CENTURIES FOR QUEENSLAND
SHEFFIELD SHIELD (17)

180	v. Victoria	Brisbane	October 1973
101	v. Victoria	Brisbane	October 1973
115	v. Victoria	Melbourne	January 1974
158X	v. South Australia	Adelaide	January 1974
159	v. Western Australia	Perth	December 1974

122	v. Victoria	Brisbane	March 1975
105X	v. New South Wales	Brisbane	October 1975
124	v. New South Wales	Sydney	December 1975
131X	v. Victoria	Brisbane	January 1976
187	v. Victoria	Brisbane	October 1976
185	v. Victoria	Brisbane	October 1979
169	v. New South Wales	Brisbane	January 1980
113	v. New South Wales	Brisbane	October 1980
102X	v. Victoria	Brisbane	October 1980
194	v. Western Australia	Brisbane	November 1980
172	v. South Australia	Adelaide	January 1981
129	v. Tasmania	Hobart	February 1984

OTHER MATCHES (4)

165	v. New Zealand	Brisbane	December 1973
122	v. England	Brisbane	November 1974
162	v. Pakistan	Brisbane	November 1981
126	v. England	Brisbane	October 1982

7. ALL SHEFFIELD SHIELD MATCHES

BATTING	*M.*	*INNS*	*N.O.*	*H.S.*	*RUNS*	*AVER.*	*C.*
For South Aust.	49	89	9	156X	3725	46.56	52
For Queensland	52	84	11	194	5037	69.00	56
Totals	101	173	20	194	8762	57.26	108

BOWLING	*BALLS*	*MAIDENS*	*RUNS*	*WKTS*	*AVER.*
For South Aust.	3447	75	1405	46	30.54
For Queensland	3978	146	1629	56	29.08
Totals	7425	221	3034	102	29.74

SHEFFIELD SHIELD CENTURIES

For South Australia	10
For Queensland	17
Total	27

8. DISMISSALS IN FIRST CLASS CRICKET

	TIMES	*%AGE*
Bowled	80	17.02
Caught	315	67.02
lbw	39	8.30
Run Out	17	3.62
Stumped	16	3.40
Hit Wicket	1	0.21
Retired Out	2	0.43
Totals	470	100.00

9. BOWLERS FROM WHOM TEST CATCHES TAKEN

G. R. Beard	1
A. R. Border	1
R. J. Bright	2
G. S. Chappell	3
I. M. Chappell	2
A. R. Dell	1
G. Dymock	4
G. J. Gilmour	6
J. W. Gleeson	1
J. R. Hammond	1
J. D. Higgs	2
R. M. Hogg	3
R. J. Inverarity	1
T. J. Jenner	2
G. F. Lawson	4
D. K. Lillee	21
A. A. Mallett	11
R. A. L. Massie	4
K. J. O'Keeffe	1
L. S. Pascoe	8
C. G. Rackemann	4
J. R. Thomson	15
M. H. N. Walker	9
K. D. Walters	2
B. Yardley	13
Total	122

10. CAREER FIGURES — ONE DAY INTERNATIONALS
BATTING AND FIELDING

PERIOD	M.	INNS	N.O.	H.S.	RUNS	AVER.	100	50	C.
1971–83	74	72	14	138X	2331	40.18	3	14	23

BOWLING	BALLS	M.	RUNS	WKTS	AVER.	B.B.
	3108	41	2096	72	29.11	5–15

CENTURIES
125X	v. England	The Oval	6 June 1977
138X	v. New Zealand	Sydney	25 Nov. 1980
108	v. New Zealand	Auckland	13 Feb. 1982

FIVE WICKET INNINGS
5–20	v. England	Edgbaston	4 June 1977
5–15	v. India	Sydney	8 Jan. 1981

11. CAREER RECORDS — AUSTRALIAN PLAYERS
HIGHEST BATTING AGGREGATES

	CAREER	M.	INNS.	N.O.	H.S.	RUNS	AVER.	100
D. G. Bradman	1927–48	234	338	43	452X	28067	95.14	117
G. S. Chappell	1966–83	321	542	72	247X	24535	52.20	74
R. N. Harvey	1946–62	306	461	35	231X	21699	50.93	67

12. TEST CAREER RECORDS — AUSTRALIAN PLAYERS
HIGHEST BATTING AGGREGATES

	CAREER	M.	INNS.	N.O.	H.S.	RUNS	AVER.	100
G. S. Chappell	1970–83	87	151	19	247X	7110	53.86	24
D. G. Bradman	1928–48	52	80	10	334	6996	99.94	29
R. N. Harvey	1947–62	79	137	10	205	6149	48.41	21

13. MOST CATCHES — EXCLUDING WICKETKEEPERS
TEST MATCHES

	CATCHES	MATCHES
G. S. Chappell (Australia)	122	87
M. C. Cowdrey (England)	120	114
R. B. Simpson (Australia)	110	62
W. R. Hammond (England)	110	85

14. CATCHES IN ONE TEST MATCH

7	G. S. Chappell	Aust.–England	Perth	1974–75
7	Yajurvindra Singh	India–England	Bangalore	1976–77

15. AUSTRALIAN CAPTAINS

	TESTS	WON	LOST	DRAWN	TIED
G. S. Chappell	48	21	13	14	–
R. B. Simpson	39	12	12	15	–
I. M. Chappell	30	15	5	10	–
R. Benaud	28	12	4	11	1

16. WORLD SERIES CRICKET SUPERTESTS

BATTING	M.	INNS	N.O.	RUNS	H.S.	AVER.	100	50	C.
1977–78 in Australia	6	12	1	661	246X	60.09	2	1	10
1978–79 in Australia	3	5	0	134	81	26.80	0	1	5
1978–79 in West Indies	5	9	0	620	150	68.88	3	2	4
Totals	14	26	1	1415	246X	56.60	5	4	19

GREG CHAPPELL

BOWLING	OVERS	MAIDENS	RUNS	WKTS	AVER.	B.B.	5 W.I.
1977–78 in							
Australia	29	4	91	5	18.20	5–20	1
1978–79 in							
Australia	5	1	9	0	–	–	–
1978–79 in							
West Indies	15	3	56	1	56	1–27	–
Totals	49	8	156	6	26	5–20	1

INDEX

INDEX